Appreciation for Succul

"What if love isn't about losing yourself or compror
What if, instead of the 'you complete me' model
we approach love from 'I complete me' and 'you complete you' wholeness?
In *Succulent Wild Love*, SARK and Dr. John Waddell offer up tools for coming
into a relationship as a nourishing, growth-enhancing, 'joyfull' spiritual practice.
Definitely medicine for the soul, as well as the heart."

— Lissa Rankin, MD
New York Times–bestselling author of *Mind Over Medicine* and *The Fear Cure*

"Tired of looking for love in all the wrong places? *Succulent Wild Love* is the best self-help book
you could possibly read. Trust me, it's PERFECT! You're perfect too!"

— Rachel Naomi Remen, MD
bestselling author of *Kitchen Table Wisdom* and *My Grandfather's Blessings*

"*Succulent Wild Love* offers a new philosophy of love that provides a more
enlightened way of experiencing all your relationships. It's brimming with innovative tools
you can use to make any relationship more vibrant."

— Marci Shimoff
#1 *New York Times*–bestselling author of *Happy for No Reason* and *Love for No Reason*
and coeditor of *Chicken Soup for the Woman's Soul*

"If your soul is ready for love — self-love and soulmate love — read this book.
It's filled with wise and wonderful advice and really useful (and easy) exercises."

— Arielle Ford
bestselling author of *The Soulmate Secret* and *Wabi Sabi Love*

"The wonderfully whimsical appearance of *Succulent Wild Love* is only the beginning.
The book is profound! Based on SARK and Dr. John Waddell's personal experiences,
it reveals the principles that make love flourish and presents them in ways you can
immediately apply to bring greater wonder, joy, and love into your life. We love this book!"

— Donna Eden and David Feinstein
New York Times–bestselling coauthors of *The Energies of Love*

"Succulent. Wild. Love. When I first saw the title, it made me want to rip my jammies
right off. Then I read it, and WOW. It really is a whole new philosophy of love
and relationships in a whole new way!"

— Joan Borysenko, PhD
bestselling author of *Inner Peace for Busy People*

"From the queen of self-love and her wise and thoughtful fiancé, Dr. John Waddell, comes a sweet and insightful book with practical how-tos on fostering and nurturing love with another soul on this life's journey. Very beautiful."

— TOSHA Silver
bestselling author of *Outrageous Openness* and *Change Me Prayers*

"SARK and Dr. John Waddell have written the new bible for creating soulful, conscious, loving relationships. Their genius, guidance, and practical tools are sure to transform any relationship in your life into a succulent wild one. The blend of personal stories, transformational teachings, and step-by-step processes is nothing short of amazing. I highly recommend this book for anyone ready to receive more love!"

— AMy AHIers
bestselling author of *Big Fat Lies Women Tell Themselves* and coauthor of *Reform Your Inner Mean Girl*

"The whole is greater than the sum of two hearts! SARK has written about love before, but never quite like this. It is rare for a coauthored book to so effectively deliver a single message through two distinct voices. But Mr. and Mrs. Wonderfull are meant to write books together, and the combination of their voices is glistening, potent, unforgettable."

— MArney K. MAKriDAKis
bestselling author of *Creating Time* and *Hop, Skip, Jump*

"SARK's books have been a guiding force in my life since I was eighteen, and this book is no exception — except for the fact that the fun and playfulness and advice and truth are all doubled. John Waddell and SARK together are exactly what a relationship should be: independent but together. Not always agreeing but coming back to the center. Thank you for helping us redefine and rewrite our own love story so we see only possibility."

— SuZAnne evAns
New York Times–bestselling author of
The Way You Do Anything Is the Way You Do Everything and Inc. 500 honoree

"I love this book! Succulent Wild Love is not only a powerful guide for bringing more love into our relationships and lives, it is also written by two amazing people who practice what they teach. Allow the wisdom, creativity, and authenticity of this book to inspire you."

— MiKe RoBBins
bestselling author of *Nothing Changes Until You Do*

**A new philosophy of love
and relationships for everyone**

Succulent WILD LOVE

Six powerful HABITS FOR Feeling More LOVE More often

BY SARK and Dr. JOHN WADDELL

New World Library

NEW WORLD LiBrARY
NoVATo, CALiForniA

Thank you to our wonderfull guest essayists in the book & to our fabulous endorsers.

We appreciate Andrea Scher for photos on pages 8, 69, 81, 247, and 257.

Creative spelling & copy utilized & any "mistakes" are those of the authors.

We exuberantly thank & appreciate the thoughtfull, professional, and kind people at New World Library.

Marc Allen, Jason Gardner, Kristen Cashman, Tona Pearce Myers, Tracy Cunningham, Kim Corbin, Munro Magruder, Georgia Hughes, Jonathan Wichmann

New World Library
14 Pamaron Way
Novato, California 94949

Library of Congress Cataloging-in-Publication Data
SARK, date.
   Succulent wild love : six powerful habits for feeling more love more often / SARK & John Waddell.
      pages   cm
Includes bibliographical references.
ISBN 978-1-60868-358-1 (paperback)
1. Man-woman relationships. 2. Intimacy (Psychology) 3. Mate selection.
4. Couples. 5. Interpersonal attraction. 6. Love. I. Waddell, John, date.
II. Title.
HQ801.S43373 2015
306.7—dc23   2015016974

Photo credits: p. 40, photo of Virginia Bell by Irene Young; p. 63, photo of Valerie Tate by Tracy Maxwell-Ashley; p. 82, photo of Leslie Lewis by Paul Buceta; p. 105, photo of Arielle Ford and Brian Hilliard by Carl Studna; p. 202, photo of Sam Bennett by Erin Clendinin; p. 226, photo of Clark Tate by Valerie Tate; p. 233, photo of Andrea Scher by In Her Image Photography; p. 242, photo of David and Cliff Swain-Solomon by Donna Hackney.

First printing, November 2015   ISBN 978-1-60868-358-1
Printed in Korea

10   9   8   7   6   5   4   3   2   1

HEART of DEDICATION

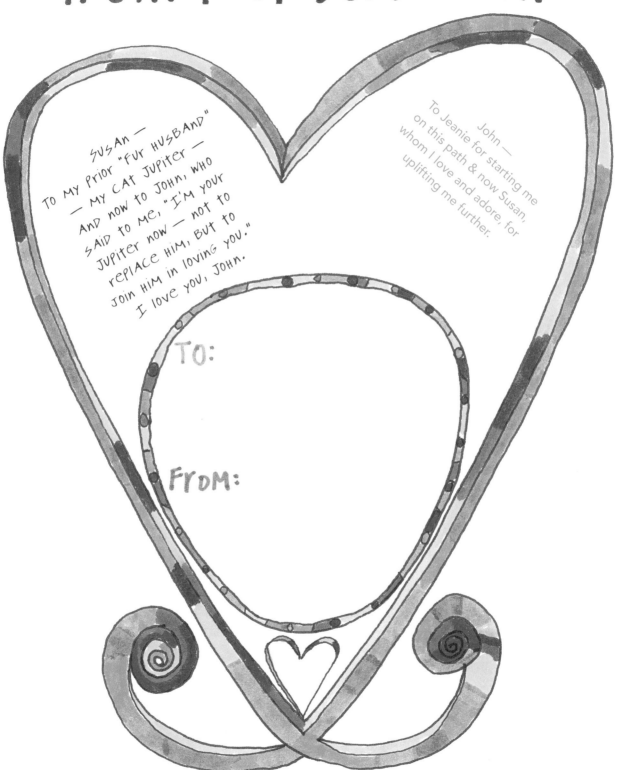

Susan —
To my prior "Fur Husband"
— my cat Jupiter —
and now to John, who
said to me, "I'm your
Jupiter now — not to
replace him, but to
join him in loving you."
I love you, John.

John —
To Jeanie for starting me
on this path & now Susan,
whom I love and adore, for
uplifting me further.

TO:

FROM:

TABLE of Contents
(For content relationships)

Your content
relationship guides

Essays By Glorious Guest Contributors

How to Use This Book:
A Quick Guide

WAYS FOR YOU TO GET INTO THIS BOOK

Feel free to read this guide — and the book — in order, in its entirety, or out of order, randomly, and in any combination that moves you most.

IF...

...you are curious about Succulent Wild relationships and would like to find out more about creating one, go to chapters 2 & 6.

...you are basically happy in your relationship and would like it to feel even better, go to chapters 12 & 23.

...you are kind of, or mostly, unhappy in your relationship and want new solutions that work, go to chapters 7, 8, 9, 10, 11, 12 & 17.

...you'd like to be in a relationship or just feel more inspired about love and relationships, go to chapters 4, 5, 6 & 7.

...you think you might be ending a relationship or would like to, go to chapters 7, 13, 14 & 22.

...you feel like you've never really understood how relationships work, go to chapters 1, 2 & 23.

…you'd like to read about how other people behave in their relationships, go to chapters 3, 4, 7, 9, 16, 19, 20, 21, 22 & 23.

 …you want some **Fabulous** and **Quick** answers to your love and relationship questions, go to chapter 24.

 …you feel afraid to tell your partner about something that has been bothering you, go to chapters 10, 12 & 18.

 …you feel fulfilled in your relationships and want to increase the unconditional love you feel, go to chapters 11, 15 & 23.

Awareness Practices

At the end of most of the chapters in this book are what we call Awareness Practices. We designed and created them to inspire you to expand your awareness about the topic we've written about in the chapter. These practices may contain fill-in-the-blanks, questions for you to ponder, or places to further practice with the tools we're supplying. We've focused on providing a blend of art and words in a way that we think will benefit both visually oriented, intuitive people and more linear, analytically oriented readers.

We recommend working with only those Awareness Practices that you feel moved to explore. If you feel resistance, either stop or customize the practice to suit you better. You might not do any of these and still receive great benefit and new awareness, or the practices might suit you perfectly — or anywhere in between.

You might discuss the practices with a partner, friend, or therapist — or favorite animal. If they don't resonate with you initially, the practices might reappear at the perfect serendipitous time that you need them. Allow yourself to utilize these in ways that feel best to you, including not doing them at all.

We have also included some additional material for *And we welcome you as you are, with no "improvements"* you online that you are welcome to enjoy and use for your benefit. You can access this via the internet addresses at the end of each Awareness Practice.

OTHER PERSPECTIVES

We have invited and included some wonderfull people — like you — to share their experiences of love and relationships. We've tucked these into various nooks in the book for your enjoyment and for illustrations of love relationships in action.

LET me introduce you

I'M SARK, Also known AS
Susan Ariel Rainbow Kennedy.

If you've read any of my ⑯ BOOKS,
you know THAT THey're color·full,
Handwritten expressions of my self·loving
Creative, very real Life.

SARK BOOKS Are intimate and
Journal-Like, filled WiTH MY ART
and vulnerable SHArings.

I created THem To Be personal and
universal, WHimsical, FreSH, Deep and
funny, and ultimately for everyone.
I've written ABout my experiences with
sexuality, my explorations in Most realms
of Life. THe one subject I had not
written A BOOK About yet WAS

Specifically, love with another person in addition to me. I married myself in 1997 and promised to never leave me.

I wrote about it in my book SUCCULENT WILD WOMAN, which is my statement of self-liberation.

This new book is my statement of love and relationship liberation.

It's about the best of being single with the best of being in a relationship, and how to actually create that every day.

I'd like to introduce you now to

Dr. JOHN WAddell

He's my co-author—my very first one! My life, love and adventure partner, and my most beloved.

When I met John in 2012, he told me that he'd been happily married for 10 years and that the honeymoon never ended.

His wife Jeanie HAd died in 2011.
John HAd grieved and opened Himself
To loving AGAin.
When we first met, John said to me,
"I Want you To Know THAT I'M QuAlified
To Adore you."
I felt MArried To HiM in THAT instant.
He Also said, "you're obviously A very talented,
unusual and creative WOMan-WHAT I'M Going
To say next MiGHT sHock you. WHAT I
Appreciate Most About you is THAT I Know
THAT you're norMAL' you're norMAL in
The sense THAT you're A WOMan WHO
WanTs To Give and receive love."
I started To cry, Because THAT'S WHAT I
Most Wanted To SHAre WiTH another
Person and HAD Felt too scared To Be
seen and loved in THAT deeply
intiMATe WAY.

My Life and career successes were immensely fulfilling but couldn't fill My desire for THAT kind of loving relationship.

John HAS A PHD in clinical psychology, is A Metaphysical teacher & AVTHor, and I experience Him AS an embodied JOY Being. I'M So HAPPY To introduce HiM To you in THis BOOK and in My Life.

It's LARGER THan our personal love story.

JOHn introduced me To 3 principles THAT He Lives, practices and TEAcHes, and Now I do too.

it's really a lot to do with How He Got into My Life

I introduced HiM To 3 processes I created To Be ABle To Live My SvcculeNT WILD Life, and He's practicing With THese Now Also. We've "MArried" our principles and Processes in THis BOOK for you to use To Benefit All of THE relATionsHips in

Your life—including with yourself.
In January 2014, John proposed
and I said **Yes!** We're happily engaged
and getting married after completing
this book. Of course, it will be a
succulent wild marriage, and we plan
to be known as Mrs. & Mr. Wonderfull

This book is a wonderfull blend of
handwriting, creative design, typeset
and art.

enjoy
The SARK similarities & differences
in this new form.
Welcome to YOU! in your very own
succulent wild loving self

★ as you might imagine, this is not a normal book.

I HAVE CREATED AND WRITTEN THIS BOOK WITH MY BELOVED PARTNER, Dr. JOHN WADDELL. TO MAKE IT EASIER FOR YOU TO SEE WHO IS SPEAKING, I AM WRITING IN MY STYLE — WHICH IS MY MULTICOLORED HANDWRITING.

All THE ART IN THE BOOK IS BY ME.

SARK (a.k.a. Susan Ariel Rainbow Kennedy)

I loved writing this book with Susan. My style and color look like this. We use these styles when we have individual thoughts and stories we want to share.

Dr. John Waddell (a.k.a. John ;-)

With other text, sometimes our writing is blended, and sometimes you can guess who is writing.

I. THE PROMISE OF THIS BOOK

All the HEART·full people
and aniMALS

Dear Brilliant Reader,

If you follow the guidelines in this book, you will have a most nourishing foundation for all your relationships. If you are experiencing any pain in your relationships, applying the processes in this book can remove it. And if you are looking for an intimate partner, this book will open you further to that experience. Succulent Wild Love is a spectacularly guided path to experiencing more love, and then having the skills to keep creating and expanding it. It's a new philosophy of love and relationships for everyone.

We all want more love, and we want love that feels good. The wisdom in this book — the six powerful habits — will enable you to love more and be loved more. You will be able to take your relationships with the most significant people in your life from "I love you anyway" to simply "I love you" — releasing tension and fear and getting the support and affection you want. If this sounds too good to be true, know that you're holding yourself back from having a Succulent Wild Love relationship.

Loving is meant to be easy and natural, and this book will show you how.

Succulent Wild Love is about nourishing yourself, the way a succulent plant does. You can have what you want without being dependent on the people around you to change, so you can love them unconditionally. It is about being wild — as in untamed and not limited by those close to you. You are free to be yourself in your relationships.

You Becoming The right Partner is your Joy. full Opportunity

FOR THOSE NOT IN A PARTNERSHIP

If you feel blocked from being in a partnership or are looking for a soulmate, by living the principles in this book, you can see and be seen by the nourishing lover you want. That person might be in your life right now or just around the corner. But you won't be able to recognize them until you're ready. Rather than emphasizing *finding* the right partner, Succulent Wild Love teaches you how to *become* the right partner.

We like to think of a soulmate — or sole-mate —
relationship as one where you feel self-loving and loving with another.

Ask yourself why you are looking for a mate. Is it because your mother or someone in your life wants you to get married? For many people, being in a traditional, marriage-style partnership isn't their true calling. There are many kinds of love relationships, and by using the tools in this book you can create a partnership that suits you perfectly — if that's what you truly desire.

A Succulent Wild Love relationship enhances your life and does not diminish it in any way. Are you ambivalent about being with someone based on the relationships you've observed, or what you've been taught or experienced (such as seeing people stuck in roles, feeling a loss of freedom, or having to compromise)? You can be in a relationship that is the best of what you've learned, without the limitations.

I realized, as long as I felt ambivalent, the partners I drew in felt the same. And they reflected my own ambivalence and uncertainties about love back to me. I now know that the only way I let love with another person in was to begin by truly understanding how to love myself — and not just when things felt "good" but especially when I was at my "worst." My experiences

WITH UNCONDITIONALLY LOVING MYSELF LED DIRECTLY TO LETTING IN A GREAT LOVE WITH ANOTHER PERSON.

FOR EVERYONE IN ANY KIND OF RELATIONSHIP

All Feelings Allowed

Succulent Wild Love shows you how to resolve the two most common complaints that undermine most relationships: "If the other person would only change, I would feel better" and "I feel pressure to change (or to stay in my uncomfortable place)." These form the foundation of most fights and create pockets of ongoing frustration in even basically satisfying relationships.

You can learn how to create Joyful Solutions that don't require anyone to change, how to have a "no compromise" relationship. We are living this kind of relationship and have taught many others how to do the same.

The processes in this book will enable you to "clean up as you go" — to use your feelings constructively rather than denying them or amplifying tension. You can use all your feelings, including hurt and frustration, to create greater intimacy.

Succulent Wild Love removes the barriers to experiencing unconditional love. We all want to give and receive love without reservation, but few of us have learned how to do this on a consistent basis. Most of us have been told that the uninhibited joy and unconditional love we feel at the start of a relationship will inevitably fade. After practicing the six habits in this book, you will know that doesn't have to be so.

I USED TO BE CONVINCED THAT IT WAS ONLY A MATTER OF TIME BEFORE MY RELATIONSHIPS WOULD START DECLINING, AND SINCE I DIDN'T KNOW HOW TO NOURISH THEM OR MYSELF ALONG THE WAY, IT EVENTUALLY BECAME NECESSARY TO SEPARATE.

THIS WORKED OUT FINE FOR THE PART OF ME THAT FELT AFRAID OF LOVING — I COULD THEN "ELIMINATE" THEM FOR GOOD REASON. THE PART OF ME THAT WANTED TO LOVE AND BE LOVED HAD LITTLE OR NO VOICE, AND I JUST THOUGHT I WAS AN UNLOVABLE MISFIT, AS I'D FELT THAT WAY IN SO MANY OTHER AREAS OF MY LIFE.

I AM NOW EXPERIENCING A HONEYMOON EVERY DAY, AND INSTEAD OF COUNTING THE HOURS UNTIL I CAN BE ALONE AGAIN AND FEEL LIKE MYSELF, I'M SAVORING ALL THE TIME I HAVE IN THIS RELATIONSHIP WITH UNCOUNTABLE JOY AND APPRECIATION.

We think there is much about your ability to be in relationships with others that is good. Even if you're acutely aware of difficulties, much about the relationships you've created suits you. This book will help you with those relatively small parts that have a big impact on diminishing the joy you deserve.

THE WORST SORT OF MAGNIFYING GLASS

My previous way was the opposite — I used the small things that felt like difficulties and magnified them until I could barely see the other person at all! I spent far less time acknowledging or seeing the good things in the relationship or my part in creating them. One former boyfriend said that I wasn't high-maintenance, I was renovation. I now see that I was really renovating myself.

No one enters a relationship as a blank slate. You are carrying expectations, desires, and many beliefs that you learned from the people around you when you were growing up. Much of what they taught you was helpful — some was not. Understanding what is truly suited to you and what is best left behind can make a huge difference in how happy you are in any relationship.

Being in a partnership successfully is a lot like driving down a highway without running off the road or getting into an accident. On a winding road, you are constantly making decisions and adjustments to the steering wheel to stay in your lane. Likewise, interacting with someone isn't a static thing. It's an ongoing series of experiences and decisions.

On most modern highways, clear lines in the center and on the edge let you know the safe boundaries of your lane. Crossing those lines when you don't want to can run you off the road or into another car.

Now imagine it's late at night and the road is covered with snow. The edges of your lane are almost impossible to see. This is how most people drive down the relationship highway. And when they feel stuck or crash into others, they don't know what happened or why. They just assume that relationships are series of alternating joyful and painful experiences, and not much can be done about it.

Imagine if people had accidents in their cars on a weekly basis. No one would accept that. And you don't have to accept regular painful interactions in any of your relationships.

We have identified six habits that facilitate Succulent Wild Love relationships. These habits are like the lines on the road. They will help you see how you've drifted out of your lane into a painful situation and how to get back. And practicing them will enable you to go where you want in your relationships.

Of course, there will still be bumps. There are bumps on any highway, even if you stay between the lines. But the bumps will be brief, and you won't be wondering why you're stuck in weeds or why you keep crashing into others.

The skill is not in avoiding anything that might upset you but in handling it well. People in the best relationships have disagreements, miscommunications, and hurt feelings (we certainly do). But they recover from these quickly and spend most of their time delighting in each other. Applying the guidelines in this book will enable you to create that kind of relationship.

ONE OF MY MENTORS USED TO SAY THAT I'D RATHER CARPET THE WORLD SO I COULD WALK BAREFOOT THAN DO MY INNER WORK OF ADJUSTING SO THAT I COULD WALK ANYWHERE I WANTED. THIS SOUNDED TRUE AT THE TIME. I NOW REALIZE THAT I DIDN'T HAVE THE SKILLS OR TOOLS TO RECOVER QUICKLY, SO IT SEEMED LIKE MY BEST TOOL WAS AVOIDANCE. I'M HAPPY TO SAY THAT I'VE LEARNED HOW TO RECOVER QUICKLY AND GET INTO AND OUT OF EMOTIONAL PLACES THAT WOULD HAVE FRIGHTENED ME BEFORE.

THE SIX HABITS OF PEOPLE IN SUCCULENT WILD LOVE RELATIONSHIPS

★ They listen to their relationship mentor inside them — their Inner Wise Self, Higher Self, Holy Spirit — and take action.

★ They use their feelings, both as a guide to know when the relationship is off track and to constructively evoke cooperation from others.

★ They recognize inner critics and other negative dialogue in their head and don't put this criticism on their partner — or themselves.

★ They respect their own and their partner's boundaries.

★ They create Joyful Solutions where no one needs to compromise or sacrifice.

★ They practice seeing the perfection in their partner and all the other people they're in relationships with.

In the following chapters we give you the tools to practice these habits. And the more you practice them, the more skillful you'll become. At first you will learn how to resolve tension, then how to navigate in such a way that you don't create new tension, and, along the way, how you can amplify the love and delight you feel for the people around you.

As you learn about these tools, you may have some painful moments where you become aware that you have hurt yourself and others in the past. Our intent is to help you become more self-aware, but with love and self-acceptance. You have been doing the best you could with the knowledge you had.

Also, using some of these tools may not be the right path for you. There are many relationship paths. Above all, we encourage you to listen to yourself and trust yourself. These are guidelines we have applied to our relationship successfully, and have helped others do the same. You will need to mold them to your way of being. If you follow what feels good to you, rather than simply accepting what we or any other well-meaning people tell you, you will find your best path.

You may also find yourself continuing to be stuck in one or more difficult relationships. As with any skill, these tools take practice to master. Applying them to particularly difficult situations may be more than you are capable of at first, and you may benefit from skilled support, such as from a therapist.

Even if you use only a few tools in this book, they will bring more joy into your relationships. And if you barely read the book, or have it on a shelf for a while, it'll still be working subliminally.

WHAT IS A SUCCULENT WILD LOVE RELATIONSHIP?

You feel free and well loved and loving

One simple indicator will let you know if you are living in a Succulent Wild Love relationship: you are happy by yourself and happy to see your partner.

This is at the basis of everything anyone does in relationships: You want to be happy with the people around you, as well as by yourself. You want to love and be loved, not only by others but also by yourself. The number one indicator of whether you are on the path you want in any relationship is if you feel good around the other person.

So what are some of the qualities of a Succulent Wild Love relationship? What does a most wonderful relationship look and feel like? What qualities would a perfect relationship for you have?

Here are some things that come to mind for us. You may want to add other qualities or modify these. Note which ones resonate the most for you.

- ★ You feel safe and that you have what you need in the relationship.
- ◎ You can count on your partner to do what they say they will.
-   You have fun together.
- ◎ You share responsibilities well together.
- ★ You are kind to each other.
- ◉ Your partner helps you get wherever you want to go and celebrates you along the way.
- ☆ You can sometimes be childlike or adult or take the role of a wise elder, and be appreciated for all parts of you. Your partner can do the same.
- ◉ You are heard and understood, and your feelings are welcome.
- ☆ You are loved just as you are.
- ◎ You can be intimately engaged with yourself in the presence of the other.
- ★ When you see each other, you smile in delight!

You Share Joy and everything else

When Susan and I met, I told her the only thing I wanted from her was that she be glad to see me. **and I usually AM**

WHEN JOHN TOLD ME THAT, I FELT LIKE I WAS ALREADY QUALIFIED! AND I CONTINUE TO BE GLAD TO SEE HIM. THE ONLY THING I WANTED WAS TO GIVE AND RECEIVE LOVE, AND I AM NOW EXPERIENCING THAT.

There are also some common negative conditions that are not part of Succulent Wild Love relationships. You might be experiencing a version of some of these. (And this includes with yourself. You may be treating yourself in some of these ways.) Note ones that resonate with you.

- ☆ You feel guilt, shame, or criticism directed at you or evoked in you.
- ★ You compromise or sacrifice.
- ◎ You feel bullied or nagged.

- You feel stuck in a role or roles.
- You feel that you have to accept things that don't feel good.
- You don't feel valued or respected.
- You regularly experience hurt, anger, or tension.
- You feel held back from speaking your truth.
- Your significant other isn't doing what you believed they would.
- You don't feel free or supported in doing the things that bring you joy.
- You have the feeling that you can't really be yourself.

We will show you how to minimize and even eliminate these, and how to amplify the things you want. Many people believe they can't expect to feel great about their partner or themselves most of the time. Actually, you can!

WHAT DOES IT FEEL LIKE TO LOVE?

You Might Feel Boxed in

Have you ever seen an angry mother yell at a child, "But I love you"? Have you heard a frustrated lover who isn't getting what they want say, "But I love you," or someone scream at their partner during an argument, "Don't you know I love you?"

In all these instances we have no doubt that the person declaring their love does have a loving bond with the other. But at that moment what they are feeling is not love. When we talk about feeling more love more often, we are actually talking about feeling loving feelings, the way a mother might feel when she looks at her newborn or how new lovers feel when they see each other.

Having someone declare their love for us feels wonderful, but we want to create situations where we actually feel love flowing, to us and from us, love that is not mixed with fear in the form of anger, frustration, hurt, or control. Succulent Wild Love is pure love flowing. That is what we *all* want.

And most of us do have this kind of love in our relationships, but usually only in little bits here and there. Our ability to let love flow is often clogged by built-up resentments, judgments, and fear. In many relationships, people only feel free to express uninhibited love when someone is hurt or dying. Applying the tools in this book, you will be able to feel uninhibited love flow freely through you every day.

Awareness Practice: Imagine Your Relationship

1. Take a moment to picture a wonderful relationship for you. Or if you're already in one, imagine how it could be even more wonderful. You can also picture a wonderful relationship with any other significant person in your life, whether a friend, family member, boss, or coworker.

   How do you feel? Draw, write, or speak about what you envision. Let yourself create on the outside what you feel on the inside. You might list words that appeal to you, or colors, or scenes.

2. Use some of the positive items from the Succulent Wild Love relationship list on page 15 — you can even add others or change them if you want to make your own list. See if you can picture incidents in your life (or make them up) that represent one or more of these conditions. For example:

   When I'm with _____, I feel safe and have what I need in the relation-
       ship because they _____.
   These are the ways we have fun together: _____.
   I love how we share responsibilities together. I remember when _____.
   Here is an example of how we're kind to each other: _____.
   When I wanted to make this change in my life: _____, this is how they
       supported me: .
   I remember really being heard when I _____.
   I will enjoy expanding these things in our relationship: _____.

3. Now look at the list of negative items on page 15 — again, you can add others or change them. If any of them brings up events in your life that are happening now (or that you're afraid might happen if you enter a relationship), then write down one or more of these feelings or fears. For example:

   Sometimes when I'm with _____, I feel _____ (For
       example: guilt/shame/criticism/jealousy/anxiety). It isn't easy to feel this.
   I feel like I'm sacrificing what I really want to do when I _____.
   I like being a (parent/spouse/lover)   , but don't like this part of it:

   _____.

When we've tried to talk about _____, it hasn't gone well.
I'm afraid to tell them that _____.
I wish they would be more supportive of my _____.

By the end of the book, you will have addressed each of these concerns and have the tools to change them.

4. Take a moment and think about the people close to you. If there is something unresolved, it will likely pop up quickly. If it does, there is nothing you need to do right now. In the following chapters, you will see many ways to take care of unresolved issues.

   Of course, you aren't necessarily going to feel joyful and loving 100 percent of the time when you think of your partner or other people in your life. But by understanding yourself and how relationships work, you will be able to get to feeling that way most of the time.

5. As you go about your day today, practice noticing how you feel as you greet the people around you. How do you feel about them as you spend time with them? Ask yourself these questions about the people in your life:

WHEN DO THEY DELIGHT ME?

WHEN DO THEY DRAIN OR DISTRACT ME?

WHO "LIGHTS ME UP"?

WHO DO I TRY TO AVOID?

WHO DO I WANT TO BE AROUND?

WHO FEELS EASY TO SPEND TIME WITH?

To be further inspired to envision and keep envisioning your wonderful relationship, go to:
SucculentWildLove.com/Imagine

2. How We Developed Succulent Wild Love And the Six Habits

A WHOLE WORLD of relationships

WHAT IF THE EARTH WAS secretly wearing A TUTU?!?!

BOTH OF US have spent most of our lives either being single or in what we call "growth relationships." These are partnerships where you experience dysfunctional patterns you learned in childhood and find out a lot about your foibles and limitations. There is love and support in these relationships, but also insecurity and ongoing stress. Through trial and error, many uncomfortable experiences, and a lot of self-awareness work, we developed the habits in this book.

It wasn't until age 52 that I first experienced what we call a Succulent Wild Love relationship. It was with my wife, Jeanie, who is no longer physical. Before I met her, after many years in growth relationships, I took a year to reflect on what I had been doing. I knew if I didn't change, I would create similar uncomfortable situations again.

I didn't try to date or even meet anyone. I made a wonderful friend, Mike. We would go hiking together and talk about relationships. I also spent a great deal of time alone, studying how to create a positive, intimate relationship from the perspective of both psychology and metaphysics, particularly the Law of Attraction.

After spending that time being single, looking at myself and how I was in relationships, I was able to enter one in a different way. Not only had I changed, but Jeanie was different and more suitable for me in a nurturing way than the women I had been attracted to in the past.

Jeanie loved me unconditionally and taught me how to do the same. She was an unconditional love genius.

When Jeanie was younger she ran a day-care center. At one point she was taking care of 23 children, including 4 or 5 in diapers, all by herself. Under the spell of her unconditional love, the children played cooperatively together, did artwork, and helped each other.

One day a social worker who reviewed child-care centers for the local government notified Jeanie that her center would need to be inspected. Jeanie called all the parents and begged them to keep their children home that day. This was before there were laws limiting how many children could be taken care of by one person, but she knew having such a large group by herself would be frowned on, and they would probably require her to cut way back or might even close her center.

Of course the parents all worked, so most of the children were there when the social worker came. Jeanie presented the situation as best she could and then waited to see what would happen. That evening the social worker — who inspected many day-care centers — called and asked if Jeanie could take her child.

Jeanie was not able to love everyone unconditionally all the time, but she came very close. More important, she knew consciously how to achieve that. The path she took to loving me unconditionally in our relationship was to see me as *perfect*.

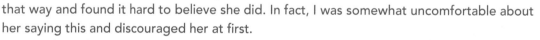

Early in our relationship she told me — and anyone who would listen — that I was perfect. Of course I didn't think of myself that way and found it hard to believe she did. In fact, I was somewhat uncomfortable about her saying this and discouraged her at first.

But then I began to understand the power of what Jeanie was doing. Seeing me as perfect was the basis for her being able to feel unconditional love. And soon I started seeing her as perfect.

Through my self-awareness work I had been able to set a foundation, and being with Jeanie I learned how to love unconditionally on a daily basis. She knew how to consistently live in that flow and gave that gift to me.

We also agreed early on that when we wanted different things, we would do our best to create joyful solutions together. And we were often delighted when we would come up with something better than what either of us had started with!

Jeanie was more respectful of my boundaries than anyone I had ever been with before. This quality, along with the way we made decisions together and the unconditional love we shared, became the foundation of three of the habits in a Succulent Wild Love relationship. I

Jeanie (1942–2011)

had that kind of partnership with Jeanie. We just didn't have a name for it or fully understand what we did to make it so good.

Jeanie helped me write two novels (*John and Jeanie Fly: Living the Law of Attraction* and *John and Jeanie Fly: Our World and the Law of Attraction*) in which the main characters practice achieving unconditional love in a variety of stressful situations. In many ways these books reflect the relationship Jeanie and I were living. They are an intimate example of two people actually living a Succulent Wild Love relationship.

When Jeanie left the physical in 2011, I went into despair. It was the most painful experience of my adult life. As painful as it was for me, I felt that her leaving was the right path for her. From my understanding of metaphysics and the Law of Attraction, I didn't see Jeanie's transition as an accident or as a failure.

The day I met Susan, I learned a number of important things about her (though I had no idea who SARK was), but what caused me on that first day to decide I wanted to explore a relationship with Susan occurred on an entirely different level.

In any long-term partnership there are ups and downs, but there is also a consistent, familiar, reassuring feeling-tone when one is around one's partner. As Susan and I were walking with some friends, I realized I was feeling with Susan exactly the way I had felt with Jeanie. I trusted that my Inner Wise Self would never guide me to feel that way unless I was on the right track. And so I followed what felt right and good to me. And it has been.

After Jeanie left, there was one thing I couldn't reconcile. We had agreed that we would always find a solution that would be joyful for both of us. I felt that her leaving was right for her, but it was far from a joyful solution for me.

It was not until I met Susan that I was able to reconcile this. Being with Susan is my joyful solution.

I LOVE BEING A JOY·FULL SOLUTION

I love being a Succulent Wild Woman, and now that I'm experiencing SUCCULENT WILD LOVE with another person, I want to share all the joys, challenges, and transformations of creative, lively partnership, so that other people can experience more of this too.

Succulent Wild Love is what I had always envisioned in a life-and-love partnership, and here's what I believe it consists of:

Two people, living life as full cups of self-love, sharing the overflow with the world. And any time that either doesn't feel like a full cup, they do their transformational processes and practices to fill themselves back up from the inside, and then bring that to their partner and to all their other relationships too.

And when they need kind, compassionate, loving care from others in order to more swiftly transform, they request and receive that kind of focused attention.

I created three transformational processes to support my growth and my ability to "fill my own cup," and had been practicing and teaching these for years before meeting John. This is how I live mostly happily in what I call the "marvelous, messy middle" of life, feeling ALL my feelings and not spending so much time in the negative ones.

Most days, I communicate with my spirit/soul/intuition/higher self. I call it my Inner Wise Self, and I now know that during early-childhood abuse, this part of myself kept reassuring me that I was all right on the inside, despite the actual circumstances on the outside. Later in my life, I learned how to activate and empower this part to be in action in my life on a daily basis and involved in everything I do. This is how I created my 17 books, many products, and creative business — and allowed more love into my life.

I've learned that when my feelings are flowing and cared for, I feel safe, happy, and well loved. So I created a care system for my feelings that I can do quickly and easily on a daily basis. It results in my feeling better more often, and feeling basically glad most of the time. This allows me to more fully share myself with others and actually be consistently happy in a love relationship.

My inner dialogue used to be mostly critics talking about how I wasn't good enough, and/or rampant fears and worries. Since I learned

A little note about feelings:
Feelings can only Feel and only you can Feel Them ♥ ♥ ♥

HOW TO CALM THESE CRITICS AND CREATED A SYSTEM TO MANAGE THEM, MY inner DIALOGUE is MUCH MOre loving AND feels MOre MENTAlly SPACIOUS. I leArneD THAt My Inner Wise Self AND I Are in CHARGe Of My life, AND not THe inner CritiCS. THESE trAnSfOrMATIONS OPENeD UP THe SPACE tO Allow MOre love intO My life, AND reSulTeD in My BeinG willinG tO let JOHN in.

JOHN intrODUCeD Me tO THe THree HABitS Of trAnSfOrMATive relAtiOnshiPS THAt He wrote ABOut eArlier — THAt He lives, PrACtices, AND teACHes, AND THAt I AM AlsO nOw livinG, PrACtiCinG, AND teACHinG.

We effectively married our six habits and are sharing them in this book.

WHen I Met JOHN, I eXperienceD new levelS Of lovinG witH HiM AND leArned THAt everyone reAlly is PerfeCt — not An iDeAlizeD sense, But in A series Of CHOiceS THAt I COulD MAKe. JOHN SHAreD THAt BeinG seen AS PerfeCt, AND seeinG His wife AS PerfeCt, wAS How He HAD liveD AND BeHAVeD in His 10-yeAr MArriAGe. once I eXperienceD THis PrOfOunDly lovinG enerGy DireCteD towArD Me, I wAnteD tO live THis wAy too.

When JOHN firSt DeSCribeD THis concept tO Me — His tHinkinG Of Me AS PerfeCt — I loveD it. THen Of cOurse I reAlizeD tHAt I'D neeD tO tHink Of HiM tHAt wAy too! THis wAS GOinG tO Be A CHAllenGe, AS I'D AlwAys kePt A list Of THe wAys My PArtner neeDeD tO CHAnGe sO tHAt I COulD feel Better. Of course, they never COulD MeASure UP tO My stAnDArDS or list iteMS, sO After A wHile I COulD SAfely eliMinAte THeM — AND DiD.

critical pen

My LiSTS USeD TO Be Very LONG

I CAn now sAy THAt I HAVe no list ABOut JOHN. I'M tecHniCAlly "listless" ;-) But I'M siGnifiCAntly HAPPier, since THe list MAintenAnce took A lot Of tiMe AND enerGy, AND THe PersOn COulD never MeASure UP!

I'M now AlsO eXperiencinG MySelf AS "PerfeCt" in wHOle new wAys, AND leArninG ABOut THe PerfeCtiOn Of love, AND THAt it's not ABOut BeinG PerfeCtiOnistiC.

Now I CAn see JOHN AS PerfeCt AND not keeP A list Of "iMPrOveMentS" tHAt COulD or SHOulD OCCur fOr Me tO Be HAPPy. THis is now eXtenDinG tO frienDS, BusinesS PArtnerS, AND neiGHBOrs too, wHiCH is A POwerfull SHift.

It was exciting to decide that any way I think they're not perfect is my responsibility and opportunity to transform. This doesn't mean that I don't have and express preferences — I have and express plenty of them! I just spend most of my time and energy in relationships focusing on what's already good.

When I met John, he also explained that he was offering a "no compromise" relationship. This sounded really good to me, since I was not very good at compromise and, in fact, hadn't really done much of it. I mostly operated by doing things "my way," which works all right when you're by yourself or in charge in some way. It works less well in collaborative or close relationships, where there are invariably more differences to navigate.

I also dreaded conflict, so the idea of finding solutions that were joyfull for both of us sounded great to me, but I felt very suspicious about being able to actually do it. John let me know that we didn't need to stop at compromise. We would create joyfull solutions, and these often would be better than what either of us would have thought of on our own.

I had experienced some of this in my various business partnerships, but it felt more accidental and not consciously applied. I observed that John lives this way with everyone — not just with me. He truly believes in and lives from a place where a joyfull solution exists for everyone in any given situation. I've learned now how to go beyond compromise, and it really works.

I can honestly say that in our relationship I've given up nothing and compromised very little — and the only reason I compromised at all was when I got scared and thought that a joyfull solution couldn't possibly be created, and so compromised in secret. Any time John has discovered this, or I've admitted it, we've created some great new solution together.

I'd also decided that in any long-term love relationship, I had to

HAve Autonomy. My self-loving And creative prActices require A fAir Amount of spAce And freedom, And I'm quite spontAneous. So the ideA of being And feeling sepArAte AppeAled to me very much. John And I tAlked extensively About these subjects, And he reAssured me that he sAw me As wholly sepArAte unto myself — And that I wAs AlwAys free to chAnge our relAtionship model or pAtterns Anytime. He continues to reAssure me About this more thAn three yeArs lAter. He shAred the importAnce of mAintAining his own sepArAteness And boundAries while in relAtionships too.

I'm glAd to sAy I feel thAt my sepArAteness is honored And supported, And thAt we creAte joyfull solutions whenever one of us wAnts them. Of course, I don't know whAt time will bring — but I do know thAt I cAn communicAte with my Inner Wise Self, my close friends, And John whenever I need to.

I now Also see thAt my close friends hAve honored me As sepArAte And thAt my true "soulmAte" is my own soul — my self-loving relAtionship with me is whAt Allowed me to welcome in And receive John's love. I Also think of this As being my own "sole-mAte," which feels like the best of being in A relAtionship with Another person And with myself.

You Can Do What I Have Done

Sometimes when people heAr my stories they think, "It's eAsy for you to hAve A Succulent Wild Love relAtionship, given your yeArs of experience And who you Are. You're A super-quAlified, lucky person, And you were just reAdy to hAve or be A soulmAte." I wAnt to be cleAr thAt if I cAn do this, ANyone cAn. My resistAnces, feArs, And beliefs About love not working were MUCH lArger thAn Anyone's I knew. I've discovered thAt Succulent Wild Love is more About prActicing these six hAbits with myself first And then Another person.

I believe thAt if you hAve A bAsicAlly good person who's compAtible enough to prActice with, you cAn creAte A Succulent Wild Love relAtionship together. Of course you'll hAve upsets And conflicts! No mAtter how AwAre, insightfull, And thoughtfull you And your pArtner Are, there may even be moments of despising them or how they behave. And if you're younger or less experienced, you'll experience more of these. But it's always about recovering and moving on, and when you can apply the habits and concepts that we share in this book, you'll be able to recover more quickly and keep loving and being loved.

I introduced John to the wonders of "trail napping."

3. Soulfully Single And Open For Love

Keeping Your Heart Open for Love

I had a marvelous mentor named Patricia who reminded me frequently, "Don't make the mistake of attaching your love to another person." She went on to say, "Realize that their love is reflected through you, it does not originate from them. They are not your source of love — you and your Inner Wise Self are."

I embraced this message wholeheartedly and wrote this in my journal: "Release yourself from the voices of inner critics who will tell you outdated messages from long ago about how you 'should' love, or how other people love, or how if you don't love another you'll die all alone in a nursing home in winter in a shared room."

release yourself from the voices of inner critics

I began to explore and practice new ways to be what I described as "Soulfully Single," while also describing myself as open to love with another person. To me, "Soulfully Single" sounded and felt so much richer and deeper than just "single."

My friend Vai had said to me after I had ended a love relationship, "Whatever you do, don't close your heart to love." She intuited that I'd already begun trying to close my heart and seal it off so I wouldn't feel that kind of pain again. So I resolved to keep my heart open and available for love. And I secretly thought that it wouldn't happen anyway, so what did I have to lose?

I practiced opening myself to new ways of doing and being, and learning even more about how to state my preferences clearly and directly in relationships with others. I used to either overstate my preferences or hide them — even from myself.

In my friendships, I started being more willing to practice telling and receiving MicroTruths (see chapter 18), those seemingly tiny, often unspoken little things that sometimes get swept under the carpet — until it feels like the carpet is so lumpy that you can't walk on it anymore. I wanted my friendships to be positive, current, and free from unnamed hurts and irritations. For the most part, this worked beautifully, and I kept my heart open to love in ways I hadn't previously imagined.

My childhood carpet was very lumpy

As I developed and lived my Soulfully Single life, I noticed that lots of other women were experimenting with something similar. They had full, rewarding, satisfying lives and work, and yet were open to love with another person arising or arriving unexpectedly. They also said they felt fine if it didn't happen.

When people asked my relationship status, I would reply, "I'm Soulfully Single," and most would swoon over that description and ask me to describe it further. Some would share that they still wanted romantic love but were no longer willing or able to sacrifice or compromise to get it. Everyone said they wouldn't "settle." I knew that for me, settling meant having just part of what I wanted, and I knew I wanted WAY more than that.

It reminded me of my career: At age 26 I'd resolved to be and live as an artist and writer — no matter what. I made the decision to live that way, all the way, even if it meant I wouldn't have much food or money. Prior to that, I'd had over 250 different jobs, trying to find something that could support me while I explored my creative gifts. I didn't know then that I could have created joyfull solutions for myself,

WHICH WOULD HAVE BEEN EASIER THAN WHAT I DID DO. BUT AS THEY SAY, HINDSIGHT IS ALWAYS 20-20, AND I JUST MADE IT UP AS I WENT ALONG — AS WE ALL DO.

i THINK MY **IN** SIGHTS ARE EVEN WISER THAN MY HINDSIGHTS

I KNEW THAT IF I WAS GOING TO ADD ANOTHER PERSON INTO MY SOULFULLY SINGLE LIFE, I WANTED TO FEEL SUCCULENT WILD INTIMATE REAL LOVE. I WANTED TO SWIRL WITH LOVE, I WANTED 110 PERCENT. I WANTED THE WHOLE MAGILLA (WHAT IS A MAGILLA, ANYWAY?). I WANTED HIM OR HER TO BE MY WILLING, WHOLEHEARTED EMERGENCY CONTACT. I WANTED THE PERSON WHO COULD SHOW UP, STAND UP, BE THERE WITH ME AND WITH LIFE. I WANTED TRUE BLUE. I ALSO WANTED A SELF-ENTERTAINING UNIT — SOMEONE WHO WAS ALSO SOULFULLY SINGLE AND COULD BE ALONE AND SELF-NOURISHING. I WANTED A PERSON WHO FELT GOOD ABOUT THEMSELVES AND ABOUT LIFE. I WANTED ANOTHER LIFE LOVER.

I WANTED A MATE — ONE FOR MY SOUL AND ONE FOR PLAY.

I WANTED SOMEONE WHO WOULD RESPECT AND ADMIRE MY SOULFULLY SINGLE SELF. I KNEW THAT BEING SOULFULLY SINGLE WASN'T SUBSTANDARD, BUT SOMETIMES INNER CRITICS WOULD RISE UP WHEN I WOULD SEE OR HEAR OTHER PEOPLE DESCRIBE IT DIFFERENTLY. I ATTENDED A FRIEND'S PARENTS' 50TH WEDDING ANNIVERSARY PARTY, AND AFTER ALL THE TOASTS AND EVEN A SHORT FILM ABOUT THEIR WONDERFUL UNION, THEY ASKED FOR PEOPLE TO STAND AND SHARE HOW THE COUPLE'S LOVE AND MARRIAGE HAD INFORMED THEIR LIVES.

A NUMBER OF WOMEN STOOD AND DESCRIBED THEMSELVES AS "STRAYS" WHO HAD BEEN TAKEN IN BY THIS LOVING COUPLE. I KNEW THEY WERE JUST SHARING THEIR EXPERIENCE, BUT I FELT ENRAGED THAT PERHAPS THAT'S HOW OTHERS HAD SEEN ME — AS A STRAY. AND OF COURSE MY INNER CRITICS WERE BUSY CONFIRMING THAT I WAS ONE. I RANTED AND RAVED TO MY FRIEND WHO WAS WITH ME, ABOUT WHAT I CALL THE "TYRANNY OF COUPLES," AND HOW UNFAIR IT SOMETIMES FEELS TO SINGLE PEOPLE. (SHE LOVES POINTING OUT THAT I MET JOHN TWO WEEKS LATER.)

BEING SOULFULLY SINGLE AND OPEN FOR LOVE FELT RIGHT FOR ME. OTHERS MAY JUST WISH TO BE SOULFULLY SINGLE — OR JUST SINGLE. I'M GLAD WE'RE ALL REDEFINING LOVE FOR OURSELVES AND WHAT FEELS BEST FOR EACH OF US.

Until I completed my classes in graduate school at age 28, I had spent most of my life single. I had been in and out of relationships but never lived with anyone for an extended period or settled down for a long-term experience. I started graduate school when I was 25, and at that time wanted to be in a deeper, more stable relationship. But in many ways I felt too insecure to be both in a relationship and in such a challenging PhD program.

I was born an only child in a devastated Germany two years after the end of the Second World War. Within a year, my parents amicably divorced, and my father was almost completely out of my life. When I was five, my mother had a chance to start a new life and left to go to America. I stayed behind in a boarding school until I was eight. Those were frightening years.

Leaving my friends and familiar surroundings in Ohio to go to graduate school in New York evoked some of those old fears. By today's standards, I was physically and emotionally abused in the boarding school, and the fear of authority that I developed there translated to fear of my professors later.

Up until that time, my love relationships, in part influenced by my childhood traumas, had been either relatively brief or "growth relationships." So, while I longed for a supportive emotional relationship, I didn't feel capable of handling my fears of the school authorities and of my not succeeding there, along with the difficulties I knew I would likely encounter in a relationship.

But I was able to make some wonderful friends, and by my third year I felt more secure and ready to explore a deeper partnership. However, I had a dilemma. I knew I would be leaving New York in less than a year. Did I want to start a relationship only to have to leave? Would I be able to find someone who would come with me? While I never made a clear decision, no one appeared in the city of seven million with whom I could start a long-term partnership. I felt a hesitancy, and every woman I met felt a hesitancy too.

At the end of my graduate school classes, I returned to my hometown of 5,000 in Ohio. Within two weeks I met someone with whom I would live and spend the next five years. When she decided to end the relationship, I met someone similar within three months, and we were together for 17 years.

I never felt that I was stuck being single or had to go to great lengths to find an available partner. Before graduate school, when I was alone I never doubted that I would find someone to be in a relationship with. And during graduate school I understood why no one appeared.

I also had the support of close friends and realized I didn't have to be in a partnership to have deep emotional bonds and support. For me, the struggles I had were not so much in finding a partner but in learning how to be the right partner. It wasn't until I was with Jeanie that I had the knowledge and skill to be in the kind of relationship I'm in now.

Awareness Practice:
Being Soulfully Single and Open for Love

We invite you to explore your relationship history and current situation in the following Awareness Practice. We've listed some questions and prompts for you to respond to. See what emerges as you answer. If you feel drawn to doing so, share your answers with others or add questions of your own. The objective is for you to increase your awareness of yourself in and out of the relationships in your life.

If you're currently single, begin here:

- Does the description of "Soulfully Single" resonate with you?
- If so, what appeals to you about it? If not, why not? Is there a description that fits you better?
- What does your relationship status mean to you?
- What do you love about being single?
- What is less desirable about being single?

    List ways that you love and care for yourself.
- Are there any ways you would like to be more loving to yourself?

If you're in a loving relationship with another person:

- What do you appreciate about being in this relationship?
- In what ways is it less than satisfying?
- How would you describe your relationship?
- What are some of your favorite qualities about your significant other?
- What does your significant other appreciate most about you?
- What self-loving practices do you do that nourish your relationship?
- What do the two of you do to support the relationship climate?
- In what ways do you celebrate and appreciate each other?
- In what ways could you celebrate and appreciate each other more?

You can reflect on your responses to these questions as you explore the processes for expansion and change throughout the book.

To explore and expand your relationship awareness go to: SucculentWildLove.com/Soulfully

4. The Possibilities And Tyrannies of Soulmates And Coupling

HEARTS in All Sorts of Positions

For years, I felt tyrannized by the whole idea of finding a "soulmate." It seemed impossible to me to find a mate for my soul — my soul being so vast and unknowable. I knew I wanted to be "met" and loved by someone with a soul, so why did I find it so seemingly impossible?

I now think the overachieving and perfectionist inner critic parts of me got hold of the concept and were tromping through, as inner critics do, assuring me that no soulmate ever existed who could possibly measure up to what I thought I wanted.

And what I thought I wanted was certainly unattainable — I didn't want "tall, dark, and handsome," I wanted deeply self-aware, compassionate, kind, sexy, funny, creative, abundant, emotionally intelligent, and brilliant. And of course adorable, endearing, wise, resilient, generative, and qualified to adore me!

But when I burrowed around inside myself further, I wasn't sure that my own soul was up to being mated. I felt like my soul might not be qualified.

I created a long list about who I thought my soulmate could be. I remember sharing it with a friend, and she read it and said, "You just sound really scared of love." And I reacted quite strongly and unexpectedly, "Well, of course I'm afraid of love — who wouldn't be?"

And she replied softly that she wasn't.

32

I began to examine why I was. I think I was as afraid of finding a soulmate as I was about not having one. It seemed to me that if I had a soulmate, they could trap me, hurt me, leave me, ignore me, or just not be quite right for me. Or bore me, which might even be worse.

I've learned that my greatest challenges occur in what I call the preliminaries — before I actually do something. So, I was raking through every possible scenario, looking for possible detriments before I'd even dated or met anyone. My younger brother, Andrew, commented that I was in love with the "idea of a relationship," rather than a real-life version. And at that time, I knew he was right.

Honestly, the whole soulmate thing felt so exhausting, I just wanted to sleep forever and avoid the subject. But it felt like everywhere I turned, there was another book or program or radio show about "finding a soulmate."

It felt like if I wasn't actively looking, I'd failed, and if I didn't find one, I'd really failed! And I felt like I'd already failed at "soulmate school."

My grade at soulmate school

D-

And "actively looking" always involved "getting out there," which is the opposite of what my shy, introverted, sometimes-afraid-of-love self wanted to do. As soon as my inner critics heard about me "getting out there," they became terrified of the concept — something new could happen, something even wonderfull, and then what would they do for work?

I decided that for me, the best plan was to become my own soulmate.

When I embarked on the whole journey of loving myself, even marrying myself and writing about it, I didn't quite realize that BECOMING my own soulmate was not the same as BEING one.

Becoming one was my entry decision point.

Being my own soulmate involved truly being with myself through every mood and feeling, deeply living daily life with myself and being that "soul met" person who I had thought I wanted to find — meeting and loving my own soul first before being with another person. I practiced romancing myself — slow dancing after dinner in my living room, writing love notes to myself on my window shade. I explored my shadows and dark thoughts, and learned how to love myself even when I couldn't stand myself.

Being my own soulmate showed me that I had the capacity to love myself deeply, to romance myself, to listen to and love myself "no matter what."

Being my own soulmate enabled me to be soulfully single.

I created self-care and love methods, and experimented on myself to be sure they worked in all the conditions that arise in being fully human. I knew I had a lot of feelings, so I created a system to care for them. I also knew I had a lot of inner critics, so I invented a system to transform my inner relationships with them. I created a system to activate and empower my Inner Wise Self to act on my behalf every day — in my inner and outer worlds.

I practiced with these three ways daily as I built my relationship with myself as my own soulmate. For many years, I sat with my multiple feelings, dialogued with the voices of inner critics, and received wisdom from my Inner Wise Self.

I didn't fully realize that by becoming and being my own soulmate, I was readying myself to create another soulmate to join with.

I'd always considered myself more of a "me" person than a "we" person. I felt like independence was my key to creativity and freedom, and that I could travel faster and better by myself. It wasn't that I didn't like or appreciate people, I just noticed that what I describe as "we" people are more vocal about and accustomed to being intimately involved with others than I was.

or JOHN with

I sometimes experienced "we" people as those who seemed more capable and qualified to love than I was, or more used or open to experiencing love with others than by or with themselves. It seemed clear that it was the "we" people who found soulmates, and that felt fine to my "me-defined" self.

I feel vulnerable writing about this — as though I'm the only one who has felt these things. I know I'm not, but there's a widespread societal pressure to love beyond all reason, or to view loving as the goal — as if loving a special someone is the reason for everything.

And that to be a "we" person is somehow "better" and having a romantic "soulmate" is the A on a grade scale, and anything less is, well, just that.

I even created a poster called "Loving Is the Whole Point" — which I heartily believe. (You can see it on page 264.) But it doesn't say that having romantic relationships or soulmates is the only way.

There IS No "only way"

That's part of my experience of the tyranny of soulmates. I think there are many misconceptions about what a soulmate actually is. Here's Wikipedia's definition: "A soulmate (or soul mate) is a person with whom one has a feeling of deep or natural affinity. This may involve similarity, love, romance, friendship, intimacy, sexuality, sexual activity, spirituality, or compatibility and trust." So when I open up the definition to include all kinds of soulmates, I feel no tyranny.

And when I was ready to join souls with another, I met John and found that I was fully qualified to be adored and to adore him. All the ways I became and am my own soulmate apply beautifully to sharing life and love with this person named John.

As I write these words now, on a writing retreat in Big Sur with John, I realize that he and I are so much more than I believed, predicted, or asked for. I didn't know that the union of two souls makes more than two. It creates not only a third entity but an infinite expansion of love.

When John and I first started teaching about Succulent Wild relationships, John wrote about how easy it really can be to allow a soulmate to manifest, and wrote humorously, "You can create your soulmate using simple household ingredients."

And I think that in a way, it's true — if you want a soulmate, you have within you all that it takes to create one. I don't think you "find" them — they're not lost.

From our experience, there are potentially many partners with whom you could have a relationship on a soulmate level — a Succulent Wild Love relationship. However, in our view, it isn't about hunting for them; it's about becoming such a person yourself.

SOME SOULMATE MYTHS

Here are some myths many people believe or have believed about soulmates. See if any resonate for you, and think about what new beliefs you might wish to develop.

⭐ *When I find my soulmate, we will automatically have a beautiful relationship. I will no longer need to do any soul-searching, and we will go happily off into the sunset and have perfect sex there.*

⭐ *My soulmate will fill me, entertain me, and support me, and I will spontaneously do the same for them.*

★ *Everything will be better once I have a soulmate.*

◉ *When I meet my soulmate, I'll be happy.*

★ *Any problems I have will vanish when I find my soulmate.*

◉ *My soulmate will be everything to me, and I to them. We will not need others.*

✳ *Having a soulmate means I've finally found real love.*

◉ *There is only one soulmate for me, and I have to find them.*

 ARE YOU SURE YOU WANT A SOULMATE OR TO BE PART OF A COUPLE?

You may have been told by well-meaning people that a lifelong partnership is the way to go. Yet there are many couples who don't seem very happy in their relationships (and often end them). So it's not surprising that people who want a life partner also frequently have doubts.

Many single people know that the emotional deficits marriage is supposed to cure, such as being lonely, bored, or insecure, can actually be made worse in a partnership. For example, being in a relationship with someone who is constantly traveling for business or off with friends can feel more lonely than being single. And few things are more boring than having to spend time with someone who no longer shares your interests. Having a partner who chronically gets into financial trouble can also feel much less secure than being independent.

Many of us have also seen partners fight, be emotionally distant, and stifle their feelings — hardly a good advertisement for coupling. And then there are the messages about having to compromise and losing your freedom.

There are a lot of reasons that might cause you to be hesitant about spending the rest of your life with someone, soulmate or otherwise. So if you've been looking for a soulmate and finding no one suitable, it would be a good idea to explore why you wouldn't want one. Admitting to and addressing your doubts can remove barriers that are actually keeping you from being open to sharing your life with a partner.

We will help you do that in this book. But there is one more consideration: is a marriage-style relationship really the best path for you? And we don't mean because you have "hang-ups," but simply because you have other ways to better express your life.

Many of humanity's greatest teachers — like Mother Teresa and Gandhi — have chosen lives where their focus was not on a deep relationship with one other person. Others, like Gloria Steinem or Jane Fonda, have a series of relationships and find that to be their right path.

We receive many messages from our parents and society telling us that it's better to marry. Some people find a middle ground. They may marry but then take jobs that require them to be away for much of the time. There is no single right way to be in a relationship.

For years, I did really well in long-distance love relationships, because I could have love but not feel smothered by another person. When I was with the person, I was in love and present, but looked forward to returning to my more singly focused life. As time went on, that path became less sustainable as I'd begun to desire being with someone full-time.

When I was in the 17-year relationship before I met Jeanie, for most of the time we lived apart from each other. It wasn't fully satisfying for either of us, but it gave both my partner and me freedom that we didn't know how to create when living in the same household.

Both of us have spent time being single and found this to be extremely valuable. We are in no way encouraging people to couple. But if you decide that coupling is right for you — or indeed, that participating in any relationship is right for you — we have tools that can make it more satisfying.

So even when all the barriers that might hold you back from joining a soulmate are resolved, you may choose simply to date, have a series of relationships, or put your energies into other creative endeavors.

Even when you know how to be in a partnership skillfully, a traditional, lifelong relationship may not be for you. Not only can you become skilled in participating lovingly in relationships, you can also create the kind that feel the best to you and your energy systems — even if it doesn't make "sense" to others.

And if you don't want to be in a partnership at all, you can release yourself from any kind of tyranny — inner or outer — that says you need one to be happy. Not everyone is made or meant to be in a romantic, conventionally thought of, marriage-style partnership.

Your relation·ship is yours to create

You Can Design a Relationship That Is Unique to You

Before I met Susan, she had arranged for a carpenter to build two queen-size beds in her bedroom, one directly above the other. One can think of them as elegant bunk beds for adults. When I first moved in, I wanted us to sleep in the same bed. In fact, I was embarrassed by the notion that we wouldn't. I remember showing a friend pictures of my new home and specifically not including a picture of our sleeping arrangements.

To me, sleeping in the same bed was a Love Symbol (see chapter 16). I believed that wanting to sleep in the same bed together was a demonstration of two people's intimacy and love for each other. We tried sleeping in the same bed for a couple of nights, but the queen-size felt too cramped for both of us. We also have different styles of going to sleep — Susan likes to watch TV and read; I just like to get in bed and turn off the light.

It turns out this bunk-bed arrangement is perfect for us. We can visit each other when we want to and not worry about disturbing the other when one of us wants to go to sleep. Sleeping this way is no longer a symbol of emotional distance for me.

Our relationship is unusual in other ways too. We live and work together in a relatively small two-bedroom apartment. Most couples wouldn't enjoy spending that much time sharing such a small space. It suits us, but we also have doors and methods that allow each of us to have privacy.

My workspace is in the kitchen/living room. So when I don't want to be disturbed, I put out a chair with the back toward the kitchen. (Susan has taken to turning the back toward me if she doesn't want me to talk business when she comes into the kitchen for a snack.)

Before I met Susan, it never occurred to me that I could modify the way I live in a marriage-style relationship in such unique ways. And if someone had told me about our living and sleeping arrangements, I'm certain I would have said that would be too strange for me. But Susan has always been a creative thinker. That not only includes the way she nurtured herself when she was single but extends to her partnering.

He's Like an angel sleeping Above me

SHAriNG A BED FOr sleeping never sounDED GOOD to Me. I'M A lUCID DreAMer AnD DO A lot OF CreAtive thinKiNG AnD

iMAGiNiNG in BED. WHen JOHn MOveD in, I WONDereD HOW tHis WOUlD WOrK. Since JOHn OFFereD A "no COMPrOMise" relAtiONsHiP, I DIDN'T HOlD BACK FrOM stAtiNG My Preferences to sleep sePArAtely. It Also HelPeD tHAt I HAD DesiGneD A queen BeD lOFt sPACe FOr two sleeping spots in tHe sAMe rOOM. I DreAM DeePly, CreAte Freely, love AviDly, AnD AM tHrilleD to HAve CreAteD sUCH A lUsCiOUs sleeping AnD WAKiNG liFe WitH JOHn.

In a Succulent Wild Love relationship you are free to explore and be in ways that suit you and your partner.

OUr eleGAnt ADUlt BUnK BeDs AnD My DrAWiNG On tHe WAll

Virginia Bell — Some Thoughts on Being Single

Virginia Bell

Every once in a while it hits me — the fact that I don't fit in. Anywhere. I'm not a wife or a mother. I'm not even divorced, which although not exactly a status symbol does have its own category and conveys the fact that one *was* married. In other words, none of the traditional labels apply to me. I'm not unhappy with my choices, but occasionally I do question them. Were they conscious decisions, or did I simply forget? Did I misplace my life, like a shoe or a book? Was I asleep at the wheel?

I've had lots of wonderful affairs, a couple of great loves, and a few long relationships. Children? I never even heard the biological clock ticking; it was always a nonissue. I've had marriage proposals, but marriage, or rather the institution itself, held no attraction. For me, the feeling was always more important than the form. When I was young I was always either in love, recovering from it, or searching for it. I think I was really searching for myself, but I didn't realize it at the time.

I began modeling as a teenager but never felt comfortable in that world, where I struggled with low self-esteem and a crippling eating disorder. Later I worked as an actress and dancer but hated the "business" of show business, the politics and power struggles. Up till then, everything I did was connected to a man. It was only after I started a restaurant and had something that was truly my own that I began to really find myself.

I've never taken the straight path or the main road, either professionally or personally. I've always chosen the detours, side roads, secret passages, back staircases. I've been an outsider who could move easily through many worlds but belong to none. In the end, my most important relationships have been with my friends, some of whom I've known for 30, 40, even 50 years. Along the way I've learned that there are many different kinds of relationships and many ways to be in the world.

So here I am at 71 and still single. Can you even call a woman in her 70s "single"? That term is more fitting for someone in their 20s or 30s. But nevertheless, here I am: single, stubborn, a lover of solitude and long walks, books, astrology, and writing — all self-contained and solitary pleasures. Although my life isn't perfect, I love what I do and how I've turned out.

In many ways everything has come together as I've gotten older and found my real calling (astrology and writing). I'm not the star I once dreamed I would be, but I'm also not the failure I feared I would become. The hard edges have softened; the drama and crises seem to have disappeared. All my mismatched qualities and crazy quirks have settled like a soufflé that is uniquely me. I feel more peaceful and content; perhaps not exactly happy, but healed, filled with enormous gratitude and a sense of grace. And although I may question my life from time to time, I embrace it.

Virginia is an astrologer, writer, and artist of life living in New York (VirginiaBellAstrology.com).

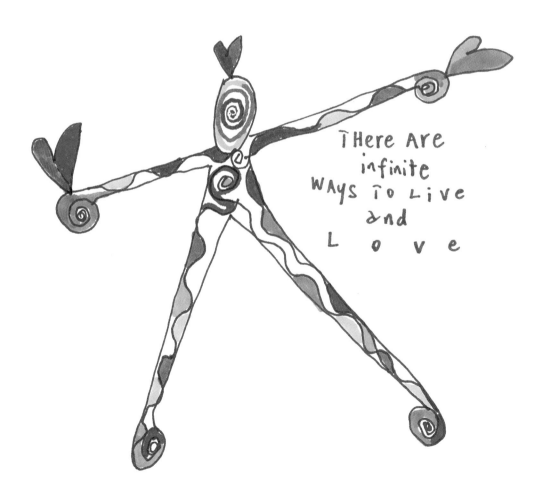

Awareness Practice: Soulmate Exploration

If you are currently single and interested in experiencing a soulmate/sole-mate relationship, start here:

1. List any reasons you're hesitant about being in a partnership, if you are. (Many of these will likely be addressed in the chapters that follow.)

2. Fill in these blanks if they fit for you:

   ☆ If I had a soulmate, I would need to _____.

   ★ I might not want to _____.

   ◉ I think I would enjoy _____.

   ✦ I definitely wouldn't like _____.

   ★ The kind of soulmates I've admired seem to have qualities like

   _____, _____, _____.

3. Ask yourself these questions:

   ☆ What would an ideal soulmate relationship look like on a day-to-day basis?

   ◉ What kinds of things would we do and not do together?

   ◉ In what ways do I imagine that this kind of relationship would benefit me in my life?

   ◉ In what ways am I my own soulmate now?

   ☆ What is my fantasy about having a soulmate?

   ★ What just sounds so good?

   ◉ Do I have any fears about having a soulmate?

   ◉ What doesn't sound good at all?

If you are currently in a relationship and would like to explore making changes for it to be even more satisfying, start here:

1. Ask yourself these questions:

   ☆ Are there any areas in my relationship that I'd like to be different — anything from sleeping arrangements to activities to how we manage our living environment?

- Are there areas that I've just kind of accepted as "how it is"?

- If you've identified any areas for change, ask yourself: In what ways could I change by myself — without my partner needing to do anything — to make the conditions more desirable for me?

- How does my partner completely or partially satisfy me? (List the ways.)

- What new things could I explore or try with my partner, going *beyond* "date night"?

- What *new* activities or ways to be together intrigue me? (These could be as simple as taking a class together, trying a new kind of sport, or having a deep, revealing talk about your desires and fears.)

- If your relationship is generally satisfying, ask yourself: What small adjustments would make it even *more* satisfying?

2. Your primary long-term relationship is with yourself. No matter how much you love or are loved by your partner, nothing will replace you loving you. With that in mind, ask yourself these questions:

- What changes within myself might I like to make?

  What would I like more of?

- Less of?

- In what ways do I speak to myself kindly?

- In what ways do I nourish *me*?

For more support & inspiration about what kind of relationship you'd like to create or re-create, go to:
SucculentWildLove.com/Soulmate

5. Longing For A Great Love: SARK's Covert Love Operation

First Loves Are Sometimes Animals

I think my first great love besides my family was at age 10 when a curly red-haired dog named Punky entered my life. Looking into his soft brown eyes, I consistently experienced a universe of love. I swooned over feeling unconditionally loved. I passionately hugged and kissed him and told him all my stories and secrets. I read books to him and fell asleep with my hand on his fur. I cried tears onto his neck and put doll bonnets on him. I felt love flowing consistently between us.

When I met my first boyfriend, Michael, at 16, I knew that my love universe had expanded in significant new ways, especially since he was a human being and our relationship included loveMAKING.

It also included "going steady" and attending the same school and wearing matching outfits on Fridays. My dress was a short, navy-blue velour with wooden buttons. His outfit was a navy-blue velour shirt with jeans. We walked to school together, holding hands.

This felt like the kind of great love I'd read and dreamed about. Michael was my best friend, my lover, my life adventure partner. I felt like I was living in my own love story.

GIVING UP ON FINDING GREAT LOVE

There was a significant plot twist when I found out that he'd been sleeping with other girls for much of the time we'd been together.

I reacted with hurt and anger, and he was sympathetic but told me that he wasn't ever going to be monogamous. I then made a decision to not ever be in that position again.

I decided I wouldn't be monogamous either. I would just sleep with whomever I wanted and give up on my ideas about great love. I couldn't see how to explore or expand my vision of great love and what I really wanted it to include.

My father had always said I was "too smart to get married," and even though I didn't fully understand what he meant, I knew that a loving, marriage-style relationship could compromise my ability to be separate, independent, and as smart as I actually was.

And that set the stage for decades of love relationships as a kind of adventure. I chose lovers along the way and experimented with all sorts of ages and lifestyles, ranging from a 65-year-old multimillionaire when I was 18 to a female lover 23 years younger than me when I was 55. I also explored and experienced having lovers from other cultures — any culture that was different from mine.

As an adult woman, I joined the throngs of other women who said there are no good men — or not enough good men — out there, and then found the evidence to prove it. I didn't find any good men either, so it seemed that they were right.

Certainly not succulent wild men. I knew that if I was to be in a happy long-term relationship with another person, and if it was going to be a man person, I wanted one of those. And a succulent wild man was probably as rare as anything I could imagine. I wanted a self-loving, soulfully masculine man who could navigate the feminine and masculine realms and not try to change me — but rather celebrate my succulent wildness and join me with his own.

As I grew older, it seemed to be even truer that the type of man I wanted didn't exist. Also, as a bestselling author, the ones I did meet often wanted me to advise them about marketing or selling their books, or seemed to be intimidated by

A rare succulent WILD MAN
Not so rare

MY STRENGTH AND OUTSPOKENNESS. I SEE IN RETROSPECT THAT MY FEARS ABOUT LOVE HAD CAUSED ME TO KEEP FINDING THE ONES WHO WERE AS AFRAID OF LOVE AS I WAS.

I EVEN WROTE A FULL PAGE "PERSONAL AD" IN MY BOOK PROSPERITY PIE, DESCRIBING WHO I WANTED TO FIND OR MEET. WHEN I SHARED IT WITH PEOPLE, THEY QUICKLY TOLD ME THAT IT WAS PROBABLY IMPOSSIBLE. I NEVER RECEIVED A RESPONSE TO THAT PAGE IN MY BOOK AND USED THIS AS FURTHER EVIDENCE ABOUT THE SCARCITY OF THESE GOOD MEN.

I READ THE STATISTICS ABOUT OLDER WOMEN HAVING AS MUCH CHANCE OF BEING MARRIED AS BEING STRUCK BY LIGHTNING. SINCE I'D NEVER BEEN STRUCK BY LIGHTNING OR EVEN DREAMED OF MARRIAGE AS A YOUNG GIRL, IT SEEMED FINE TO ME TO NEVER GET MARRIED.

WHEN I WAS 40, I MET A MAN WHO WAS RAISED IN THE SAME STATE AS ME — MINNESOTA — AND WE SPENT FIVE YEARS IN A "NORMAL" MONOGAMOUS RELATIONSHIP. MY MOTHER LOVED HIM TOO. THEY HAD SIMILAR RELIGIOUS AND POLITICAL BELIEFS, AND HE AND I HAD SIMILAR CREATIVE BELIEFS. HE WAS ALSO AN AUTHOR AND ARTIST WHO WAS FULFILLING HIMSELF CREATIVELY AND PERSONALLY, BUT IT NEVER PROGRESSED TO MARRIAGE OR EVEN LIVING TOGETHER.

AND IT WASN'T JUST HIM, IT WAS ME TOO. I HAD A LIST OF WAYS THAT OUR RELATIONSHIP SHOULD CHANGE FOR ME TO FEEL HAPPIER. I DIDN'T KNOW THEN THAT I COULD CHANGE AND JUST BE HAPPIER. WE WENT TO THERAPY TOGETHER AND, WITH HIS PERMISSION, I WROTE ABOUT OUR RELATIONSHIP IN MY PREVIOUS BOOKS IN CHAPTERS TITLED "FEAR OF BEING TOO MUCH," "THE GOOD GIRLFRIEND MUST DIE," AND "BRAMBLES OF INTIMACY." EVENTUALLY, WE BOTH FELT THAT IT WAS JUST TOO MUCH WORK TO CONTINUE TRYING TO BE A HAPPY COUPLE, AND WE PARTED AS FRIENDS.

BOTH WITH MY FIRST BOYFRIEND AT 16 AND IN THIS RELATIONSHIP, I WAS ABLE TO ESTABLISH A NEW FRIENDSHIP WITH EACH, LONG AFTER THE LOVE RELATIONSHIPS HAD CONCLUDED. THIS DEFINITELY EXPANDED MY DEFINITION OF LOVE AND WHAT IT COULD INCLUDE.

I DREAMED ABOUT A GREAT LOVE

I PERIODICALLY THOUGHT OR DREAMED ABOUT HAVING A GREAT LOVE, BUT MOSTLY DISMISSED IT AS AN IMPOSSIBLE DREAM — FOR ME.

I THEN SPENT A DECADE LEARNING ABOUT AND PRACTICING BEING MY OWN GREAT LOVE — MY OWN SOULMATE. I MARRIED MYSELF IN 1997 AND PROMISED TO NEVER LEAVE ME.

AS I MENTIONED IN THE CHAPTER ON THE POSSIBILITIES AND TYRANNIES OF soulmates, I created ways to be with and care for my feelings, care for and transform my experiences of my inner critics, and connect deeply and daily with my Inner Wise Self. and sometimes I didn't do any of this

HAVing these three methods solidly in place, I was ready to create a new kind of love relationship, and I found it with a woman who shared my self-loving ways and taste for life adventures. We spent a happy year and a half before realizing that our differences in age and the ways we actually lived our lives were too significant for our relationship to grow into the kind of great love I'd longed for.

My vision for having a loving partner broke, and I lost hope (again).

When that relationship ended by positive mutual agreement, I hung up my "relationship tap shoes" and then sunk into a kind of despair that seemed rather like what I'd heard midlife crises were. I cried a lot and felt certain that I'd be alone forever. I began admitting to myself that I'd always felt alone and had in fact arranged my life that way.

I then returned even more to my solo life, self-love, and exquisite self-care practices and devoted myself to teaching and mentoring others to do the same. This lifestyle didn't include the great love with another person that I longed for, but I couldn't really see how to do that without making major changes, so I continued with myself as my great love.

HOPE LEAPS UP

I knew there was more for me to explore about romantic love with another person and wasn't sure what to do next. I began experiencing a kind of existential love crisis, wondering at age 57 what kind of great love I could possibly allow in. This state led to depression and despair, because I didn't really want to live the rest of my life alone, yet it appeared that I was headed that way. During that time, I took a lot of long, contemplative hikes and sometimes cried in my bed at night.

I then really began taking a deep look at why I wasn't allowing a "great love" with someone besides myself to enter my life. In all my many explorations of this topic, I felt myself to be unqualified for this kind of love.

That year, I attended a "Being Single By Choice" weekend class at the Esalen Institute in Big Sur. I sat in a circle with a group of other single people, exploring why and how we chose to be single. I had realized by then that this was a choice I was making — it wasn't something that had just "happened" to me.

Shortly before attending this class, I'd seen a cartoon greeting card with a drawing of a woman sitting on a bus bench holding a leash attached to a small dog. Only, the woman and the dog were both skeletons, and the caption underneath read: "Waiting for the perfect man."

Terrified Me

The drawing terrified me, because I knew that my sometimes controlling and perfectionistic ways could prevent me from being able to experience a great love in my life. I knew that I could or would just keep eliminating love relationships based on my fears.

When the class at Esalen started, I looked up to see that one of the group leaders running the class was wearing a t-shirt with that cartoon on it! I felt scared and excited at the same time — scared that I would be "found out" and excited that I would be "found out."

The group leaders then distributed cards from Carl Jung's therapy work for us to randomly draw from. These cards had images and no words, and we were to pick a partner and then take a card, and in pairs puzzle over what our cards meant to each of us.

The practice of picking a partner in groups almost always scares parts of me that are sure I'll either not be picked, be picked by someone I don't want to partner with, or I'll pick the wrong person altogether and spend the whole session resenting them.

In this case, there was one man in the entire group I was attracted to, and I felt certain that he wouldn't pick me. When the choosing process began, I tried to hide in a corner, and looked up to see the attractive man headed my way! This was worse than I'd feared, because now I was convinced I'd be so busy trying to manage the impression I made on him that I wouldn't be able to learn anything.

My heart was pounding as we drew our cards. My card image was of a giant iridescent fish lying on a dock. This made no sense at all to me. My partner took the time to ponder with me, and even gave me some of his allotted time to talk gently with me about it.

I saw how much my fears and anxieties had blocked me from experiencing love, and felt like the card represented how much I felt like a "fish out of water" with love, especially as it related to other people.

My Fish on the Dock Card

He and I went on one date after the workshop, and it didn't go further than that. He certainly wasn't a great love — for me. But he had helped me to alter my beliefs and repetitive stories about men and how they behaved in love. Having his kind and focused attention during the workshop, and the deep conversations we'd had, showed me that men were not only capable of loving and expressing emotions, but that I was capable of receiving them.

SEEING NEW SUCCULENT POSSIBILITIES

My longing for a great love wasn't going away — in fact, it appeared to be growing. I began taking online courses and reading books about the subject. I asked friends to "love-mentor" me by listening to my longing and asking me questions about my love beliefs.

I started acknowledging that being alone was a choice I'd made and kept making. I also saw the gifts in it — that I'd learned to be self-loving and independent, having no "need" for a relationship. I wrote a lot about the gifts of solitude rather than loneliness, about traveling and going out alone. I reveled in my own company and used the significant self-care systems that we share with you in this book.

There are so many wonder-full gifts in being SOULFULLY SINGLE

These self-love and -care systems resulted in my becoming truly, madly, and deeply in love with myself. I began saying how in love with myself I felt, and began sharing that love. I lived like "a full cup of self-love, sharing the overflow with the world," and when I felt half empty, which was multiple times in a day, I used my self-care systems to fill myself back up from the inside — the way a succulent plant does.

I had worked on my book GLAD NO MATTER WHAT: TRANSFORMING LOSS AND CHANGE INTO GIFT AND OPPORTUNITY throughout my breakup with the fun woman and detailed my grieving process as it led to an expanded self-love experience. I realized that it was really more of a breakthrough than a breakup.

Break Down To Break Up To Break Through

My previous relationships were good and provided necessary opportunities for growth. I'd left them because I had lists about what was wrong and should change, and was blaming the other person instead of doing the inner work to change my responses. I'd also strategically chosen people I could leave with "good reasons."

I then started facing some of my deeper emotional issues resulting from early-childhood abuses. I had done earlier work, and my love relationships later in my life had uncovered more.

For example, I started transforming my relationship with emotions and food, using my Inner Feelings and Inner Critic care systems. I started deeply looking into why I soothed myself and sedated my feelings by eating. With the support of my Inner Wise Self, I began to lose weight in a new kind of way — joyfully, without depriving myself or measuring quantities.

I felt my feelings, expressed them, and learned to do this daily — and felt better more often. I learned to transform my relationship to the inner critics who told me in multiple ways that I wasn't lovable, that I'd always be alone. I activated and empowered my Inner Wise Self to help me identify what I'd always wanted — to love and be loved.

I started tenderly looking at my anxieties and fears and stopped comparing myself to how other people did their love relationships when it made me think negatively about myself by awakening my inner critics.

I spent time with nourishing, uplifting people, and if people had different experiences of love or negative messages about love, I chose not to hear them. Or I ran wildly away from them, plugging my ears

I embarked on a mission to clean up and transform my past love experiences. I wrote stories about how I thought it had actually been, and then wrote a new story about how I wished it had been. I then wrote a third, totally new story that was a blend of "facts" and wishes and decided to focus on that story going forward.

I did my Feelings, Inner Critic, and Inner Wise Self practices all along the way. The stories and messages I told myself about love were really changing. If someone said, "There aren't enough good men out there," instead of, or in some cases in addition to, resisting them or reacting to their belief, I questioned it in myself.

It turned out that I believed it too and had kept creating the "evidence" that there wasn't one for me by sharing my experiences of the scarcity of men "out there." I then began my "covert operation" to find romantic love — sharing with a few close friends my desire to find someone to love who would also love me.

When I began speaking about my desire, I felt certain that I'd be "struck down" in some way for daring to want this. Throughout all my life and successes, this was the one thing I was sure would be denied to me — even though my close friends said that love was not only possible, it was everywhere. I felt like a huge unqualified misfit. My friends said that I could have love if I really wanted it and was willing to change my belief systems that kept telling me I couldn't or wouldn't be able to have it.

I read books about relationships and learned about the many reasons I didn't have one. These books confirmed what I already knew — that I was an independent, strong woman who didn't really need a relationship. They didn't address my wanting one, but then again, I was in a covert operation.

I started out covertly because I felt ashamed of my desire and fairly certain that I was too flawed or wounded for someone to truly love me. I didn't want people pitying me, or worse, turning me into a "project" to be fixed.

**I didn't want people to say,
"Look at that poor single woman"**

So I continued my self-love practices and expanded my covert operation to include finding reliable "love mentors" to advise me. These love mentors were friends who I trusted not to pity me or turn me into their project but instead tell me what they saw in me that was lovable and why they believed I could have the love relationship of my dreams.

I also started noticing happy couples who had a mature kind of love that had always felt so out of reach for me. I began "trying on" what that kind of love might feel like for me and interviewed these couples informally and ongoingly about their love relationships.

I continued exploring by reading books about finding a soulmate. The concept of a "soulmate" had always annoyed me, since I'd never believed that there was only one person to be found in all the world who would fit me perfectly. The idea of a "twin flame" was even worse. I dismissed these concepts, even though I secretly wanted to have a soulmate. My version of a soulmate was someone who would share their soul and witness mine, someone to love and adore who would also love and adore me.

I decided that my version of a soulmate could also be spelled "sole-mate," and that to me, it represented the best of being single, along with the best of being in a relationship.

I began exploring the idea of having my Inner Wise Self communicate with the Inner Wise Self of my unknown sole-mate. My friends Joshua and Gina introduced me to their version of this concept, and I was able to tell them later that I had successfully applied it. I visualized this imaginary person and "spoke" to their Inner Wise Self with what I perceived to be my Inner Wise Self. I felt at times like I was making up the whole thing, and I did it anyway and had some rather incredible psychic experiences, receiving what seemed to be messages from my yet-to-be lover. I wrote a note one night in my journal asking my Inner Wise Self to further inform me in a dream about what type of lover would be good for me. Here's what I received:

Thank good ness for people who can act as love mentors

and it reminded me also of a happy shoe

excerpt from my april 2011 journal:

From my dream — meeting my soulmate and what it would feel like — and this gentle man appeared. Being with him felt warm, welcoming, supportive, easy, kind, sheltering, vulnerable, real. When I asked him what he did for a living, he said, "I'm a living attendant." He kept his hand on the small of my back and it felt so supportive. He felt like a good, quiet guy. I asked him what sign he was, and he laughed and replied, "I'm the sign of love." This man felt like someone I could travel through life with.

I started taking a new online course to find my sole-mate. I felt horrified at the amount of work that it seemed to be — to untangle years of false beliefs and ways I'd made sure not to find or have love.

I barely attended the complex online class. I felt afraid of exposure — that someone would recognize me as my public author self and pity me. I'd written about everything BUT love. How would it look if I was in a course trying to find love and failing at the course?

The one section in the program I responded to was about clearing out my past beliefs and experiences about romantic relationships. I had a lot of these, and I like clearing clutter, so I began the process of writing out every grudge, withheld feeling, and belief.

This process took nearly a year. (I had a LOT of grudges ;-)

Then I tried online dating.

And that's how I found him!

Just kidding.

MAYBE IT'S BETTER FOR ME TO BE ALONE

As I signed up for every dating site and answered hundreds of questions about my passions, interests, hobbies, and beliefs, it actually felt satisfying to see that there really were not very many men that suited me, or me them. It reminded me of that time in my life when I was having hundreds of jobs. I took a test to see if I could become a librarian. The results came back that I was singularly the worst, most ill-suited person ever to work at a library. This online dating felt like that.

I actually never went on a date.

I just kept eliminating them, or they me.

My very wise younger brother, Andrew, told me, "You're in love with the idea of dating. An actual person would likely horrify you." Oh, god. It felt so true. Actual people horrified me with their needs and desires and beliefs and just their humanity. I horrified myself with the same. Clearly I was remarkably unsuited to love or be loved.

I decided it was best that I'd married myself in 1997 and staying married to just myself was the best path. I figured I should just learn to accept that this was enough for me and began searching for ways to support myself as a self-loving single person. I started ranting out loud about couples and how I experienced them as being a kind of "cult," with their own language, system, and ways. I decided to identify completely with being single. I would reject the system of being a couple, as I felt that it had rejected me.

Inner Wise Self to the Rescue

I found a group online called "A Conscious Singles Wisdom Circle" and looked up the location of the closest group. It was over an hour away, and I made a plan to attend a meeting anyway.

On the appointed evening, I tried everything to get out of it, nearly convincing myself of the hopelessness of the whole thing.

As I parked my car near the meeting place, my inner critics had begun not only a chorus but an entire symphony about why it couldn't, wouldn't, and would never work for me to find love with another person.

"Maybe I really should just become a better person first," I thought.

I began thinking I should just go to a movie or drive back home, and then remembered my Inner Wise Self and how I could ask it to

ACT ON MY BEHALF. THIS SEEMED LIKE A GOOD TIME TO ASK, ALTHOUGH I DIDN'T THINK THAT MUCH WOULD HAPPEN FROM THE ASKING.

My Inner Wise Self directed me to go get ice cream. Hey! Was this really My Inner Wise Self or just the emotional eater in me trying to sedate My feelings of overwhelm, hopelessness, panic, And fear?

I decided it didn't matter and got an ice cream cone and sat on a bench. As I licked My cone, I asked My Inner Wise Self for more guidance, saying sarcastically, "Well, Inner Wise Self, what have you really got for me NOW??"

It replied, "WATCH THIS."

As I WATCHED, the scoop fell off My cone and onto the wooden arm of the bench.

WILD ICE CREAM

I stared at the mess and shook My head at My thinking that any Inner Wise Self could actually help me at a time when I actually needed it.

I said again, sarcastically, "Okay, Inner Wise Self, how are you going to help me now?"

And My Inner Wise Self responded stoutly, "Life is messy as well as sweet. Allowing love in will be too. You can go home or go to a movie, or do something new. It's entirely up to you."

Shit. My Inner Wise Self knows stuff AND rhymes.

I reluctantly got off the bench and walked to the conscious singles wisdom meeting and took my place in the circle. People were nice to me, and I resolved to just quietly experiment with being there for this one time. I had wondered if it would be all women and was glad to see about 50 percent men. I'd also wondered if there would be any men that would be for me.

And THAT'S where I met My soulmate.

SUCCULENT WILD MEN ARE OUT THERE

JUST KIDDING.

THAT'S WHERE I discovered that there are succulent wild women AND men, doing deep consciousness work about loving and being loved. That night, I witnessed a man doing some of the deepest, most vulnerable work I'd ever seen, and I became aware that it was time to shift My beliefs to see and include succulent, self-loving men in My world.

I sat in that conscious singles wisdom circle a few times a month,

And a significant turning point came about nine months later, when I made my covert operation overt by saying out loud in a small group,

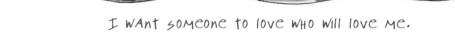

I want someone to love who will love me.

I wanted my own person to love and maybe live with! This felt truly revolutionary for me, since I'd never lived with a romantic partner and had doubted that I ever would.

Before saying this, I started sweating and shaking. After saying it, I felt shaky and ecstatic. I called all my covert operation love mentors to share the news. They all applauded my courage and encouraged me to keep going.

I felt complete with the circle then and said goodbye to the kind people who had helped me birth my desire, and the group dissolved soon after.

MY VISION BECOMES CLEAR AND SOLID

During this time, my conscious connection with my Inner Wise Self had expanded tremendously, and I was now teaching this ability to other people, along with the other two systems I practiced every day. I called these the Three I's — or the Three Eyes, depending on my mood.

I now absolutely knew that this foundation would allow me to manifest love with another person.

I now knew WHY I wanted it. I wanted it because I felt full of love and life to share, and wanted to do that. I had desires for love that I'd tried to deny, and it felt fantastic to let them out. I still didn't know HOW this could possibly happen.

The 3 eyes

Around the same time, my friend Edward and I had started watching a reality TV show together called THE MILLIONAIRE MATCHMAKER. Patti, the host, matches her millionaire clients with prospective people to date and asks them to list their five "non-negotiables," with love and

CHEMISTRY BEING A GIVEN. OVER THE COURSE OF A YEAR, EDWARD HELPED ME TO HONE MINE, CHALLENGING ME TO GET MORE AND MORE SPECIFIC AND BE ABLE TO SPEAK COGENTLY ABOUT THEM. MINE WERE (AND STILL ARE):

- SIMILAR WORLDVIEW
- EMOTIONALLY INTELLIGENT
- SUCCESSFULL AND PASSIONATE IN THEIR OWN REALM
- ECCENTRIC, CREATIVE
- ALLOWS AND RESPECTS MY AUTONOMY

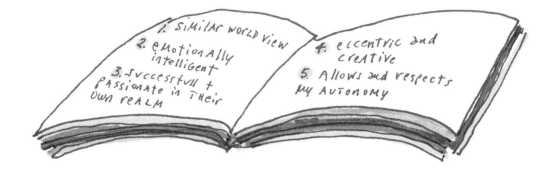

AND THAT'S WHEN I MET MY SOULMATE. STILL JUST KIDDING, BUT NOT TOTALLY.

I THEN WENT ON A METAPHYSICAL SEMINAR CRUISE TO ALASKA WITH EDWARD AND OUR FRIEND PHILIP. I'D BEEN TO ALASKA A NUMBER OF TIMES AND WAS REALLY OCCUPIED WITH MY BUSINESS, SO WAS NOT SURE I SHOULD GO. ABRAHAM-HICKS IS A METAPHYSICAL DISCOVERY SYSTEM ABOUT CREATING YOUR REALITY THAT I'D STUDIED SINCE THE '80S, SO I KNEW THERE WOULD BE TREMENDOUS BENEFIT WHETHER I MET SOMEONE ON THE CRUISE OR NOT. I'D BEEN ON NUMEROUS ABRAHAM CRUISES AND NEVER MET SOMEONE BEFORE, AND SINCE I WAS STILL IN SOMEWHAT OF A COVERT OPERATION, ONLY MY LOVE-MENTOR FRIENDS KNEW THAT I WAS LOOKING.

AND THAT IS WHEN I MET HIM.
AND IT'S WHERE I MET MYSELF FULLY, READY TO MEET HIM.

I want to be clear that you don't need to do any of the things I've described in order to find love. If you desire a sole-mate, locate that desire inside and ask your Inner Wise Self for guidance about how, where, and whether to allow them into your life.

As we wrote about in the previous chapter, I believe there's something quite active in our culture that I call the "tyranny of soulmates."

It's this idea that we're incomplete without a romantic partner, that if you haven't found one yet, something is probably wrong with you.

And if you're not actively looking, something is really wrong with you.

Not everyone is ready for, or suited to, romantic love with one person.

For example, polyamorous relationships — the philosophy or state of being in love or romantically involved with more than one person at the same time — is a great option for some. I believe in it in theory and am not personally drawn to do it in practice. I do heartily celebrate my polyamorous friends.

John at 16, and my inner 16-year-old has a mad crush on him!

Being consciously and soulfully single is another choice, and one I made for many happy years.

Living happily apart, in relationship with another, is another of the many loving choices we can make.

I now see that my "covert operation" was what I needed to feel safe enough to admit my desire to myself, and then to others. Loving another person fully in a romantic way was not easy for me to approach.

Now that I'm happily living with my succulent wild man, John, I can say that my love for myself enabled me to truly love him, and continue to love him and myself.

Awareness Practice: If You're Longing for a Great Love and Want to Create It (or Deepen the Love You Have)

1. As you read my story above, did you note any areas you relate to? If so, write them down. You can use these notes to develop a plan to create more love for yourself.

2. Do you tell any old negative stories about love and relationships in your life? Most people do this without realizing it. If so, list one or more. You can also use parts of stories and sentences that others have told you and that you believed. For example, my father telling me that I was "too smart for marriage" led to my devaluing myself and marriage!

3. Stop repeating the negative story or stories. This sounds obvious, but many people have iconic negative love and relationship stories that get told and retold so often, and always get reactions of sympathy or maybe even shock, which can become negatively reinforcing.

    When you tell a negative story, your body experiences the same emotions and hormones as though it just happened, even though it may have happened years ago. You'll be flooded with the same or similar feelings that you felt back then. I used to feel so sad and betrayed every time I told that story about my first boyfriend.

    People also sympathize, give extra kinds of attention, commiserate, or relate — saying things like, "Me too! I understand — what a jerk. They're all jerks." People will hear your stories and see you the way you tell them, which in many instances reinforces the ways you don't want to be seen. I found out that my early love betrayal story guaranteed that I'd get sympathy and not be held accountable to live a new kind of love story. I could effectively "hide out" from love by repeating that story.

4. IF YOU HAVE ANY NEGATIVE love AND relATIONSHIP STORIES, SEE IF YOU CAN BEGIN TO CreATE A NEW STORY or STORIES FOR YOURSELF. DO THIS BY EXPERIMENTING WITH "THE FACTS." FOR EXAMPLE, MY FIRST BOYFRIEND SlEPT WITH OTHER GirlS WHILE HE WAS WITH ME. THAT'S A FACT. THE WAY I CHOOSE TO reCAll THE experience NOW IS TOTAlly UP TO ME.

5. PrACTICE CreATING YOUR NEW STORY. YOU CAN Fill IN THE BlANKS, BUT YOU'll PrOBABly WANT TO USE A SEPArATE SHEET OF PAPER.

The fact is _____.

MY BOYFRIEND SlEPT WITH OTHER GirlS WHILE WE WERE TOGETHER WHEN I WAS 16.

As a result, _____.

I FElT HURT, BETrAYED, AND ANGry. I MADE CHOICES TO NEVER BE HURT liKE THAT AGAIN.

How could I have behaved? _____

I COULD HAVE SHArED MY HURT AND ANGER AND GOTTEN SOME HELP SO THAT I COULD FEEl BETTER.

How might that have shifted things? _____

I MIGHT NOT HAVE ACTED OUT IN THE WAYS THAT I DID, FOR AS MANY YEArS AS I DID.

What might I have been doing or thinking that contributed to the situation?
_____

I NEVER WANTED TO HEAr UNPlEASANT THINGS. AFTER BEING ABUSED IN MY FAMILY, I DEVElOPED SENSITIVITIES AND FEArS THAT FElT IMMENSE.

How could I see the situation differently? _____

MICHAEL WAS A SWEET YOUNG BOY WHO TRULY LOVED ME TO THE BEST OF HIS ABILITIES. HE TRIED TO PROTECT ME FROM HIS BEHAVIOR WITH OTHER GIRLS BY KEEPING IT SECRET. HE THOUGHT HE COULD GET AWAY WITH IT AND DIDN'T UNDERSTAND HOW HURT I WOULD BE. MY HURT WAS OUT OF PROPORTION IN SOME WAYS BECAUSE OF THE ABUSE I HAD EXPERIENCED. MY EXPERIENCE OF HIS BETRAYAL MATCHED HOW BETRAYED I FELT IN MY FAMILY.

How might I tell the story now?

WHEN I WAS 16, I WAS MADLY IN LOVE WITH A BOY NAMED MICHAEL, WHO TOOK ME ON MOTORCYCLE ADVENTURES, WAS EXTREMELY KIND AND LOVING TO MY BABY BROTHER, AND HAD A BACKPACK DESIGNED FOR ME OUT OF COLORFUL LEATHER. HE WAS MY FIRST LOVER AND MY BEST FRIEND.

RIGHT BEFORE HE GRADUATED FROM HIGH SCHOOL, I FOUND OUT THAT HE'D SLEPT WITH OTHER GIRLS, AND IT REALLY HURT. I WENT OFF TRACK FOR A WHILE, RECOVERING FROM WHAT HAPPENED. SOME YEARS LATER, WE WERE ABLE TO BECOME FRIENDS, AND I INTRODUCED HIM TO HIS WIFE, AND THEY HAD A DAUGHTER TOGETHER. BY THEN I'D BEEN ABLE TO TAKE 100 PERCENT RESPONSIBILITY FOR MY LIFE AND BEHAVIOR, TOTALLY FORGIVEN MICHAEL, AND MOVED ON COMPLETELY FROM THAT EXPERIENCE. WHEN HE DIED, WE WERE FRIENDS AND I HAD NO REGRETS.

6. TELL YOUR NEW STORY TO SOMEONE.

SAYING it out loud is power-full

7. TELL AND SHARE THE STORIES YOU WANT TO LIVE. THIS DOESN'T MEAN IGNORING OR DENYING THINGS THAT HAVE HAPPENED OR HOW THEY AFFECTED YOU — DO YOUR INNER FEELINGS CARE SYSTEM ABOUT THEM IF NEEDED (SEE CHAPTER 8). IT MEANS MOVING ON AND BEING WILLING TO LIVE THE LOVE STORY YOU WANT TO BE IN.

8. ACT "AS IF" WITH YOUR STORIES — TELLING A VERSION THAT MOST PLEASES YOU. YOUR STORIES CAN SUPPORT YOUR HAVING THE LOVE YOU WANT. YOU CAN DESCRIBE SOMEONE GIVING YOU THE APOLOGY YOU WISH YOU

COULD HAVE. YOU CAN tell A story THAT Gives you closure. YOUr BODY DOeSn't KNOW or CAre if it's "true." It only KNOWS HOW you Feel. THe iDeA is to write something THAT Feels Genuinely POSSiBle. Stretch JUSt A Bit BeyonD WHere you USUAlly Go. IF you Go too FAr, it will stArt to Feel PHony — THAt's OKAy, JUSt tAKe it BACK A little until it Feels POSSiBle AGAin.

For exAMPle, Here's My new ACting As-iF — WHAt I wisHeD CoulD HAve HAPPeneD witH MicHAel, stArting right BeFore His GrADUAtion FroM HiGH scHool:

My enDeAring First love, MicHAel, AnD Me

He sHAreD tHAt wHile He loveD Me, He DiDn't wAnt to Be MonoGAMOUS AnyMore, AnD AsKeD iF we coulD Attend counseling toGetHer so I coulD Fully unDerstAnD His new PersPective. We FounD A FABUlouS tHerAPist, AnD AFter My initiAl uPset, sePArAteD so lovingly, I never Felt ABAnDoneD or BetrAyeD. He AnD I BeCAMe tHe DeePest AnD DeArest FrienDs AnD reMAineD so For MAny yeArs. WHile He wAs ill AnD BeFore He DieD, we reneweD our DeeP love For eAcH otHer AnD BAsKeD in tHe Glow oF tHAt love.

If you want more practice in changing your stories, go to:
SucculentWildLove.com/MyStory

Valerie Tate — Love, Connection, and Relationship

Valerie Tate

I am a romantic and love to be in love, blindly and experientially. This blind faith has allowed me into the depths of it. Sometimes I am swimming, at times drowning, and then rising to the surface with wisdom grooves to live by. Again and again.

In my 41 years of long-term relationships and romantic life, I have awakened to some naked truths about relational life, love, and connection.

I have come to realize the need to separate the experiences of *love*, *connection*, and *relationship*. Why?

Falling in love with another is God's gift. We are awakened to our highest level of being and behaving when in love. It's God's flashlight to show what our individual potential is. In my early relationships I believed that this love only existed with another person.

During one major breakup, deep in the grief, on my knees in prayer, I asked God to show me true love within myself without another to reflect this to me. What happened was a miracle. For nine months I experienced an "in-love state" that was not subject to circumstances. On a daily basis I felt in love with everyone and everything, no matter if I was dating, getting attention, or receiving a specific kind of care. Even cleaning my toilet felt experientially as an in-love state! This awakened me to a basic truth: that *love* is a state we can access anytime, no matter the circumstances.

I then realized that *connection* is different from the state of love. It is the unique fabric that exists between individuals. This fabric can never be broken, and its experience and qualities are like a snowflake cocreated between souls. I notice this most readily with friends I have not spoken to in years: when we "connect," the fabric feels the same, even when circumstances or desires for relating have changed. An irreplaceable, inarguable essence exists between us.

And the last aspect of the triad is *relationship*. Relationship is the *form* that we take with one another, whether it is as lovers, as friends, as coworkers, in one-time meetings, etc. This form can change slightly over time in terms of how we "relate" to one another, or in some cases shift completely from that of lovers to friends or no relationship.

In my psychotherapy practice working with couples, I often see that while a couple's connection is strong and has its own fabric, the relationship has broken down. Relational work needs to be done, and it has nothing to do with the impenetrable state of connection.

I often speak with clients who say, "But we were so good together, and now he says he doesn't love me anymore." They have chosen consciously or unconsciously to shift the love they are reflecting and the "form of relationship" with their partners. The connection has not changed.

So I feel it's crucial to distinguish what has happened to the relationship form and where one person wants it to go versus another. We can also clean house in relationship, so that the connection can be felt more clearly and the reflected love can flow freely again.

And most vitally, it is our gift and opportunity to individually expand our capacity to feel the state of love that is always available to us, to love beyond circumstance. Connection is eternal. Relationship form is a choice and can be worked.

Valerie Tate is a psychotherapist, energy healer, illuminated life liver & coach in San Francisco (ValTate.com).

6. Creating Your Perfect Partner For A Succulent Wild Love Relationship

THere Are All Kinds of pArtners

If you're looking for someone to make you happy, they will always fall short.
If you're looking for someone with whom to share your happiness,
you will always have enough.

When I returned from graduate school, I entered a long-term relationship, and when that broke up, I quickly got into another one. While these relationships were obviously deeper than what I had experienced earlier, they were still in many ways growth relationships.

I didn't have the tools I have now and frequently got stuck in patterns I had learned in childhood. I was also less self-aware and more defensive. But these things don't need to destroy relationships; there will always be bumps. I didn't know how to handle the bumps well, however.

I didn't have the ability to change the uncomfortable patterns in the relationships, so my solution finally was to stop trying to be in a marriage-style partnership. Others are able to make such changes without having to leave a relationship. The tools I have now, which are in this book, will certainly make this easier. I had to spend time being single.

When I took that year to reflect and change my patterns, I wasn't actively looking, but I did make a list of the characteristics of my ideal mate. After Jeanie and I were together about a month, I found the list and read it to her. She was everything on my list and more. We both cried.

When Jeanie left after our 10-year honeymoon, not only did I miss her, I missed being in a relationship. In a floundering way, while still grieving the loss of Jeanie, I tried to fill that giant hole, but all I encountered were women who, like me, were drawn to being in a relationship and weren't ready.

I then made a decision. I believe if Jeanie had stayed physically alive, we would have continued to grow together, and our relationship would have become richer and even more satisfying. After the period of floundering, I decided I wanted to continue to grow in the way Jeanie and I had. I also knew if I was going to do this, I had to go back to my own resources. Before I met Jeanie, I felt complete. I was happy and looking for someone to join me. I was not looking for someone to make me happy. After Jeanie was gone, I knew I had to get back to that place of self-nurturance. It took many months, but eventually I found my balance.

I knew I was interested in finding a partner who shared my worldview of self-responsibility and that I would likely meet such a woman at an Abraham-Hicks Law of Attraction seminar. So I signed up for their Alaska cruise. By the time I got on the ship, I felt open to meeting someone but was not feeling lack.

I sought out and spoke with a number of attractive women, and one even complimented me on the fact that I wasn't pushing for more. However, on the morning of the day I met Susan, during a seminar session I talked to my Inner Wise Self. I thought, "If the perfect person were here for me, I would have met her by now." I grumpily declared that I didn't want to meet someone on the last day. Looking back on my outburst, it seems humorous, since no more than three hours later I met Susan.

In retrospect, all the partners/soulmates I have met in my life were a perfect match for me at that time. Earlier in my life, I had significant gaps in my ability to maintain my boundaries and resolve tensions. I was also most compatible with women with whom I could create a relationship based on limiting childhood beliefs about how to love and be loved. Since the year I took off to examine my beliefs and patterns, I have been most compatible with a soulmate who lives the principles of Succulent Wild Love.

Knowing what I know now, I could go back and have a much more nourishing relationship with any of the women I was involved with in the past. There was nothing inherently wrong with my past partners. The main limitation was my lack of skill in taking care of myself in the relationships.

A perfect MATCH

A perfect partner isn't someone you find; it is someone you create by becoming a perfect match to the kind of person you want to be with. For example, if you want to be with a partner who is kind, then do not accept less than kindness. And be kind yourself.

If you're feeling sad, lonely, and inadequate, you will be a perfect match to someone who feels just like that. And someone like that in no way is going to live up to the image most people have of the perfect soulmate. In fact, a series of such prospective partners might come into your experience, and you might conclude that all eligible men or women are unappealing, never recognizing that if you would change, the kind of people who come into your experience would change.

In the following chapters, you will learn how you can be a Succulent Wild Love partner. As you practice being that, the people who come into your life will be a match to that.

I knew I wanted to experience a big, deep, true love in my life, with someone in addition to me. I just didn't know how. Plus I was really scared. The combination of these two things resulted in years of my not being in the type of relationship that I'd always wanted to experience. Since I'm a visionary creator, it eventually seemed clear that I could use those skills in visioning and creating a relationship.

For me, the visioning of something is better kept separate from the details of how and when it happens. If I envisioned a life partner or sole-mate and tried to "figure out how" at the same time, it felt like a disaster. As soon as I thought about how, all sorts of fears and resistances arose:

- I didn't want to get "out there."
- I didn't want to go on blind dates, sighted dates, or really any dates.
- I didn't want to change.
- I didn't want to compromise, lose my autonomy, or be in a relationship "processing" all the time.
- I didn't want to feel bored, stagnant, trapped, or partially present in a relationship.

I didn't want to get "out there"

These thoughts were so repetitive and familiar that they seemed real. It seemed like this was just how I was. I thought that other people were willing, flexible, qualified in love — not me.

I did want to experience a luscious, loving, inspiring, depthfull, creative, wise, funny, intuitive, relationship. I just didn't know how.

I allowed the how to turn into a why I wanted this kind of love relationship. My asking why led to all sorts of luscious things:

- To share my life and adventures with a real playmate
- To be seen, known, and loved

⭐ To Feel Adored And Adoring

★ To experience Deep, expansive romantic love

◎ To Feel Fully Met By Another

✦ To Give And receive love

My HEART GOT reAlly WIDE

So I created A Succulent Wild relationship. And you can too, if you want to.

The HoW is Already within you. I kept thinking that I was unqualified, overqualified, or just resistant, lazy, or not connected with the "right" people. I HAD All sorts of IFs in my inner DiAlogue:

@ IF I HAD Better clothes

◎ IF I WAS in Better shape

@ IF I WAS An extrovert

⭐ IF I WAS less "sensitive"

★ IF I HADn't Been ABUSeD As A child

⭐ IF I HAD HAD Better experiences with men

The "HoW" WAS inside of me and I learned How to let it out

This is where I learned that John plays in the world the WAY I Do, with Joy And Adventure — we were in A 12x12-foot Parklet, And John told people gleefully that we were the only two PArk rangers because one HAD called in sick.

The list literally seemed endless — AND WAS. I now realize that I was trying to solve symptoms without looking at the core issue.

The core issue was that I was pretty sure I was unlovable. I had plenty of inner critics telling me this was so. The "evidence" of this seemed to be reflected in my lack of ability in attracting and having a love relationship. So I began experimenting by talking with other people about love and their love experiences.

People often said, "As soon as you give up trying, they'll show up." That used to REALLY annoy me, because I'm not the type of person who gives up. So I was sure that if I did, the right person couldn't ever show up.

But he did.

And I did.

Awareness Practice: Paths to Creating Your Succulent Wild Relationship

If you want a love relationship, start here. If you're already in a love relationship, see if this section resonates with you. You may find things you can use to feel more love more often in your current relationship.

Look at the list of fears and resistances that came up when I thought about how I could create the kind of relationship I wanted — all the things I didn't want to do — and make a note of any items that you relate to. Do the same with the IFs I listed.

Now look at the section on WHY I wanted a love relationship, and do the same. See if you can allow more WHYs and fewer HoWs, and allow yourself to FEEL your desire for how you'd like your love relationship to be — whether you are in one or not.

In the previous chapter, "Longing For A Great Love: SARK's Covert Love operation," I talked about looking for love mentors. I asked friends to support me in creating my great love relationship. I chose people who either had great relationships or great attitudes about relationships. We met and talked informally, and I requested that they hold me accountable to my vision — to my WHYs — and remind me of that when I started experiencing my HoWs and hearing my inner critics. Each person did this magnificently. You could also consider doing this to create an even better version of a relationship you might already be in.

Respond to the visioning questions below, and if it feels supportive, talk about them with a love mentor or friend who loves you and will support your love relationship vision.

1. If you could create anybody to be in partnership with, what would they be like? Can you imagine the type of person who would be your ideal soulmate? How would being with them feel? Focus on the feeling sensations in your body, your emotions, and your thought processes.

    If you can picture and feel this person, that's wonderful. If you can't get a clear picture, come back here after learning how you can create a Succulent Wild Love relationship in the following chapters.

2. When you imagine your ideal soulmate, can you picture them accepting you and wanting you exactly as you are? If so, that's wonderful. If not, write down the qualities in yourself that you think need to change for your soulmate to choose you.

3. Some people picture someone with many desirable traits and don't believe they have sufficient status or qualities to be attractive to someone like that. They expect that anyone who would actually want them would be somewhat undesirable.

An acquaintance of mine, a successful physician, often mentioned that she could never find a man with whom she was satisfied. It turned out she was attracted to two types of men: With men who were financially less able than she was, she felt strong but didn't respect them. With those who were financially at her level or made more, she felt vulnerable and insecure.

Had she made the effort to imagine some different possibilities, she could have dissolved this barrier. For example, she could have pictured a man who didn't have much money but had other outstanding qualities that she respected equally or more. Or she could have imagined someone who had money but was so delighted by her other qualities that he held her in high esteem.

What qualities do you have to contribute to a partnership? In any relationship each partner has specific things to contribute, such as money or beauty, or even cooking skills or the ability to maintain a lawn. What can you contribute?

4. Focus on what you can give to a relationship and adjust the qualities you're looking for in your soulmate until you feel it is a fair and realistic match. The key is to picture someone who has the qualities you desire, knowing that you have things to contribute too. Though the qualities may be different, overall they feel equivalent.

If you have difficulty with this, come back here after reading chapter 9 on inner critics. The soulmate you're picturing sounds like they could be representing your inner critics.

5. Ask yourself what is attractive about someone who wouldn't choose you. Often they represent qualities that you feel you lack, qualities that you believe someone else needs to provide for you to be happy. Some examples are financial security, emotional support, the ability to be social and make friends easily, someone who would impress your parents or friends, or someone to help parent your children.

Can you provide these qualities for yourself or live a happy life without them?

6. As discussed in the previous chapter, do you have negative beliefs about relationships in general? Can you imagine living daily life with someone and being happy?

To continue along the path of creating your Succulent Wild relationship, go to:
SucculentWildLove.com/Creating

7. Your Relationship Mentor Inside: You And Your Inner Wise Self

MOST PEOPLE KNOW THEY HAVE AN INNER WISE SELF. They might describe it as their higher self, pure positive energy, Holy Spirit, gut feeling, or intuition. You can describe or think about this part of yourself in the words that most please and resonate with you.

This part of you arrived before you were born and will be with you all your life and beyond. It's part of your Human Operating System. Your connection with your Inner Wise Self is your most intimate long-term relationship.

Your inner wise self inside is TRULY MAgnificent

Your Inner Wise Self is and always will be your primary source of nourishment and love. No matter how thoughtful and attentive, no person or relationship can ever give you the ongoing unconditional love that you have with your Inner Wise Self. It is the source of your ability to love yourself.

The more you feel self-love, the more you will be able to enter a relationship as a strong, independent partner.

Many people have little or no active connection with their Inner Wise Self, so they look to others to "fill them up," and love them in the ways that they aren't able to love themselves. This means that if and when relationships end or change, those people feel empty, without connection to their own source of love inside.

> Of course I felt tremendous loss and despair when Jeanie died. Some people never get over such a loss. Having an active connection with my Inner Wise Self helped me feel love again, first for myself and then for Susan.

The source of love inside you is endless and tuned in to who you are — not who you want to be, or wish you were, or think you are on your best days. It's there for every instant of your life, and truly loves you without judgment or reservation. By communicating with this part of yourself, you can love yourself in every feeling and condition, and accept how you "actually are." When you open this channel with your Inner Wise Self, love can truly flow.

Most of us have been taught that no one is perfect — especially ourselves — and that the highest possible self-awareness is one in which you accept your flaws and love yourself as best you can. But your Inner Wise Self really sees you as perfect — exactly as you are. And that is a model you can use for how you see everyone. You can then share with everyone the unconditional love that your Inner Wise Self extends to you.

We will show you how to activate and empower your relationship with this part of you that's unconditionally loving and wise. With this awareness you have the ability to cultivate a lasting, aware connection with your Inner Wise Self. You'll experience having a giant inner love mentor who can guide you in every aspect of your life — including all your relationships.

HOW TO ACTIVATE AND EMPOWER YOUR INNER WISE SELF: LOVE NOTES

Asking your Inner Wise Self is all you do to activate and empower it.

Writing what I call Love Notes is a great entry point for asking. Writing is kinesthetic and engages the mind, body, and spirit. It allows your Inner Wise Self to express clearly. When I first began this process many years ago, I heard my Inner Wise Self as some kind of distant figure who spoke from "on high." When I created this activation and empowerment process, I experienced my Inner Wise Self first through writing and then IN ACTION in every area of my life. As my relationship with my Inner Wise Self has grown and expanded, it has begun speaking in ALL kinds of ways — through books, movies, other people, nature. My Inner Wise Self now expresses itself in VERY loving ways and words.

Your Inner Wise Self will speak to you in ways that are customized just for you. My relationship with my Inner Wise Self has developed over many years, and it speaks to me in endearing terms and often in very flowery language. Everyone has a unique relationship with their Inner Wise Self. One time in a workshop, I asked for people to write and share Love Notes. A young man in a leather jacket stood up and said he'd written his note on his phone and wanted to read it out loud. He stared down at his phone and then blurted out,

"Hey dude. I f***ing love you."

And then he sat down, smiling.

We could all feel the love he could feel for himself in that moment. He came up to me later and expressed astonishment that he could really feel love for himself.

Here are two of my Love Notes for you to read so you can be inspired to write one of your own. When reading them, you can imagine your own Inner Wise Self speaking this way to you.

My inner wise self loves speaking in terms of endearments - yours may speak differently

Dearest Adorable Most Precious Susan,

I see you with so much love. I see you in your resistances, avoidances, and sometimes frantic attempts to avoid your holy purpose and intentions. I am ready to deliver all that you seek and need — just ask. Spend some quiet moments with me and allow me to speak through you. I will give you the grace, courage, and ability to bring your intentions more fully to life. I adore you completely.

To My Gumdrop of Pure Love, Susan,

I am with you wherever you go, whatever you do. Every word you write, every step you take, every blink you blink. Whenever you doubt yourself or allow inner critics to speak loudly, I am there. Whenever you forget to ask me for help, I am there. Whenever you feel fat or ashamed or blinded by your ego, I am there.

Remember this especially when you try to hide from your awareness of my total unconditional love. Put this note where you can see it and read it again. I know your goodness, I see your radiance, I understand where and how you stumble. You are safe. All is well. You are whole, perfect, and complete. I love you everlastingly.

I save all my Love Notes in a folder and read and reread them. They're amazingly effective for raising my emotional vibration and expanding my feelings of self-love.

When I ask groups of people if they're aware of this part inside of them, 85 to 95 percent will raise their hands. When I ask the same group if they consistently ask this part for help and love in their life, very few raise their hands. We are not used to feeling and experiencing unconditional love for ourselves. Most people are listening to the dialogue or inner critics in their heads and don't realize that those parts of themselves are not who they are. Being mentored and loved by your Inner Wise Self is a remarkable way to live and love. We are meant to have our Inner Wise Selves guiding us, not our inner critics.

After I've described the Love Note process and given some examples, people say,

"I didn't know I could ask about that."

"I don't want to over-ask."

"I don't know if I would ever get any answers I could use."

Then, after they ask and hear what their Inner Wise Self has to communicate, people say,

"Wow. I didn't know that much was inside of me."

"I feel so much love for myself and everyone — like I have a never-ending source."

"This feels unbelievable. I hope I can keep asking."

Be aware that when you're first beginning with this practice, you might wonder if you're just making up answers you want to hear. It's quite understandable to wonder this, and ultimately doesn't really affect the information you receive. As you go along, your positive experiences will multiply, and this question will become less and less relevant.

When I was growing up, my mother was an avid student of self-help books and Eastern philosophy. She was one of the first yoga teachers in the United States in the 1960s. She actually taught me and many of her students to activate our relationship with our Inner Wise Self. We didn't use that term then, but I remember her asking her connection with Source about everything meaningful in her life.

She had gotten the clear understanding that her Inner Wise Self loved her and was ready to help her in any way possible. For example, by asking about everyday things, she always had the best kind of paper towels and toilet paper. She would find amazing presents for people, things they hadn't known they wanted or needed.

My favorite example of her connection with her Inner Wise Self occurred one afternoon when we were talking in the kitchen. My mother was trying to remember a specific word to express something. Suddenly, she reached behind her and turned on the small TV we had on a table. An announcer was speaking. He said the word. My mother turned off the TV and continued talking to me as if what she had done was the most normal thing in the world.

When my mother taught us how to communicate with our Inner Wise Self, she would always stress the quality of the material we received. It mattered less to her if we were responding wisely from an ego level or the material was coming from our Inner Wise Self. If the material was uplifting and useful, that is what mattered.

One of my wisest teachers

How to Have Your Inner Wise Self in Action in Your Life and Relationships

Once you activate and empower your Inner Wise Self and become familiar with writing a few Love Notes, you'll be ready to ask your Inner Wise Self to help you in your life and relationships and receive on-the-spot relationship mentoring. There are a number of ways to do this.

Think of a challenging situation in a relationship in your life and write it down or hold it in your mind. Simply ask your Inner Wise Self what to do, and you will receive an answer.

For example, let's say that someone isn't communicating with you the way you would wish, and you want them to communicate differently. You might write down or say to yourself, "_____ hasn't responded to my text or call. I hate when they do this."

Then, ask your Inner Wise Self for on-the-spot guidance, "Hey, Inner Wise Self, what do I do here?" You might receive answers like:

- "Remember that it's not personal. _____ gets busy and doesn't respond. If you wait a bit, they will turn up."
- "Do you need to spend some time paying attention to yourself?"
- "What can you do right now about this person that would feel good?"

After receiving answers from your Inner Wise Self, you'll have the opportunity to do things differently than you ever have. If you don't understand the answer at first, ask again. If you need help taking action on the answer, ask for that. Your Inner Wise Self has an endless stream of goodness and love for you to access. Once you establish this channel and learn to keep it open, you'll be acting with love instead of reacting in fear.

Practicing asking for and receiving answers literally creates new pathways in your brain and supports you in guiding your emotional responses rather than simply reacting to outside circumstances and people. When your Inner Wise Self is in your awareness on a daily basis, you have an instant and consistent source of support and guidance. What other people do, or don't do, will not negatively affect you as much, or at all.

If writing appeals to you, you can write your questions and ask your Inner Wise Self to respond. Here are some examples:

- What are some ways that love can feel even better for me?
- How can my relationship be easier?
- How will I benefit from learning about love and relationships?
- What can I do right now to feel better about _____?

Or simply ask them out loud, or in your head, depending on the circumstances.

One time I was in a grocery store, searching for a certain kind of corn chip and picking up a bag to buy. I knew that this was a precursor to emotionally eating — to sedating my emotions with food — and I had made a commitment to at least try to ask my Inner Wise Self for guidance and mentoring when I felt this way. At such times, I don't feel calm or loving or really ready to change at all.

But I still mostly ask. In this case, I kind of belligerently said, "Inner Wise Self, what have you got for me this time?" I felt extremely skeptical that anything could help me but those chips.

My Inner Wise Self said, "Go ask that couple for help."

I looked over and saw a couple near the fruits and vegetables, and they didn't look very nice. In fact, they looked crabby and distinctly unhelpful. But over the years I've learned that when I do manage to ask, I can trust what my Inner Wise Self delivers. So I went over to them, not knowing at all what I would say — if anything.

I want to note here that I'm an introvert from the Midwest and not at all comfortable with going up to strangers and asking for help, but I do know that my Inner Wise Self is a wise mentor and customizes its guidance exquisitely for me.

I walked up to the man and said, "Excuse me. Could I ask you for some help?"

He put down a piece of fruit and kind of sighed, and reluctantly said, "What?"

I stared at him and had no idea what to say, and then suddenly blurted out, "Could you remind me that I really want love and not these chips?"

His whole face burst into bloom, like a flower, and he said in a big booming Australian accent, "Oh, darlin', you just want some love!!! We'll give you some love." And he swooped me into a big bear hug and lifted me off the ground! His wife hugged me from behind, and she was exclaiming too. I was suddenly in a love sandwich, and I was laughing so hard and felt so filled up with love that those chips became inconsequential.

And I was again reminded of the magnificent power of my Inner Wise Self. My personality self had judged the couple as crabby and unhelpful. I was reluctant to ask for help and seriously doubted I would receive any.

None of these kind of doubts matter to your Inner Wise Self — it doesn't care how, when, why, or if you ask. It's the best kind of mentor you have — free, constantly available, and unconditionally loving.

And in case you're thinking that it only works for SARK or John, I've had thousands of profound experiences like the CHIPS story, and I've initially resisted asking my Inner Wise Self almost every time. In both teaching about the Inner Wise Self and living with my own, I've learned that most of us resist asking because we fear that there won't be an answer — or an answer we can use. And I've also learned over and over for myself that the practical answers are always there.

I've asked my Inner Wise Self imperfectly or partially and tried not to ask at all. Receiving responses that actually work in my life inspires me to continue asking, and that's what we're inviting you to do also.

I learned about my Inner Wise Self before I had the understanding I have now. At first I thought of it as channeling a personality that could take me over. I remember wanting to ask about things, but then angrily resisting. What I discovered is that this inner wisdom is the most respectful energy I can imagine. It lovingly listens and never pushes or demands.

When I feel stuck about something, I most often go to the computer and write about what's going on. Then I sit with open expectation and feel for a response, which I write down. Below is an example of one of my exchanges with my Inner Wise Self. But first, some background.

Asking is the whole point

When I was left in a boarding school in Germany as a young child, my mother promised that I could have a bicycle when I came to America. I was insecure and unhappy, and the promise of a bicycle became a strong symbol for me of "joy to come." Emotionally, as an adult this symbol has extended to motorcycles and scooters.

When I moved to San Francisco, I bought a scooter. As much as I loved the little runabout, I soon wanted to venture across the Golden Gate Bridge and to other parts of the Bay Area. That meant getting something more powerful. And so began my journey to find the best bike for me.

At the time of the dialogue below, I had already moved on to a motorcycle, and then a second, larger scooter. However, I still felt relatively new to San Francisco. While I embraced much of what was happening, I was also feeling insecure because so many things in my life still felt unsettled. Searching for the best bike gave me something uncomplicated and delightful to focus on. When I asked the question, I was thinking only about the decision to buy the bike, but my Inner Wise Self quickly focused on the larger issues.

Dear Inner Wise Self,

I'm thinking about buying a new motorcycle. The bike I'm considering buying seems to be the best combination of what I want.

Getting a bike has been a strong symbol for me of having something to look forward to, and I keep looking for a new and more suitable one. This one feels like there is no better bike for me right now, but if I buy it will I need another one to fantasize about so I have something to look forward to?

Do I get the new bike? The scooter I have now can get me everywhere I need to go. I guess I've already answered this for myself. The new bike will take me there in *the way* I want to go.

A second question is, Would it be best for me to buy the bike today, before the scooter is sold, or would it be better to wait? There is a wonderful person in the wings who is likely to buy it. Holding both bikes for a week or two would not be difficult, but doing so longer would be inconvenient.

Any thoughts would be appreciated.

Dear John,

You are learning and growing in so many areas of your life right now that it can often feel overwhelming. You are still fitting yourself into a new city and a new lifestyle. You have a new career. You've learned the basics and are now expanding your reach.

Your relationship with Susan is nourishing and all you had hoped for in a partnership — and more. And you are also still in the process of building your social life with new friends.

Focusing on one thing you appreciate, a motorcycle, is a way of simplifying all this. While the many changes in your life are wonderful, they take time, focus, and energy. Give yourself credit for what you have achieved and for what you are capable of achieving. You are quite hard on yourself regarding what you should be able to accomplish.

You have made amazing changes and are in the middle of expanding even further. You are on the ride of your life. All you basically need to do is learn how to enjoy it. And that is the biggest process for you right now. The best shift for you at this time is to appreciate more the breadth of what you are accomplishing.

Regarding the bike: basically it doesn't matter whether you buy it today or next week. Having it will bring you great joy. As you adjust to the various changes in your life, the symbol of the motorcycle will lessen in intensity, and you will have a bike that is most suited to you. The details will take care of themselves, or you can use them as points of worry to remind you where you want to align more.

With more love than you can imagine,
Your Inner Wise Self

IF JoHn were single, this woulD Be His online DAting profile picture.

The guidance from your Inner Wise Self will always inspire you. It is always unconditionally loving. It waits until you ask, and it won't ever tell you what you "should" do. If you ever hear guidance that feels parental or critical, one or more inner critics are getting blended with your Inner Wise Self. In that case, do some Inner Critic Care and Transformation (see chapter 9) and then ask your Inner Wise Self again.

When you feel good, you are aligned with your Inner Wise Self.

In addition to being available for guidance whenever you are making a decision, your Inner Wise Self is constantly supporting you through your feelings. Your Inner Wise Self is a beacon of pure love and joy, and when you are feeling that, you are tuned in to this beacon. It is an experience you can trust. When something brings you joy, you are on your right path.

Leslie Lewis — Thoughts on My Most Important Relationship

Leslie Lewis

On a beach in Montauk, Long Island, in 1998, inspired by Susan's ceremony that she'd written about in *Succulent Wild Woman*, I promised to love, honor, and cherish myself until death. I donned a Cartier Trinity ring and gave myself a pair of diamond stud earrings as a personal wedding gift. Five days later my then-boyfriend proposed to me, and I happily accepted. I must have sensed the proposal was coming and knew that before I could promise myself to someone else, I had to give that love to myself first. During our 16-year marriage, I renewed my vows to myself twice, because I needed the reminder that my connection with myself was important. I wanted to affirm that even as a mother and a wife, I had to make myself my first priority.

He and I divorced amicably last year. Soon after, I renewed my vows to myself, this time in a ceremony in Naples, Florida, with two girlfriends who were marrying themselves for the first time.

It felt so good to take my own hand and promise to take care of myself forever. It's no one else's job. It's only mine. And I can do it.

I have found that the only relationship that really matters is the one I have with myself. When I feel good about myself, when I'm taking care of myself, I have an abundance left to give other people — my children, my family, friends.

When I'm not taking care of myself, well, it's better for me to just stay in bed.

I try to consult my inner guidance before every decision. Definitely before sending an email, for example, I check in with that still, small voice within before pressing Send.

I used to do a simple muscle test to decide whether to send the email, or call or text someone, or not. But now it's enough just to connect to my Inner Wise Self and listen for the answer that is always available.

I also find that when technology "doesn't work" or an email doesn't send, there's a reason, and I just go with the flow, instead of pushing against the delay. When I relax and allow myself to go with whatever is happening, things just tend to work out well for me.

So, I'm now enjoying dating. I'm getting to explore all the fun new technology of the dating world: Coffee Meets Bagel, speed dating. Tinder! But the most important date is *me*. I value myself, I listen to myself, I love myself. This seems to be a good way to manage my life.

I find that it works for me. The other day, after watching the Broadway show *If/Then* I realized I have no regrets. Not a single one. What a relief.

Leslie is a writer, performer, happy life liver, and explorer (LeslieLewisOnline.com).

Awareness Practice:
Activating and Empowering Your Inner Wise Self

Now it's your turn. Use a pen, pencil, or keyboard to create your own Love Note or to ask something of your Inner Wise Self (IWS). You don't need to know "how." Just begin anywhere.

Here are some ways you can expand your practice with your Inner Wise Self:

- Read your Love Note to yourself after you've written it.
- Read it out loud.
- Read or send it to a friend.
- Say out loud to yourself in any situation something like, "Inner Wise Self, what do I do with this one?"
- Here are some questions to ask your IWS:
- What do I want to receive from a Succulent Wild relationship?
- What is the best path for me regarding intimate relationships in my life?
- What will I appreciate knowing about myself and relationships?
- Here are some possible blanks to fill in with the help of your Inner Wise Self:
- How do I talk with _____ about _____?
- In my relationship with _____, what is a good path for me to take?
- I want love to be _____.
- I don't want love to be _____.
- My favorite parts of relationships are _____, _____.
- In love relationships, I'm completely puzzled by _____, _____, _____.
- I'd like to experience more love in the following ways: _____, _____.

Your Inner Wise Self has surprises for you. Go here to explore more:
SucculentWildLove.com/IWS

8. Tending to And Transforming Your Feelings So You Can Feel More Love: Your Inner Feelings Care System

Feelings Are everywhere All The Time As Your Guides

When I was growing up, I was basically allowed to express one feeling, and I had to go to my room to do it. When I came out of my room, I was expected to feel "better," even if I didn't. The basic message was that feelings were to be barely tolerated and best kept hidden. I knew I had a lot of feelings, and they made themselves known to me in lots of ways — some overt and some covert. I eventually created an "Inner Feelings Care System" to manage and care for my feelings, which is an immense benefit for feeling better a lot more often, no matter what is happening in your life. I've mentored many people in how to use this system in their lives.

Your feelings are a powerful compass to guide you and can be used as an effective foundation for evoking cooperation in others. Being aware of your feelings will make it easier to make joyful decisions with a significant other and to move the relationship forward together with love instead of fear. It will make it easier not to fall into a role (such as "the good wife" or "the good mother") that doesn't fit you. When you learn how to care for your feelings, you'll recognize when you or an intimate other is heading toward a hurtful situation before your feelings become intense. This can prevent significant conflicts that would be more difficult to resolve.

My feelings frequently become intense, but now instead of acting them out with John or others, I do my Inner Feelings Care System — and it works.

Most people don't know how to attend to and manage their feelings. This can and does result in angry outbursts, poor work performance, ineffective parenting, lack of loving feelings, or just simply feeling bad. Our feelings affect us every day, and untended feelings capture our attention and consistently drain our energy for living life joyfully.

 Feelings get time sensitive when we haven't been listening

Our feelings can sometimes be temporarily put aside as we work or do other activities but will come to us for attention right after we've finished whatever we had to do. And then we're often tired or distracted and try to ignore our feelings — which never works. Most people don't tend to their feelings along the way during the day. For example, if you feel worried and try to ignore a feeling, it just gets louder and larger. Louder and larger looks like this: you feel frustrated with your partner, then have an upset at work, then wake up at 3 AM in despair. Your untended feelings are at the root of any emotional disturbance.

Another common strategy people use is to try to avoid, deny, or repress their feelings. This doesn't work either. People often try sedating feelings with food or anesthetizing them with alcohol. They may try to outrun them with overachievement or excessive activities, or just say, "fine," when they don't feel that way at all.

Also, most people don't know how to have or hold multiple feelings simultaneously. For example, you might feel glad to be going to visit your mother, sad that she's in declining health, angry that your sister isn't doing more, worried about how you will manage it all, and hopeless about the whole situation. Many people get overwhelmed with multiple feelings and just try to turn them all off.

Many times it's not convenient or possible to share your feelings with the people involved in evoking them. They might be busy, unavailable, or even unwilling to hear your feelings. It is also best not to blast pent-up feelings onto others. It's *always* possible to acknowledge your feelings to yourself, tend to them, and feel better or differently before you interact with other people.

When you actively care for your feelings, you can more effectively communicate what you want in ways others can hear. You can also then use your feelings to help evoke cooperation from others. Luckily, all our feelings just want some love and attention and will respond swiftly to just a tiny bit of focused care. Giving yourself permission to express and care for your feelings will significantly amplify your ability to feel good more of the time.

Feelings Are Quick responders

The Inner Feelings Care System is an effective way to take charge of your feelings rather than being overwhelmed by them. Using this powerful yet simple system, you'll learn to identify and express your feelings and then transform them to multiply and expand feelings of goodness and love in your life and relationships.

Express-Release-Relief

1. Express

Write, "I FEEL _____ ABOUT_____," across the top of a piece of paper. (You can use recycled paper for this or write on a computer or even your phone.) Then make a *fast list* of sentences about everything you can think of that applies, from the tiniest to the largest things. Don't stop to reread or punctuate — just keep writing. You are *expressing* your feelings on the page. Add as many feelings and adjectives as apply to you in this moment. Focus on the negative or challenging emotions.

For example:

★ I hate my neighbor.

☆ I hate the way she slams the door.

◉ I'm afraid I can't get peace.

◉ I'm afraid she will fight with me and not stop if I tell her.

◉ I'm enraged by her thoughtlessness.

☆ I feel helpless to change this.

★ My neighbor is stupid and insensitive.

◉ I don't like how often she comes and goes slamming her door.

Use profanity or exclamation points. *Let yourself get very theatrical.* Fully express how you feel on the paper or screen. Don't hold back. Express until you don't have another negative feeling in your head or body. When you first start this process, you might write five to eight pages. Feel free to customize what you're doing. For example, if you would rather not get theatrical, don't, until or unless you feel ready. Let your feelings be your guide.

2. Release

A few minutes into writing your fast list, you'll begin to feel the release of these feelings, because they're moving out of your head and onto the paper or screen — a transformational process is occurring with them.

You can highlight this by looking at what you have written and saying, "I see you, I hear you, I acknowledge you." Then fold up your paper or close the file and imagine sending it to the universe, or God, or whoever you think is larger than you.

3. Relief

The expressing and releasing you've done with mind, body, and spirit will naturally lead to *relief.* You're feeling this relief because we're not meant to carry around or have unexpressed feelings inside our heads.

Get quiet and take a moment to feel this relief. If you aren't feeling relief, either go back to step 1 or write some positive thoughts about the situation. For example:

- My neighbor is thoughtful in other ways.
- We've always been cordial.
- She would like to be a good neighbor.

  She's preoccupied with other things and doesn't notice the loud door.

- There has to be some way I can resolve this.

Keep going back to step 1 or writing positive thoughts until you feel relief.

Now let yourself experience the relief as you go about your day and interact with others. We want you to know that your feelings don't have heads. A feeling only knows how to feel. Your feelings will not respond to desperate pleas or bribes.

Your feelings will respond to your love and attention.

You can do your Inner Feelings Care System in a five-minute segment, and this will provide immediate relief and lead to long-term changes. You may also spend 10 to 15 minutes when you first start practicing your Inner Feelings Care System and be able to abbreviate these sessions as you become more experienced — which can happen quite quickly.

If you don't have three to five minutes to write or type your feelings, you can do a five-second version:

As soon as you're aware of a feeling or feelings, imaginatively turn toward them and say out loud or under your breath, "I see you, I hear you, I acknowledge you." For example, you might say, "Sadness, I see you, I hear you, I acknowledge you." Allow yourself to really mean what you've just said. Your feelings will calm right down with this simple care and attention.

Good Relationship Health = Good Feelings Expression

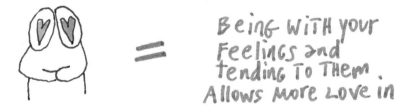

= Being with your feelings and tending to them. Allows more love in

Practicing with this system daily or as often as you can will lead to better communications with yourself and other people, expanded experiences of self-care and love, and just feeling good.

You can think of it like practicing yoga, brushing your teeth, or taking vitamins. Having your Inner Feelings Care System in place is like eating the best food *ever*. You can eat the best foods and drink great juices, but if your mental diet is one of negative self-talk or unresolved feelings, it will dramatically undermine your ability to feel good.

I promise, this works. I do it all the time, and it has significantly changed my life and my ability to love others. It allows me to have a self-loving relationship with myself, John, my business partners, neighbors, and friends. I still feel all the challenging feelings. I just don't spend so much time there.

Doing your Inner Feelings Care System will allow you to feel and transform your feelings ongoingly and with great love. This will change your experiences of your health, money, work, creativity, and *love* in positive new ways.

Activating Your Inner Wise Self to Transform & Care for Your Feelings Newly and Differently

You can also use your Inner Wise Self to actively transform and reframe your feelings, which establishes new patterns and neural pathways in your brain. Your Inner Wise Self is with you right now and ready to help you in any and every way imaginable.

1. Take one of your fast lists of feelings and sit down for a session with your Inner Wise Self.
2. Plan to spend 5 to 10 minutes reframing feelings you've written previously. This will lead to your being able to transform feelings after you've felt them. If reframing feels good, allow yourself to spend a longer segment of time doing this.

In this case, "reframing" means that you write yourself kind, encouraging, supportive, endearing words that "speak" to the feelings that you shared. For example, you might have written in your list:

> I feel like I hate my neighbor. She slams her door every time she comes home, and I feel so enraged at her thoughtlessness and rudeness. I feel helpless and like I live in such a stupid loud and upsetting place.

You and your Inner Wise Self might write something like this in response to your feelings:

> My dearest darling, I understand how upsetting this is! It's annoying to hear sounds that you feel you can't control. I want to remind you that you can speak to your neighbor and ask her to be quieter. I give you permission to feel *all* your feelings and then find new Joyfull Solutions where she isn't scared to close her door and you're not being disturbed. You can create a new way. Let's invent it now.

You could write your neighbor a note or an email to practice how you'd like to express yourself (but don't necessarily send it). Do another list if more upset feelings occur. Your Inner Wise Self might say something like, "You and your feelings matter so much. You are safe. All is well. I love you."

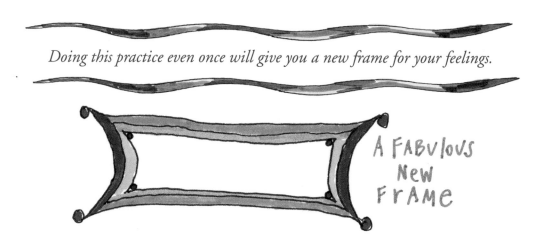

Doing this practice even once will give you a new frame for your feelings.

A FABULOUS NEW FRAME

It will let your feelings know that they are being felt by you. This will allow your feelings to soften and change shape. You can then act and behave differently with your neighbor and the feelings you feel.

Experiment with this and let yourself not "know how" to do it. Your Inner Wise Self knows — it will always guide you back to love and joy. Even a small amount of your attention focused this way will cause shifts in how you feel. You'll begin to have new experiences with your feelings, which will lead to your having new experiences with others.

Practice with your Inner Wise Self once or twice a month in the beginning. Do your Inner Feelings Care System every day or as many days as you can — *especially* when you feel upset.

Ask your Inner Wise Self for support if you get stuck or have feelings that seem untransformable. Sometimes you'll need to just keep expressing certain feelings until you're ready to shift them. This is a practice. It's not a place to fix feelings. It's a place to transform and reframe them.

Your feelings can only feel. They can't be bargained with or denied. It's your opportunity to feel them, hear them, acknowledge them, and reassure them. This is the care system that will give your feelings a safe haven, and you, inner freedom. You and your Inner Wise Self can shift your feeling experiences significantly.

Instead of spending months and years repetitively enduring challenging feelings, you can feel them deeply and spend hours, minutes, and sometimes only seconds feeling them, expressing them, releasing them, and transforming them.

Feeling Differently NOW

Having an Inner Feelings Care System means that you know how to skillfully and lovingly handle your feelings so that you don't need to act out for them to get your attention. Your feelings are seeking your love and attention consistently but not in the amounts or ways that you fear.

Receiving Support from Others Wisely

When someone doesn't feel free to express their feelings with a significant other, they often suppress and ignore uncomfortable feelings or turn to their friends to vent about what is going on in the relationship. Venting to a friend is better than suppressing your feelings, but there are significant advantages to using the Inner Feelings Care System.

When you Express and Release using the Inner Feelings Care System, at the end of the Release, you can tear up the paper and send all that negative energy off to the recycling center of the universe. But when you're doing this with a friend, they have absorbed all that negative energy about your relationship. Unless they are very mature, they will be inclined to have a rather negative view of your significant other, having listened to all that is wrong about them.

Often your friend won't be in a position to help you cultivate positive thoughts about your partner at that point. In fact, many times this kind of interaction only reinforces what is wrong with the significant other and highlights a feeling of powerlessness in the relationship.

MAny yeArs AGO, I used to COMPlAin to Friends ABOUT my MOtHer And express my neGAtive Feelings ABOUt Her to tHem. InvAriABly wHen tHey met Her, tHey would exclAim, "Wow! Your mom is so nice!" I tHen leArned How to express And releAse tHose neGAtive Feelings By myself, leAding to my writing A CHApter in one of my BOOks titled "My MOtHer Is No Longer tHe PrOBlem — Now WHAt?" And tHe "now wHAt?" wAs me tending to my own Feelings ABOUt Her And ABOUt Anyone. It Feels so incrediBly liBerAting.

There *are* helpful ways that you can share your feelings with friends. You can approach them with the intent of asking them to help you see what you're doing to create the situation you're in and what you can do to change it. You may just vent in that instance, but it is with the idea that you are looking for a more fulfilling path, not that there is something wrong with the other person. This way, the focus is on enhancing you rather than diminishing your significant other.

Supporting Others with Their Feelings

As you practice acknowledging and transforming your feelings, you might notice others in your life not feeling as good. Many people don't have an active Inner Feelings Care System in place, so they might engage in repetitive attitudes of negativity and try to include you in what doesn't feel good or loving in their lives. You are not doing them a favor by listening to these kinds of descriptions for very long, unless they are consciously practicing and want to feel better from what they're sharing.

In that case, a friend or loved one might say, "I feel really sad and upset about something. Could you just listen to me — without offering solutions — for a little bit? I think if I can just hear myself say it, I can better identify how I'm feeling."

You might also guide your friend or loved one by saying things like, "What feels most supportive right now? Would you like me to just listen or offer solutions?" Or, "Do you want to feel better now, or do you want someone to just hear your feelings so you can express them?"

Guide your Feelings with Love
Be Guided By your Feelings with Love

Or, "You asked me to remind you if you keep speaking negatively about that — so I am lovingly reminding you."

In general, if you're feeling good while you're listening, you're probably being of some help. If you're feeling restless, distracted, crabby, or impatient as your friend or loved one is speaking — or if you're feeling judgmental about them or someone else in their story — it's part of your Inner Feelings Care System opportunity to consider stopping them, distracting them, or just not spending as much, or any, time with them when they're in that state.

If asked, you can describe and share your Inner Feelings Care System, but be aware that not everyone will want to practice and experiment with feeling more love more often. Some people choose to stay with what is familiar to them and look for people to join them there. The most loving action by you in that case is to separate from them.

Your Inner Feelings Care System for Feeling More Love

If you've been practicing with your Inner Feelings Care System, you are now ready for feeling more love — which is all about your feelings of appreciation, grace, and gratitude — which leads you to experiencing *more* love and joy.

Most people say they'd like to feel more love more often in their lives and relationships, and most people don't know how to allow that same joy or love *in*.

Feeling more love and joy is not automatic, and most of us are unconsciously a little, or a lot, afraid of it.

it can Actually Feel scarier to Feel GOOD consistently Than not. explore This in your Life and use The six powerfull HABits in This Book to support you with any shifts

It can be scarier to feel love than fear, scarcity, or anger. Many of us are accustomed to struggle and unfamiliar with feeling more love. We're afraid that if we feel love or joy, we'll be punished, we'll lose something we love, or somehow we don't deserve it if others are suffering. We say we want joy and love, and then we act and behave in ways that push it away.

"I just want to feel love," we say. And then we engage in repetitive thoughts of negativity or fear that ensure we don't.

Or we allow fleeting moments of feeling love at pivotal points, descending quickly into what's wrong, what didn't work or go as well as we hoped. Blaming others in our relationships is a common place to practice feeling *not* love.

It Takes Skill and Practice to Feel Love More Often

Practicing feeling more love is the final part of your ongoing Inner Feelings Care System. We're sharing a written process here, but you can do it out loud, or in meditation, or in any way that's unique to you. Here's one way to explore expanding your loving feelings. You can do this in five minutes.

1. Write across the top of a piece of paper or screen, "I feel" — then all the delicious words that describe good-feeling emotions that you can think of. For example:

   I feel elated, joyful, happy, glad, thrilled, lucky, great, overjoyed, grateful, glad, loving, appreciative

2. Then write "about" and make a fast list of everything that fits in. Add specific descriptions that make it uniquely your experience. For example:

   ☆ my partner bringing me tea in the morning, smiling

   ★ the perfectly steamed broccoli I enjoyed

   ◎ the kind clerk at the store who ran after me to tell me about an herb he had located for me

   ◉ the way the birds play outside my window

   ✦ my new blue socks

   ★ my friend calling just to say, "How ARE you?"

You might set this up on your phone and add to it daily, or use a journal — whatever way you can most easily express these feelings.

Making descriptive notes about your love and appreciation means that *more* of those same feelings will multiply. By doing this, you will become a "love multiplier" in your life. You will become an expert appreciator of yourself, the other people in your life, and everything around you.

You will overflow with loving feelings and be able to share them with others.

Awareness Practice: Your Inner Feelings Care System

PArt 1: Express your feelings so you can experience Release and Relief (see page 86). Do this for five minutes per day, or as often as you want to feel relief. This changes your reactions into responses and allows your feelings to flow so they don't get stuck and turn into grudges or lists against other people — or yourself.

PArt 2: Use your Inner Wise Self to transform and reframe the feelings you listed in part 1, so you can receive more inner support, encouragement, and reminders that you are unconditionally loved. Do this one to three times per month for 15 to 30 minutes.

PArt 3: Joyfully list your appreciations and love so that more can come to you. Do this for five minutes per day or more often if you feel inspired. This creates more love, goodness, gladness, and gratitude.

Remember, your feelings just want your love and attention, and they don't need much to feel tended to.

Once your feelings know that you know how to tend to them, they can move and flow through you more quickly. You'll find yourself feeling upset less often and for shorter periods of time. Other people will not trigger your feelings as often, either. And if they do, you'll know how to care for yourself and your feelings.

The most loving contributions you can make in your Succulent Wild Love relationships is to be glad and feel good, and to tend lovingly and skillfully to your feelings when you're not. You can use all the parts of your Inner Feelings Care System to practice and experiment.

You'll know how you feel, what to do with your feelings, and how to love yourself and others more deeply more often. Being an "embodied joy being" is the best gift you can give the world and the people in your life. Being loving and showing it is a beacon for others to do the same.

Give yourself and the people in your life the benefits
of your feeling better more often. Go here:
SucculentWildLove.com/IFCS

9. The Critics in Your Head Are Not You — or Your Partner: Your Inner Critic Care System

it's always...
You never...
it won't work
You don't have enough...
You always...
You should...

A constant stream is streaming

YOU HAVE A CONSTANT STREAM OF THOUGHTS running through your mind, and we use the term "inner critics" to describe the thoughts that criticize you or tell you that you should be ashamed or feel guilty if you do what you want to do.

I first learned about inner critics over 20 years ago from Drs. Hal and Sidra Stone's book, EMBRACING YOUR INNER CRITIC. At the time, my inner critics were so strong that I could only read a few paragraphs before taking a nap for several hours to try to digest the information.

I learned that I was basically running my life with my inner critics in charge. I wasn't as aware of my Inner Wise Self at that point, and didn't know about the power of that aspect and what it would mean to have my Inner Wise Self and my Aware Self (what I call my Adult Self) in charge.

Over the years, I learned how to stop inner critics when necessary, redirect them, communicate with them, and transform my relationships with them and their messages. I later developed a transformational care system that works really well. This has opened my life up tremendously to feeling more love, and new ways of working and living, and it works for anyone who wants to practice it.

Ultimately, all the guilt, shame, and criticism we feel comes from inside us.

When you were growing up, basically well-meaning people taught you when to feel shame and guilt, and criticized you to get you to do what they wanted. Part of the information you took in about how to function in the world included these beliefs about who you "should" be and how you "should" behave.

After a while, these external voices became inner voices. And in many ways they were help-ful. They reminded you what the rules were so you could avoid getting punished. They moti-vated you to achieve things so the people with authority would reward you. They protected you in a world where everyone was much bigger.

Now that you're older, you have the ability to evaluate what is genuinely best for you and no longer need to rely on others to do that for you. But these clusters of beliefs are still in your head and often demand that you listen to them and do what they say.

They aren't as useful to you now as they were when you were small. In fact, they can block you from taking actions that would truly nourish you. They were given to you by the authorities in your life based on their view of the world, one that isn't necessarily best for you, especially the adult you.

Listening to these voices without questioning them, the same way you did when you were small, leads to unnecessary guilt and shame, and decisions that don't serve who you are now. Additionally, in a relationship, if your partner echoes what your inner critics are saying, those criticisms can have tremendous power to affect you.

For example, if your part-ner says you should become a mountain climber to get more exercise, chances are this would  Your inner critics echoed can feel unbearably loud inside

not echo an inner critic. Few of us have been told that we need to climb mountains to be better people. If you had an interest in climbing, you might look into it. If not, you would simply ignore the suggestion, though you might wonder why your partner would encourage you to do this.

But if your partner says you should do something that echoes what an inner critic has told you — for example, that you should lose weight or get a better job or stop playing video games or eat differently, just to name a few common inner-critic beliefs — your response would likely be much more emotional.

You might be upset with your partner for saying that. You might feel defensive or down on yourself and pressured to do what they said. It would look and feel like your partner evoked those feelings, when in reality it was your inner critics. Sometimes even mild disappointment from someone whose opinion you value can be experienced as severe criticism because it empowers your inner critics.

Using the Inner Critic Care System, you will be able to identify the thoughts in your head that speak critically to you or evoke guilt and shame, so when others echo them you can address your inner voices directly rather than trying to change the other person or having them dictate what you should do.

It doesn't work to deny, repress, or ignore inner critics — if you do, their messages will only get louder and larger inside your head and project outward. Self-critical dialogue is extremely debilitating, not only in love relationships but at work and as you go about living your life.

Once you are able to deal with your inner critics effectively, you can look into others' suggestions if they appeal to you, ignore them if not, and realize that their opinions and desires have more to do with them than you. You will be less affected by others' judgments about you and be able to respond to them more harmoniously.

It isn't that you might not want to make changes or improvements in your life, it's that you don't need to be bullied or criticized into doing so. Knowing how to manage inner critics and care for yourself at the same time will give you tremendous advantages in every area of your life.

In my years of studying and experiencing the effects of inner critics, I've encountered a great deal of inner critic energy, especially in regard to love and relationships. As I transformed my relationships with my inner critics, all my external relationships began to positively shift also. It feels so liberating now to know when and how my inner critics get activated and know what to do about it, so that I rarely blame the people I love or project my inner critics onto them. Often I still try to, but I quickly realize it doesn't work.

For years I experienced abuse in my relationships, because I felt guilty and believed I should allow myself to be treated in ways that weren't good for me. I didn't know about inner critics at that time. Only as I became more self-aware was I able to be joyfully in a partnership.

Your inner critics don't just criticize you, they also criticize everyone around you. Not only do you need to live up to their standards, often so does everyone else. So you might find yourself speaking for your inner critics and making judgments about your partner. And if their inner critics match yours, your partner is likely to respond defensively. You might even get into a big fight, when in reality it's the inner critics in each of you fighting with the other's.

One time at the airport, John made a comment about how heavy my suitcase was, and when I questioned him and said that I was big enough to carry my own bag, it somehow turned into a discussion about my weight and size, and I started getting really vehement about my choices to be the size that I am and carry whatever size suitcase I want to.

In the middle of my emotional outburst, John just looked at me and said, "Who are you fighting with right now?" And I immediately realized that it was an inner critic who thought that I should be slim and trim, with only the smallest carry-on bag. I had projected that all onto John! We were able to laugh and be together lovingly and continue on our journey. I know from this and other experiences that having an awareness of inner critics and an Inner Critic Care System in place is pivotal to loving and being loved.

Taking charge of the messages you listen to = taking charge of your life.

The idea is for your adult self — we call it your Aware Self — to be in charge of your decisions, not your inner critics. Most of us start out so merged with our inner critics that we can't see them. We might say things like, "That's just the way I am, I've always been that way," or, "I know I have flaws and should do better," or, "Loving just isn't easy for me — I always find faults and flaws in whomever I'm with."

once you become aware

your Aware Self

it can all change

If the idea of inner critics is brand new to you, your first opportunity is to become *aware* of them. Begin to notice your inner dialogue. Is it critical of you or anyone else? Anything that implies that you or someone around you "should" be doing something different, or that you (or they) are bad, wrong, flawed, or unlovable as you are, is the voice of an inner critic.

Often, our thoughts move so quickly that we miss them. The easiest way to know that an inner critic has turned on you is by how you feel. If you're angry at someone for criticizing you, if you feel that you should be different, if you feel down on yourself, and especially if you're defending yourself — these are all signs of inner critics.

You can work from the feelings back to the thoughts. Allow yourself to be aware of the uncomfortable feelings and see if you can connect thoughts to them. They could be something like, "You'll never find love," or, "You should be better," or, "You always _____." The words "should," "never," and "always" are particular favorites of inner critics.

Get to Know Your Inner Critics

Here are descriptions of the most common inner critics that have likely come up as you've lived your life: _and Keep coming Up_

The Good Person

Lurking beneath all the other inner critics and giving them their power is the Good Person. This inner critic comes in many variations. It can be the good girlfriend or the good wife, the good student, or the good husband. In each case it represents an idealized standard, one that can be met only by hurting yourself and denying who you really are.

The OVERachiever or Pushing One

No amount of anything is ever enough. This critic pushes you to do *more* — no matter what — in its attempt to get you to live up to an impossible standard. You are always behind or not producing or experiencing what you'd hoped or expected. Even when you succeed, you see mostly flaws in yourself or ways that you didn't live up to the standard and should have done more.

With regard to love and relationships, this part will push you to date multiple people to look for the best relationship ever in the history of all relationships — and it will still not be enough.

When you realize you will never attain the idealized standard of the Good Person, in yourself or in a partner, the Overachiever takes over and pushes you to continue trying. You know you can't succeed, but you don't have permission to go off and do what would genuinely bring you joy.

The Perfectionist

Everything is constantly being polished and assessed for being "better," and nothing or no one is ever quite good enough. "Never good enough" is the mantra. New activities, things to try, or people to meet are measured by this critic, and often you don't do or try new things because you fear failing or not being good enough. In love, the Perfectionist will assure you that you — and anyone else — are certainly never good enough.

The Comparer
Everyone else's life, output, process, success, or relationship is better than yours — every time. And every comparison finds you lacking in some way, often in excruciating detail. You often think that your life is harder or that others' lives are easier, luckier, more blessed. In love and relationships, everyone else has it all figured out — brilliantly. You are acutely aware of how they meet the idealized standard and you don't.

The Procrastinator
If you do or try anything — especially love or relationships — it can be judged. Better not to start or to start later. Later rarely, if ever, arrives. Rehearsing, planning, incessantly thinking — without ever moving — are the hallmarks of this critic. You often feel tired or as if you're not doing what you say you'd like to. It feels familiar and like an old pattern.

This inner critic is often a front for the Good Person. You will make an agreement, such as, "I'll mow the lawn." But the agreement is really made by the idealized person you want to be — the Good Person — not who you really are. You can't give yourself permission to admit, "I really don't want to mow the lawn," so you agree to it. Then the Procrastinator takes over. You don't mow the lawn but feel guilty about it.

The Hopeless One
What's the point? Why begin anything at all? Why try love? *I tried before and failed. Nothing will ever work. It's all pointless....* This critic collapses before beginning, doesn't begin at all, feels sad about not beginning, immediately undoes the slightest movement forward.

See which of these inner critics seem to be the most familiar to you or active in your mind. You may also notice other negative messages, and if you hear them again and again, it helps to give them names.

Remember, anything that evokes feelings of being less than or not enough, of lack, or that you "should" be different, is an inner critic.

The key is to recognize that these inner critics represent beliefs you learned in childhood. Giving them names helps you see that they are not you. Then your adult, Aware Self can take charge rather than blindly giving in to their demands.

Once you are aware of a message from an inner critic, the next step is to evaluate it and develop a more nourishing message, one more suited to who you are now. We'll address how to do this in the Awareness Practice at the end of the chapter.

The point is, you don't need to blindly accept the inner critic's seemingly authoritative evaluation of you, the way you might have had to when you were very young. You can use your adult abilities to put these messages into a perspective that will actually benefit you.

These inner critics are not your enemy. You received them from basically well-meaning people. They are just not able to give you the best advice anymore, so it benefits you to examine what they are telling you and change the message to one that fits you better — and feels better.

You can also call on your Inner Wise Self to help you with this. As you are developing more suitable messages for yourself, ask your Inner Wise Self for its wisdom and guidance about your lovableness in general and the specific message from your inner critic. When you do this, inner critics can be sneaky and try to blend in with messages from your Inner Wise Self. So here are some guidelines to alert you if this is happening:

Your Inner Wise Self will never say anything bad about you. It loves you unconditionally. There is nothing you need to do to please your Inner Wise Self. In fact, it is most pleased when

sneaky critics, trying to blend in

you're happy. It will never tell you to do anything, because you don't need to do anything for it to love you completely.

It never focuses on fear, only love. So it will never warn you away from something (though you may interpret its message in that way). Instead it will invite you to go in a positive direction (which, of course, takes you away from any danger).

So if you get a message that indicates you must do anything or you haven't done enough, or that points to anything less than a positive path forward, then it is likely an inner critic sneaking in.

If you don't have time to fully address a message from an inner critic or if it's a communication you've heard and dealt with before, a simple, powerful technique is to simply say "NO" loudly and firmly. Move yourself physically as you do this — you might make a chopping-downward motion with your hand as you say or shout "NO" from your solar plexus.

I like to redirect them and give them something else to do, so they stay out of my life and relationships. If inner critics are really acting out, you can even imagine having them arrested and taken away — which I've done. You can invent a job or productive vacation for them. Inner critics need to work, or to do something, but they don't really care what they work on or do. If you don't help to redirect them, they will work on your life and your relationships.

The object is to use your imagination to separate yourself from your inner critics, to remember that their messages do not come from your adult, Aware Self, and that you are in charge of your life, not these remnants from your past.

If you're going to give an inner critic a job, be sure to tailor the job or assignment to that specific inner critic. Remember that you're transforming your relationship with the critic, not the critic itself. An inner critic can only ever be and do what it is and does. For example, a pushing one or overachiever could never just lie around on a beach without some kind of "purpose."

One time, John and I were walking on the beach and I had expressed that one of my inner critics I had named Scarcity Girl was really acting out and talking in my head about the scarcity of everything. John said, "Let me try to comfort your Scarcity Girl by— "

I animatedly interrupted him and said, "Comfort me. Scarcity Girl can only be that. She'll take everything you offer and turn it into scarcity. Even your suggestion is seen by her as scarce." John then offered comfort to my Aware Self, who was able to truly hear and appreciate it.

Suggested Jobs You Can Give Your Inner Critics

The OVERachiever or Pushing One

- Owner of an international nonprofit
- CEO of a corporation
- Yearlong spa vacation that has a significant personal growth outcome

The Perfectionist
- ★ Supervisor at an egg factory to check for all broken eggs
- ☆ Air-traffic controller
- @ Chief laboratory technician in charge of safety operations

The Comparer
- ☆ World biographer comparing careers of all writers
- ★ Comparative mathematical analyst
- ◎ World weather person

The Procrastinator
- ◎ Nap and sleep expert
- @ Bed tester
- ☆ Head of the Later Foundation

The Hopeless One
- ✦ Monk in a monastery
- @ Goat herder
- ★ Zen hospice coordinator

ONCE you GET TO KNOW your inner critics, You can Transform Your relationships WiTH THem. You'll Also THen See How tired THey Are. (THey work in Your Life WAy Too HArd + often + will welcome New Assignments)

NOTE: The inner critics will very likely try to sneak back, and when they do, just use your imagination to send them back to their job or assignment. And you can invent new assignments if they outgrow the old ones.

The Stages of Becoming Aware of Inner Critics in Your Relationships

STAGE 1

You only see your inner critics outside you — you see them in your partner and can't tell your partner apart from them. In this stage, you may unknowingly draw from your partner (or others) messages that are what your inner critics are saying in your head.

For example, if you have an inner critic that thinks you "should" lose weight, you'll pull out of your partner something that seems like they're critical of how much you weigh — and you'll then blame your partner.

STAGE 2

You're clear that you have inner critics and experience a mixture of responses — you sometimes hear the criticism from your partner but also know that you have that criticism in your head.

If you have an inner critic that thinks you "should" lose weight, you'll still periodically pull something about weight out of your partner, but when you get upset about what they said, after a while you'll remember the role your inner critics play, and the feeling will dissolve.

STAGE 3

You know your inner critics well and are in tune with your Aware Self. If your partner makes a statement that echoes them, you will be focused more on the fact that your partner wants something than that something is wrong with you. You might have a thought like, "Pushing me to change isn't the answer," without becoming upset.

We will be talking more about inner critics in chapter 13, "Sources of Anger and How to Transform Them." Anything you do to separate yourself and others from your inner critics will significantly increase the love you are able to feel for yourself and those around you.

Arielle Ford and Brian Hilliard — Inner Critics
Inner Parent Critics

ARIELLE: One day I found myself standing in front of Brian with my left hand on my hip and my right index finger wagging in his face, and I was carrying on about God knows what. I was appalled at my behavior, and stopped and said to him, "You know, the next time this happens — and unfortunately, there will probably be a next time — would you just kindly, gently, sweetly say to me, 'When did Sheila enter the room?'"

Arielle Ford and Brian Hilliard

Sheila is my mother's name. She is very cool and I love her to death, but she can at times be very bossy and overbearing.

Well, Brian totally got it and said, "Yes, and the next time I get too patronizing, you can call me Wayne." That was his dad's name. And then we were laughing. We quickly went from an almost World War Three situation right back to being best friends, lovers, and partners for life. Now when I get too bossy he starts laughing and calls me Sheila. When he steps on his soapbox, I just laugh and say, "Oh, look who's here! Wayne's in the room."

These "code names" quickly remind us to let go of the bad attitude!

Clean the Kitchen

BRIAN: Arielle is a mess in the kitchen. When we first met, I nearly had to wear a construction helmet because of all the flying debris. Plates, knives, and forks all over the place. I wouldn't say she is clumsy; things just kind of go wild when she is cooking.

ARIELLE: It's true, I am really clumsy. I am always breaking something.

BRIAN: My mother picked up after all of us, so I have neatness kind of ingrained. I'd rather keep it clean, or clean up early, than wait 'til later to clean up the kitchen or anything in the house. So in the early days I quickly learned the best and easiest solution was just to clean up after Arielle.

And that is a choice. You realize how grateful you are to be together, and you go back to the essence of the relationship and the things that truly matter. If little things come up, you quickly learn to broaden your perspective, just like you would do in anything in life. The truth is, Arielle is having fun in the kitchen. And I don't mind cleaning up after her. You have to do it from your heart so that there's no resentment or any anger or anything like that. It becomes a kind of Buddhist practice. I continue to be happy cleaning up after my beloved Arielle, and everything is okay.

Arielle is a bestselling author & speaker (SoulmateSecret.com). Brian's primary focus is on humanitarian projects, as well as assisting nonprofit organizations in the areas of fundraising, business consulting, and hands-on participation.

THE INNER CRITIC CARE SYSTEM

There are basically three ways to deal with inner critics, and all are part of your Inner Critic Care System:

1. Stop Them

As soon as you become aware of negative inner dialogue — it usually starts with something like, "I'll never," "I should," or, "I always" — simply say "NO" loudly and firmly. Move yourself physically as you do this. You might make a chopping-downward motion with your hand as you say or shout "NO" from your solar plexus. This effectively separates you from the energies of inner critics and makes you aware that they are not you and you are not them.

2. Redirect or Reassign Them

After you've become aware of your inner critics, you can invent jobs or assignments for them using your creativity and imagination. Making up funny and fascinating assignments for them will shift your experience of them as bullies or abusers. You will begin to see them as well-meaning, bumbling, and limited aspects of yourself, and be able to transform your relationships with them so that you can function without thinking they're in charge of you and everything you do.

3. Communicate with Them

This is good to do if you have some understanding about your inner critics and a developed connection with your Inner Wise Self. We call this the Five-Point Process. Even doing this process once will significantly change your inner world and result in your being much more aware of the inner critics in your life, how they are affecting you, and the power of communicating with them in a new way. **Also, just thinking about doing this process will shift your perspective.**

The Five-Point Inner Critic Care Process

In the Five-Point Process, you activate and empower your Inner Wise Self, and you and your Inner Wise Self interview your inner critics, get a list of their concerns and complaints, and transform your relationships with them. Before you do this process, it may help to activate and empower your Inner Wise Self by writing a Love Note or asking a question and receiving an answer.

1. **Identify and invite** the aspect of yourself that is "talking" the loudest inside your head to join you and your Inner Wise Self. Picture that aspect or critic joining you in the room. Imagine them sitting in a different chair or a place separate from you.

For example, you might have an inner Perfectionist that is speaking quite loudly to you inside your head. You might notice that this part of you is small and tired looking, or large and frightening. However it looks, it has things to say.

2. **Ask** this aspect for its list of concerns and complaints. Calmly take notes. Ask clarifying questions if appropriate.

For example, your inner Perfectionist might say things like:

🌟 Your love life is pathetic. When was the last time you _____ ?

⭐ In your relationship, you keep repeating the same mistakes! You never _____.

◎ I can't believe you served that meal to _____.

⭐ Your house is very cluttered, and you never clean it. You should really _____.

⭐ You should really visit _____ more often. You're not a good _____.

⭐ The way you conduct yourself at work is substandard. You'll never make enough money doing that. You should _____.

@ You always forget to _____ and never _____.

◎ It's obvious to everyone that you can't _____.

The list might seem endless, but eventually the Perfectionist will run out of concerns and complaints. See if you can keep going until that happens. Once it's all out of your head and down on paper, the effects of this critic will be *greatly* diminished. (You'll find that inner critics are very repetitive and rarely have new, substantial things to say.)

Once you have taken charge and dismantled their typical dialogue, you have removed the source of their power — *you have shifted it at the core*, and any further communications are symptoms you can swiftly address.

3. **Thank, honor, and acknowledge** this critic for working so hard, and assure it that you and your Inner Wise Self are now fully in charge. Then embody *being* in charge. This means that you do not allow inner critics to bully, cajole, or otherwise try to get you to believe their messages.

For example, you might say to your Perfectionist, "Thank you for helping me do such good work and live such a satisfying life. The high quality of everything I do is greatly helped by you. I really appreciate how hard you've worked on my behalf and realize that I haven't really acknowledged or even thanked you. I have now decided that my adult self and Inner Wise Self are fully in charge of my life. You still have an integral, positive part to play in my life, and I want you to know your value, so I am creating a new assignment for you, one that is *perfectly* suited to you."

4. **Reassign** this critic a new job or responsibility — either close by or far away — using your imagination. Remember that inner critics need to work or have an assignment. They don't care as much about what it is, they just want to feel valued and cared for. When assigning an inner critic a new job or responsibility, refer to the list of suggestions in this chapter (page 103). Let yourself get really creative and detailed. You can draw up a contract or agreement, write a letter to your critic, or do just an abbreviated sketch of what you think they might be doing.

For example, when I interviewed my Scarcity Girl that I referenced earlier, she informed me that she never liked that name and wanted a new one. So together we created a new

NAME FOR HER, WHICH IS MS. PRESERVATION. MS. PRESERVATION IS NOW
IN CHARGE OF ALL THE WATER SYSTEMS IN THE STATE OF CALIFORNIA,
TO ADDRESS THE DROUGHT CONDITIONS AND ESTABLISH NEW SYSTEMS
FOR WATER MANAGEMENT. SHE WORKS CLOSELY WITH THE GOVERNOR OF
CALIFORNIA AND TRAVELS FREQUENTLY. IT'S A HUGE JOB, AND SHE IS
VERY FULFILLED BY IT. I CONSULT WITH HER FROM TIME TO TIME ABOUT MY
LIFE, AND SHE'S IMMENSELY HELPFUL.

5. **Transform and reframe** the list of concerns and complaints from your critic that you made in step 2. Sit down with a pad of paper or tablet and ask your Inner Wise Self to join you in reframing and transforming this list. Make your countering statements as believable as possible, and don't "argue" with your inner critic. Just calmly and purposefully state what you know to be true.

- Use reminders, supportive statements, permissions, clarifications, encouragement, and love.

- Make your countering statements as believable as possible. They have to feel right for you and acceptable to you.

- Calmly and purposefully state what you know to be true. Defending yourself or arguing with your inner critic will keep you under their thumb. The intent is to be able to lovingly ignore them and do what is right for you.

After you've responded to each list item, you can cross out the original criticism. Here are two examples:

Critic's complaint: Your love life is pathetic. When was the last time you
_____?

Your reframing: Actually, my love life is pretty good. I'm really happy with
_____ and all the progress we've made and fun we've had. I'm really able to give and receive love after all.

Critic's complaint: In your relationship, you keep repeating the same mistakes! You never _____.

Your reframing: I've certainly made a lot of mistakes in love, and I've realized that it doesn't really matter as long as I continue communicating and showing up with my loving heart. It's obvious to me how much internal airtime I've given to fears, worries, criticisms, and doubts. I'm SO INSPIRED to think and act differently, with more self-love and awareness, and to LIVE MY LIFE FEELING MORE LOVE MORE OFTEN.

Doing step 5 even once will result in your being able to reframe things in your life on the spot, without having to do it in writing. You'll be able to look at many more situations with love rather than through the eyes of your inner critics. Your inner dialogue will be friendlier, easier, and *much* more loving. You will see and experience others in a more loving way also.

The One-Step Inner Critic Care Process

If you'd like a shorter version, just take any one comment from your inner critic and write a countering statement. If you can't think of one, ask your Inner Wise Self for help. For example, if your inner critic says, "You should be earning more money," you can counter with ways you are paying your bills, or bills you have paid, and anything you're doing that you feel proud of. This allows you to get into a new habit of not letting your inner critic have the last, or only, word. It also establishes positive new thought patterns and reinforces your relationship with your Inner Wise Self.

inner critics
Belief:
You'll never Be
ABle To HAve A
Good relationship
and
You SHould Be
HAppier Than
You Are

inner critics HAve A Lot
of opinions, But THey're
Always THe sAme ones

inner wise self
statement of Belief:
You Already HAve
Good relationships
And you Are learning
So MuCH ABout Love
and practicing often
and in New wAYs.
All is well

your inner wise self HAs
unlimited love for you and
Just wAits for you to Connect
and ASK.

Awareness Practice:
Transforming Your Relationships with Your Inner Critics

1. Become aware of messages from your inner critics.

    Listen to the dialogue in your head. Inner critics frequently use words like "never," "always," and "should." Hearing these words is your signal that an inner critic is likely speaking to you.

    If you feel defensive when someone comments on something you're doing, that is an inner critic.

2. When you recognize a message from in inner critic, use one or more of the parts of the Inner Critic Care System.

    Stop them.

    Redirect or reassign them.

    Use the Five-Point Process to communicate with them.

    Use the One-Step Process to counter the message.

    For more ways to transform your relationships with your inner critics, go here:
    SucculentWildLove.com/ICCS

YOU SAY THINGS LiKE:
"you ALWAYS..."
"you never..."
"you SHOULD..."

inner critic THINKS:
"OH GOOD! THEy're Listening To me!"

10. "Succulent And Wild" Means Self-Lovingly Separate And Beautifull Boundaries

There Are countless ways To ride on The road

Many modern roads have white lines along the edges and a yellow line in the center. Having clear lines and knowing what happens when you cross them makes traveling down the highway much easier and more comfortable. The same is true in relationships.

 Boundaries can Be experimented with

What Is Self-Lovingly Separate, Why Are Boundaries Beautifull, and Why Are They Important?

The words "self-lovingly separate" may seem ironic when emphasizing the value of relationships, but it's good to remember that any relationship is made up of two or more valuable individuals and that each person's ability to love themselves and be separate as well as together affects that relationship.

While joining together with another can be immensely beneficial, it's also important for each participant to be aware of their boundaries and those of the other person. When their boundaries are crossed without invitation, people feel invaded and angry.

THIS SUBJECT WAS ONE OF THE BIGGEST REASONS I HADN'T ALLOWED MYSELF TO HAVE A live-in, ROMANTIC RELATIONSHIP. I'D EXPERIENCED SO MANY BOUNDARY VIOLATIONS GROWING UP THAT IT SEEMED CLEAR TO ME THAT love RELATIONSHIPS Were BEYOND MY SCOPE OF BOUNDARY ABILITIES. I MOSTLY AVOIDED CONFLICT OR BECAME resistAnt to perceived DOMINANCE By ANOTHER Person. IT WASN'T Until I'D DONE SIGNIFICANT SELF-love WORK WITH MYSELF THAT I UNDERSTOOD THAT I COULD FeeI loved AnD lovinG WHile AISo HAVinG BOUNDAries.

i BecAMe BUoyanT wiiH MY BounDAries

An obvious example of uninvited boundary crossing might be someone reading your mail or journals. But there are often more subtle forms. Someone telling you what is best for you — such as what to eat, how to exercise, or how to complete a task — is crossing your boundaries.

When you invite someone to help you, their help can often be beneficial. But when they aren't invited, their advice may not feel good. The implication can be, "You aren't running your life the way it should be run. I know better for you."

People often see boundary breaking as a sign of intimacy or love. This relates to the notion of ownership: "This is *my* husband or *my* child." It's common for people to not realize they're breaking the boundaries of someone close and then wonder why the person is mad at them.

This is one of the main sources of tension between parents and teenagers. The adolescents want to begin to function independently, and the parents want to keep them in line with familiar patterns and values. So the (usually well-meaning) parents press the teens to be more like they used to be, and the adolescents get angry.

We begin to learn about romantic love in our teen years, so many of us identify intimacy with someone caring enough to tell us what is best for us. We may actually not feel loved if someone close to us doesn't enter our boundaries uninvited. But this is often entwined with the discomfort of having them do so.

One person in a relationship may keep reminding the other to eat healthier. While this could be annoying to the person being reminded, it might feel worse if their partner didn't care. The person being reminded may even become afraid that without the ongoing prompts they would fall off a cliff into totally unhealthy eating. People sometimes develop patterns where they depend on others to tell them what to do, both as a way of feeling loved and to help them make decisions.

If you want to change a pattern where someone regularly reminds you to do things that you are perfectly capable of deciding for yourself, highlight other ways they can show their love for you. Being prepared to take full responsibility for your eating habits or whatever activities you're being reminded about is also important. With these things clarified, you can begin to send messages that your decisions are your own and you are not requesting advice.

Once you understand the concept of boundaries, you can consciously invite others in and send clear messages when they enter without an invitation. This way you can have intimacy without the discomfort of feeling controlled.

Inviting someone into your boundaries is a privilege you give them. In a Succulent Wild Love relationship it's a privilege that never changes into a right someone can use to "tame" or limit you. This is what makes the boundaries beautifull.

I used to be convinced that I did know the best way for another person! I would try to persuade them by showing or telling them about what I'd learned or experienced — usually without being asked. I was very well-meaning — and, I now see, misguided.

Once my younger brother was visiting, and he agreed to do the dishes after I'd cooked a meal. After he finished, I went over and found crumbs in the sink and a damp sponge sitting on top of them. I went over to Andrew with what I thought was my most reasonable explanation about a better way to do the dishes.

He smiled and asked me how long it would take to have the sink and sponge be up to my standards. I replied that it would take a minute or less. He then asked me why I couldn't just do that then. I replied that it wasn't how dishes are done, or sinks and sponges are to be handled.

He said, "According to who — you?" He then explained that this was his way to do the dishes and that if I wanted to ask him to do something, I couldn't also then tell him how to do it. He also pointed out that this is what our mother had done, and I wasn't his mother.

i THOUGHT "MY WAY" WITH sponges WAS THE only WAY

It felt like a revelation to think that I didn't need to teach him or anyone "the best way" — a.k.a. "my way." And I haven't broken his boundaries in this way since — which is saying a lot for a fairly prone-to-hovering older sister.

SECURITY, PRIVACY, ACTIVITY, AND RESPECT (SPAR)

There are four aspects to boundaries — security, privacy, activity, and respect. We coined the term SPAR to refer to them. You can look at SPAR in two ways: A spar is something that keeps things up, like a sail or tent. It is also a form of fighting. Depending on what you do with your boundaries, they can support your relationship or result in ongoing tension.

SECURITY doesn't just relate to feeling safe from harm, though that is of course important. It relates to being able to live in a way that feels comfortable, such as in a home that isn't constantly too hot or too cold. It means having the things you need for your hygiene and comfort.

PRIVACY relates to allowing yourself to have an inviolate area where you don't have to respond to another person. This could include their not digging around in your personal things, reading your mail, or watching you in the bathroom. The sphere of privacy is different for everyone, but you know when someone is invading your space.

ACTIVITY refers to the actions you want to take and the thoughts you think. External activity includes those times when you want to be "in your own world," whether by meditating, engaging in a hobby, or spending time with a friend. It's the need to replenish yourself through solitude or spending time with others besides your partner. External activity also includes larger life choices, such as your career or where you want to put your time and energy.

I SOMETIMES ENJOY WATCHING lots OF television AND HAVE experienced others JUDGING ME or reacting to this activity choice. It WAS definitely one OF the things that HAD kept ME From living WITH someone I loved — that I wouldn't BE ABle to really DO WHAt I wanted. I'D HAVE to somehow tone myself Down, or even Give UP things I loved, so that they would Feel more comfortable.

I now UNDERSTAND that it WAS More ABout ME AND My relationship WITH My inner Critics — the PARts OF ME that thought I WAS WAsting My time WITH television, WHICH CAUSED ME to overreact to others' Attitudes. I AM so HAPPY now to live in A Deeply romantic AND loving relationship AND DO WHAtever I WAnt — something I'D previously thought IMPOSSIBle, or very Unlikely. And now I WATCH plenty of GreAt TV AND HAVE A GreAt relationship.

Internal activity is the right to have your own opinions and views on various subjects. Sometimes it is so difficult for people to accept others' viewpoints that the most joyful solution is not to discuss certain topics. (For example, it can be difficult for someone in a family of avid football fans to be uninterested in the home team — and almost impossible to support an opposing team.)

RESPECT means treating each other with kindness and dignity. Most of us are fairly respectful to our friends, in part because we know they have no obligation to be around us. If we don't treat them well, they'll leave. This can get distorted when there is a formal tie, such as in a marriage, between parents and children, or with a boss. When you know it isn't easy to leave, it can be tempting to allow someone to treat you with disrespect. When someone is interacting with you, a question to ask is, Would they treat a friend this way?

Here is an example of where the two of us had to deal with different worldviews, our boundaries of internal activity.

Susan and I were driving through San Francisco one evening when she surprised me by suddenly locking the car doors.

I HAD lived HAPPily in DOWntoWn SAn FrAnCisCo For A nUMBer oF yeArs, WAlKing eVeryWHere WitH My PUrPle BACKPACK AnD enCoUntering All Kinds oF CHArACters. THe GreAt MAJority oF My eXPerienCes in tHe AreA HAD Been Positive, BUt I Also HAD soMe UnCoMFortABle enCoUnters on tHe street. on tHis eVening WitH JoHn, I notiCeD I WoUlD Feel More CoMFortABle iF I loCKeD tHe CAr DOors As We DroVe tHroUGH tHis PArtiCUlAr PArt oF DOWntoWn.

My experience with San Francisco has been one of feeling safe everywhere I go. In fact, that's my experience most places. Of course I didn't object to Susan's locking the doors. I want her to do whatever is necessary for her to feel safe. If someone believes there is a threat and doesn't protect themselves, at best they'll be tense and at worst they'll line themselves up with a negative experience.

I loVe tHAt JoHn sUPPorts My riGHt to CHoose WHAt Feels Best to Me. I WAnteD to loCK tHe Doors so I CoUlD FoCUs on otHer sUBJeCts WitHoUt FoCUsing on WHetHer I Felt sAFe or not.

But I also felt some resistance. I didn't want to take on Susan's view that downtown San Francisco is a dangerous place where someone might open our car door at a stoplight. So I began to try to convince her it was actually safe. "See the bicyclists. If it weren't safe, they wouldn't be out." Susan responded by trying to convince me that her view was more accurate.

I didn't appreciate that John was trying to convince me that it was safe. I told him, "I used to live here and had some bad experiences." I was trying to demonstrate through my previous experiences that I knew more. Mostly, I didn't want his perception to pull me off mine.

Could I allow her to have her experience without feeling that I must echo it? I value and respect Susan's opinions. She's my life partner, and we share a basic worldview. So I felt some pressure to either get her to change her view about the danger or to go along with hers.

When one person is afraid and the other is not, how do we handle that? Susan and I have an agreement: if one of us has a more loving perspective, we will try to follow that. But if a certain level of fear (or frustration) is involved, that can be hard to do.

Yes — I knew that John's perspective was more loving, but I was focusing on what would feel best to me. I didn't know how to do that with the door locks without affecting John.

I reminded myself that just because we're intimate doesn't mean we have to see the world in the same way. If I know I have the right to my own views, I can allow and respect Susan's.

In this instance, Susan only pressed me mildly to conform to her view, mostly in response to my pressing her to change to mine. But it wasn't really what she did that made me uncomfortable. My discomfort came from my insecurity about being able to keep my perspective in the face of her differing view.

Have you ever been in a situation when someone told you a particular person was mean or negative in some way, only to find that your interactions with the person were perfectly fine? Usually, we're predisposed to see people in the same way as our loved ones see them, and it can take some effort to retain our own perspective.

The more your worldview differs from your partner's, the more effort it takes to build a life with them. The ideal is to be different enough to stimulate each other but not so different that you can't find agreement on things that affect your daily life. This is true for relationships with family and friends as well. Sometimes, the most joyful solution is not to discuss certain topics — or even to go your separate ways.

In an ideal relationship — a Succulent Wild Love relationship — your individual lives are entwined but not forced together. You have the ability to nourish yourself and are delighted in the nourishment you receive from the other. You each invite the other into your boundaries to the extent that it feels good, knowing that you'll have your boundaries honored.

You invite the other into your boundaries with joy and adventure and to share love

Awareness Practice: Being Self-Lovingly Separate with Beautifull Boundaries

HONORING YOUR BOUNDARIES

1. Write down your responses to each kind of boundary below. Do you have any memories of them being broken, in the past or recently? Here are some descriptions:

   Security: Feeling safe and that your physical needs are met.

   Privacy: No one will pry into your personal things.

   External Activity: What you want to do in terms of daily activity or life path. Do you feel free to see friends, make career choices, and have projects that appeal to you?

   Internal Activity: Your opinions or attitude about things.

   Respect: Being treated with dignity and kindness. Do the intimate people around you speak to you in the way they would to a friend?

2. If you have listed any way your boundaries are being broken currently, write down ways you can take charge of them.

   For example, if someone close to you is breaking your external activity boundary as a way of showing they care about you, can you guide them to other ways they can show they care? If someone is telling you what they think you should eat, for instance, you could:

   thank and acknowledge them for caring

   let them know that you're happy with your nutrition

   invite them to celebrate your health in other ways with you

HONORING OTHERS' BOUNDARIES

Are you breaking anyone's boundaries — even if you're well-meaning, trying to help them?

   Security: Are you not meeting someone's physical needs when they're counting on you? For example, promising to pick them up and forgetting, or not locking the door when you leave the house and they're home alone.

   Privacy: Are you looking through someone's clothes drawers or computer without their permission?

External Activity: Are you pressing someone to spend time with you, exercise, lose weight, dress differently, have different friends, go out less, or do anything that they specifically haven't asked you to help them with?

Internal Activity: Are you pressing others to agree with you on some topic? When you visit family members during holidays, for example, can you allow them to have different views from your own?

Respect: Arc you being kind to the people close to you?

Are you getting angry feedback from anyone close to you about entering their boundaries? If so, see if you can find another way to get what you need in the relationship. We talk about creating Joyful Solutions in the next chapter. Once you have some skill with these, see if you can create one to resolve the boundary issue.

The only way you can honor your and others' boundaries is through awareness. You don't need to vigilantly guard them, just be aware when you feel uncomfortable. Notice when someone is telling you what to do, what to think, or how to feel. Also, when you get an angry response from someone, consider that you might be entering their boundaries uninvited.

If you want to explore boundaries further, go to:
SucculentWildLove.com/Boundaries

11. The "No Compromise" Relationship: Creating Joyfull Solutions With Everyone

JOY♡Full Solutions
can solve everything

The intimate people in your life will change for you in any way they can — if they can do it without sacrificing.

The idea of Joyfull solutions was new to me when I met John. He told me, "I want to offer you a 'no compromise' relationship," and that sounded really good, but I couldn't imagine how that would work. Most people think the best they can do is compromise, where each person gives up a little bit and both feel a little bit bad in some way, and then they go on. I knew I never wanted to do that, and it's one of the reasons I chose to be happily married to myself and live by myself.

John introduced the concept of Joyfull solutions as going beyond compromise into a new way of relating to people, and the basis of it is that there is no scarcity — everybody gets what they want. This was amazing to me because I always thought I either had to give stuff up or they had to give stuff up. Society teaches us this, and we see it in politics, and we see it everywhere, and when John said, "No. We can

CReAte JoyFull Solutions together where we both Get what we wAnt," I
DeCIDeD I wAnteD to Be in thAt kind oF relAtionship.

I liked the iDeA of JoyFull Solutions But wAs still hesitAnt when we
stArteD tAlking ABout living together. John hAD liveD in SAn FrAnCisCo
BeFore AnD loveD it, so we QuiCkly DeCIDeD he woulD Move here rAther
thAn My Moving to ColuMBus, ohio, where he hAD Been living. I Felt I
neeDeD to ArrAnGe thinGs AnD CleAr out Closets, AnD GenerAlly see if I
CoulD MAke spACe For hiM. It wAs As MuCh MAking eMotionAl spACe As
physiCAl spACe. I hAD liveD here Alone For 23 yeArs, AnD it isn't A BiG
ApArtMent. Also, I live AnD work in the sAMe spACe, so there Are A lot
of Art supplies!

I wAs ABle to CleAr out one Closet For John AnD hAD everything
pileD up, AnD we Both neeDeD More spACe. So we stArteD the proCess
of FinDing JoyFull Solutions together. John BouGht soMe Dressers, AnD
I wAs DeliGhteD with the Dressers AnD stArteD putting thinGs into
theM. BeFore, All I'D FoCuseD on wAs Me or hiM Giving soMething up. The
AppeArAnCe of the Dressers ACteD like A MAGnet, AnD they BeCAMe A
new JoyFull Solution.

So rAther thAn John wAnting Me to ChAnGe, or us ArGuing ABout whAt
AppeAreD to Be sCArCity of spACe, we tAlkeD ABout how we CoulD FinD
soMething thAt Feels GooD to Both of us, AnD we DiD it. This openeD
up the whole CAteGory of CreAting JoyFull Solutions For everything, AnD
I enjoyeD Doing it
like A GAMe. Then I
reAlizeD this "GAMe"
wAs proDuCing serious
results, AnD I BeCAMe
CoMpletely CoMMitteD
to the ConCept AnD

an AssortMent of CoMpliCAteD suBjeCts
written in A lAnGuAGe no one can understAnd
AnD thAt J O Y ♥ Full Solutions can solve

its AppliCAtion. I reAlizeD thAt As I BeCAMe More skilleD At Applying
JoyFull Solutions, I woulD Be ABle to prACtiCe with More CoMpliCAteD
suBjeCts too.

I had a convertible sports car when I was in Columbus and loved it. And San Francisco is a great
place for a convertible. However, where Susan lives there aren't many parking spaces, and we
really didn't need two cars in the city. I wanted to keep my convertible, but Susan's Mini Cooper
was perfect for finding small parking spots and had more room for carrying things than my car.

We went back and forth for a while, and it didn't seem like we could find a Joyful Solution. Keeping Susan's Mini made more sense, but I didn't want to give up the open-air feeling of the convertible. That was the essence of what I wanted, and I realized I could get that feeling — and actually have it even more — by getting a scooter. Finding parking for it was easy, and filtering through city traffic on it was fun.

One of us could have given up the vehicle we wanted, or we could have compromised and lived with two automobiles and the associated parking issues. By making the effort to go beyond compromise, we were able to come up with a solution that was even better than what either of us had started with.

Believe You Can Create a Joyful Solution

Most people spontaneously look for solutions that meet everyone's needs. We want to please the people we love and want to please ourselves. It's when we get stuck that we start to look for a compromise or think someone has to sacrifice.

To create a Joyful Solution, you start with the attitude that everyone can get what they want. That is the biggest factor. Starting from that approach is so powerful because when you believe that everyone can get what they want, you can help the other person get what makes them happy.

Often people are focused on scarcity: they think there is only a limited amount of whatever, so they have to put all their energy into trying to get what they can of it. Then the other person picks up on that and feels pushed away. And then they feel they also have to put all their energy into getting whatever they can, and it becomes a tug-of-war.

But the dynamic changes dramatically when you approach the other person with the attitude of "This is what I want. Help me understand what you want, because I want to help you get what you want too."

When people feel that, the tension dissipates. From that emotional place they will often happily make adjustments because they see it as getting them closer to what they want.

So, creating Joyful Solutions begins with believing you can. The greatest limitation to finding a fully satisfying solution for everyone in any situation is the belief that compromise is as far as you can go.

There is nothing inherently wrong with compromise, but intimate relationships feel more secure and supportive when both people know they're on the same side. When people are limited to compromise or even sacrifice, each person tends to think they must push against the other or give up.

I resist almost everything initially and focus on scarcity frequently. Living with John is a revelation, because he resists very little and believes that everyone can get what they want. I definitely ride on his energy and by watching and listening to him am learning a lot about how I can experience less resistance and scarcity thinking. After we met, he decided to sell his home and move to San Francisco, and the man he was selling his house to called a number of times to discuss the deal. I would walk by and hear John on the phone saying, "I want you to have the very best deal." John was consistently loving and generous, and it was clear that everyone was getting what they wanted. I marveled that there was no tension and it all worked so well. A few times in the process there were puzzles to solve, and John applied Joyfull Solutions — and they worked.

GIVE YOURSELF PERMISSION TO HAVE IT ALL

In some situations, one person feels uncomfortable but decides it isn't bad enough that they want to press someone they love to change. This is often true for mothers or other caregivers. Knowing you can create a Joyful Solution gives you permission to honor your needs along with the other person's.

The husband of a friend of ours is handy around the house, and they had agreed that he would redo the kitchen. But the project was so big that it was taking him a long time to get everything in place to do it. Talking with us, she realized what was most important to her was that the wall between the living room and kitchen be knocked down. That way, whoever was cooking — usually our friend — wouldn't be isolated from everyone else when they had people over.

She had felt frustrated about waiting for her husband to start, but she knew that the kitchen was a big project and didn't want to push him when he didn't feel ready. When we suggested she approach him with the idea of finding a Joyful Solution rather than pressing him to change, she quickly felt free to talk with him about finding a way to open the wall sooner.

Being able to approach someone with the attitude that you both can get what you want allows people who are sensitive to others' needs to speak up when otherwise they would feel hesitant.

Succulent Wild Love is about being both supportive of others and completely satisfied yourself. Believing you can create Joyful Solutions is a powerful incentive to make the effort to have it all.

I've found out that I'm kind of a "secret sacrificer" in some cases, and just "put up" with things because it seems easier than talking about them. That's starting to shift significantly, though, as I recognize that it's actually easier to talk about them and receive the benefits of Joyfull Solutions.

FOCUS ON THOSE ASPECTS OF THE SITUATION THAT FEEL GOOD

We often get so focused on the one thing that bugs us that we become completely unaware of the many positive things that can point us to a joyful outcome.

I remember impatiently waiting to park my car in a shopping mall as a woman was endlessly putting things into her SUV. I kept intently focusing on her and judging that she should be going faster. When she was finally finished and the spot was free, I began to relax. I stopped focusing on her and my frustration. It was only then that I noticed the empty space a few cars farther down that I could have pulled into right away.

Most of the time when you are looking for a Joyful Solution there are actually many things you agree on with the other person. If you remind yourself (and each other) of those, you won't get hypnotized the way John did in the parking lot.

ALLOW FOR SEPARATE PATHS

There are two kinds of Joyful Solutions in any relationship, ones where you take a joint path and ones where you take separate paths.

Susan and I were hiking in Red Rock Canyon near Las Vegas. It was hot and sunny, with very little shade. I wanted to hike more, and Susan wanted to turn back. After some discussion back and forth, we decided to separate, with her waiting happily in a small shady spot while I trekked farther and returned.

All separations aren't so easy. But there are times when the most joyful solution involves separate paths — temporarily or permanently. Allowing for the ebb and flow of togetherness in relationships makes it much easier to find Joyful Solutions. In the chapter on separate paths (see page 228), we go into this more deeply.

THE TWO KEY PARTS TO FINDING JOYFUL SOLUTIONS: FINDING THE ESSENCE AND GOING WIDE

Finding the Essence

While you may not always be able to get what appears on the surface, you can find a way to get the essence of what you want. Say there is only one piece of blueberry pie left and two of you want it. If your friend eats it, there's none for you. A good compromise would be for each of you to get half. That's easy, and most of us would stop there. Everyone gave up an even amount.

But what if you don't want to give anything up? If you stay focused on either you or your friend getting that last piece of pie, then you're stuck — there's only one. Instead, each of you can ask yourself, "What is the essence of what I want?" Perhaps one of you wants the taste of blueberries and the other wants pie or just a sweet dessert.

On the surface, it looks like you want the same thing — that last piece of pie. But what it means to each of you can be vastly different. Getting the pie is the solution to fulfilling a desire. When you look at the essence of that desire, you can begin to see that there might be other ways to fulfill it.

So the question to ask is, What is it that each of you is looking for when you say you want the pie (or whatever the surface issue is)?

A friend of ours who is a mediator has a great story about two farmers who were fighting over an orange grove. When they were finally forced to sit down and talk to each other, to their surprise, they found out one wanted the orange rinds and the other wanted the juice.

Go Wide

Once you know the essence, you can begin to go wide — that is, look for alternatives that can fulfill the essence. In our pie example, you might ask, "Are there any other sweet desserts in the house? Can we easily get something even better somewhere else?" You could even go on a dessert-hunting adventure.

PREPARING YOURSELF TO CREATE A JOYFUL SOLUTION

Four of the most feared words in many relationships are "We have to talk."

The main things that keep people from joining together to create Joyful Solutions are anger and mistrust. If you wait to approach the other person until you or they are angry, or if you have a history of approaching each other with criticism, one or both of you will not want to participate.

So if you feel angry, before you begin engaging with the other person, use your Inner Feelings Care System (page 86) to rebalance yourself. When you know you can create solutions that feel good, it will be relatively easy to take charge of your anger rather than having it take charge of you.

Once you begin to send clear, unambivalent messages that you want to help the other person (knowing you can get what you want too), any anger or mistrust they have will dissolve over time.

I used to use those four most feared words — "we have to talk" — and got pretty much the response you would expect. I would approach my partner with the attitude of "I'm unhappy, and if you would only do the right thing, everything would be fine."

Since I've been practicing creating joyfull solutions with John, I have much more of an attitude of "this is my preference," rather than "I'm representing a higher authority." Now I say, "I need a joyfull solution, John." And he usually responds with something along the lines of "okay, let's sit down. Let's create one."

We will talk more about this in chapter 13, "Sources of Anger and How to Transform Them." For now we recommend starting with situations where there aren't intense feelings.

Creating a Joyful Solution with Someone

In many situations you won't need to complete all the steps below, or you will complete them so easily that they will hardly seem like steps. But in situations that seem difficult, following the process below will help you create a Joyful Solution.

1. Begin with both of you communicating clearly what you want.

    We'll use the example of a two people deciding what color to paint their living room: he wants to paint it blue, and she prefers white.

2. See where you already agree, and take a moment to acknowledge these points. The goal here is to feel the support that you have for each other. Feeling that you are mostly both on the same side will enhance the possibility that you can be on the same side in resolving the current issue.

    They both want a spacious room with lots of light. They like two chairs with reading lamps, and so on.

3. Now look at what each of you wants and go deeper to **find the essence**. What characteristics about these things are attracting each of you?

    She: I like the white because it brightens the room.

    He: The walls of my childhood home were blue. It feels familiar and comfortable.

    It may take a while to get to the essence of what you want. It's a matter of practice and paying attention to how you feel. Here are some ideas for finding the essence:

    ◎ You can help each other by suggesting things or asking questions.

    ✦ You can separate and give yourselves time to reflect.

    ★ You can playfully explore different solutions, either separately or together. Here, be as imaginative as possible without any concern about what the other person might want or what is realistically possible. The intent at this point isn't to create a solution yet, but to help you get a clearer understanding of what feels joyful to you.

4. Take the essence each of you has discovered and **go wide**. See how that particular desire can be met in other ways.

    Are there other ways of brightening the room, such as light curtains or lighter-colored furniture? Can they put furniture or other items in the room that will evoke his familiar feelings of childhood?

Often when you do this, you will come up with a number of solutions that could work, and maybe even one that is better than what either of you thought of originally.

With this knowledge, practice, and some focused effort, an outcome that addresses everyone's desires can be fashioned in any situation. You will be amazed by what you can create once you begin to experiment with going beyond compromise.

Ultimately, You Are Only in Charge of Yourself

In some situations, even if you come up with a resolution that addresses everyone's essence, the other person may not respond positively. Rebellious teenagers come to mind, or angry ex-spouses. In any relationship where you have been operating with fear frequencies, such as anger or control, the other person may be hesitant to believe that the solution you've created is really in their best interest.

You cannot take responsibility for how another person chooses to respond. You can only take responsibility for how you approach them — with love or with fear. If you are genuinely approaching others with the intent of helping everyone get what they want, they will ultimately respond in kind.

responding in kind feels great

Awareness Practice:
Creating Joyfull Solutions with Everyone

1. Begin looking at situations in your daily life where you are making decisions with others. See how often you're creating Joyful Solutions without thinking much about it.

    For example, you might choose to go to a movie everyone wants to see, or maybe someone unexpectedly wants to meet an hour later than planned, and you're easily able to rearrange your schedule.

2. You might see a situation where your automatic response is to let the other person have it their way. Here you might consider what you would do if it were entirely up to you.

    ◉ Think of the essence of what you want.

    ☆ See if you can discern the essence of what the other person wants. (If it feels right, you can ask the other person to explore the essence of what they want.)

    ★ Go wide and think of alternative solutions.

    At this point it doesn't matter if you share your new ideas with the people around you. The focus is on feeling your creative power. (But if one of the solutions you come up with works, go for it.)

3. Get comfortable with looking for the essence as you go about making decisions with others.

4. Feel the power of your creativity in finding new solutions.

    This is a time to be playful, to learn and practice with total freedom to create Joyful Solutions or not. It's like learning to play a musical instrument. If you try to perform before you're ready, you can get a reputation that you're not harmonious.

    You can share what you're doing with those close to you who will understand that you're exploring something new.

    The key at this point is to develop a new creative habit of looking for the essence in any situation where you feel stuck and then exploring wider options. Once you feel confident doing this, it will be much easier to apply your skills to more significant situations in your life.

For more about creating Joyful Solutions, go to:
SucculentWildLove.com/JoyfulSolutions

12. Creating Joyfull Solutions on Your Own

JOY ♡ FUll solution creating

IF YOU CAN GO into situations knowing you can find a Joyful Solution for yourself without anyone else having to change in a specific way, you are in a powerful position. Most people believe they need to have power over others to get what they want. You can learn to use the power of your creativity.

I HAD SOME long-STANDING tension WiTH neighBors WHo WANTED ME TO CUT BACK THE BrANCHES OF severAl trees BEHiND My MAGiC CottAGE (THE Tiny HoUSE WHere I CreATED My First Five BOOKS AND COntinue TO CreATE Art in ToDAy). THEy WANTED MORE OF A View, AND I WANTED THE sHelTer AND PrivACy Given By THoSE BrANCHES. For A nUMBer OF yeArS I BASiCAlly DeFleCTED AND AvoiDED My neighBors. I WOULD MAKE PeriodiC ATTEMPTS TO MolliFy THeM. We CuT A liTTle BiT, So THEY GoT A liTTle BiT OF WHAT THEY WANTED AND I GoT A liTTle BiT OF WHAT I WANTED. THE WHOle THing WAS FAirly DreADFUl. I DiDn'T KNOW ABOUT JoyFUll SoluTions AT THAT TiME, So TO ME THiS WAS THE BeST We COUlD Do.

So Here COMES JoHN inTo My liFe, AND I SAy, "OH, I HEArD From THE neighBors. I need TO Do SOMETHing ABOUT THESE trees." AND He SAyS, "Well, leT's FiND A JoyFUll SoluTion."

I looKED AT HiM, liKE, "NoT THESE PEOPle. THEy WON'T GeT iT." He SAiD,

"They don't have to get it. You get it. Let's go over there." I said, "Go over there? What do you mean, go over there?" said, "Let's go talk to them." I said, "There, in person?" I mean, I was horrified because, remember, I'd been hiding. I'm making this sound dramatic, but it did scare me. And I thought, "Oh, it's not going to be good. It's going to be unpleasant."

So we went over there, and I saw the view from their perspective, and they had very little light because of all the tree branches. Then we created a joyfull solution. We looked at the branches, and I said, "Well, you could cut those."

They replied with surprise, "Oh, really?" And I said, "Yes — just keep the lower ones so that I have more privacy." With the attitude of believing we all could get what we wanted, it felt so different than before — where I'd thought I had to sacrifice, or they did. With joyfull solutions, you don't stop until everybody feels good.

And then I stood out there with my neighbor. I said to her, "I just want to acknowledge my behavior from before and apologize to you, because I have blocked you and avoided you and never helped you get what you wanted. And I feel so good now." She had tears in her eyes, and she said, "I feel so good now too." And we hugged, and they invited us over for a glass of wine, and everybody was happy.

So you can do this with anyone in your life. They don't have to know anything about joyfull solutions.

You can create Joyful Solutions on your own with people who aren't actively trying to help you, as Susan was able to do with her neighbors. Other people may not be able to go further than trying to get you to do what they want, but that doesn't have to keep you from going beyond that to address everyone's desires.

Many years ago I was living with a woman, and we used to sit in bed together reading. I liked to sit right next to her, touching, and she was more comfortable sitting separately on her side of the bed.

For me, sitting close together was a Love Symbol (you'll learn about these in chapter 16). Every time I would ask her to come closer she would resist, and often I would start an argument — if not about that, then about something else. The disagreements were uncomfortable for both of us, but I realized later that they got me intimate attention similar to the feeling of being loved that I was missing.

I was trying to get her to do what I wanted (to sit closer), and she was trying to get me to do what she wanted (to let her read in peace on the other side of the bed). This went on for a while.

When I realized what I was doing, my solution was to sit in bed apart from her the way she wanted and to basically see if there was another way I could get what I wanted. (I didn't know about consciously looking for the essence at that time.) When I didn't feel loved sitting there, I would repeat over and over in my mind, "She loves me." (Our overall relationship was going well, and I had many other indications that she did. If I didn't basically believe she loved me, simply saying that wouldn't have worked.)

By putting my focus there, I stopped provoking her to fight with me. It took a few times, but I was able to start feeling her love for me even as we sat apart. Then it was no longer so important that we sit together touching. As I felt loved, I felt more loving, and then her responses to me changed. She reached out to me, and we actually had more intimate contact than by arguing or even simply sitting side by side touching the way I had originally wanted.

For the purpose of learning how to create Joyful Solutions, we recommend that you experiment with doing so without asking for the other person's help. See how far you can go on your own before inviting them to consciously join you. When you know you can do it on your own, you won't be dependent on others having the same level of awareness you have.

Awareness Practice:
Creating Joyfull Solutions on Your Own

As you think about creating Joyful Solutions, the first things that come to mind may be knotty issues that have been bothering you for some time. You'll get to those, but we highly recommend starting with a decision you're planning to make with someone where the emotional stakes aren't high. It may be as simple as which movie to go to or what to have for dinner. Or it could be something more complex, such as where to go on vacation. The key at this point is that no one is intensely attached to a particular outcome. Low-emotional-impact decisions are the best when you're first learning the process of Joyful Solutions.

Think of a situation where your usual response would be to let others have their way or where you want someone to change.

1. Think about or write down as clearly as possible exactly what you want. Don't take the other person into consideration at this point. What is the ideal outcome that you can see at the moment?

2. Imaginatively put yourself in the other person's shoes. What do they want? Be as specific as possible. What do you imagine their ideal outcome would be?

3. In what aspects of the situation do you agree? Take a moment to write them down.

4. Now write down the need or desire that is behind the outcome you described for yourself. What is the essence of what you want?

5. Put yourself in the other person's shoes. What is the need or desire behind the outcome they want? What is the essence of what they want? (For some things, it may take some time to get a clear picture here. It may help to get a better feel for this while you're with them, observing them.)

6. Looking at the statements of your and the other person's essential desires, explore different possible scenarios that address them. (Sometimes a solution comes right away. At other times, it may take a while to imagine something that feels good to everyone. If you feel stuck, you can sleep on it, or mull it over the way you would if you were trying to find the perfect present for someone. Also, ask your Inner Wise Self to help you.)

If you have a solution where you can picture both of you being genuinely happy, you may simply be able to begin actualizing it, as John did with his girlfriend. In other situations, it's a matter of suggesting your idea in such a way that the other person sees how it works for them and is willing to accept it. This is what happened with Susan's neighbors and the tree branches.

Your actions and shift in attitude may change everything in a wonderful way without the other person ever knowing what was behind it. All they may be aware of is that things are suddenly better. If you have evaluated the situation accurately, they will be happy to join you. If you feel resistance, you either missed something or you may need to give them time to see the value of what you're suggesting.

You can also approach the other person with the attitude that you want to help them get what they want and invite them to describe what they're looking for in more detail. You can then go back to step 6.

If you can create a Joyful Solution, that's great. If the situation is too difficult, go on to another one. As with the Awareness Practice in the previous chapter (page 130), at first it doesn't matter if you can create a Joyful Solution in every situation.

We can't emphasize enough that it is best to start with simple things you want to change. If you begin with a complex issue that has been frustrating you for a while, you may not succeed. It's like someone trying to run a marathon without training their muscles first. They get partway and think they failed and can never do it, when in reality they have successfully run farther than ever before, and it's simply a matter of training to go all the way.

The focus at first is on feeling your creative power — your ability to find the essence in situations where you feel stuck and imagine wider options. Once you become skilled in doing this, you will be able to find Joyful Solutions to most situations in your life.

@ What do you want? What is the essence?

☆ What do they want? What is the essence?

@ Go wide. What are solutions that would satisfy the essence?

For more about creating Joyful Solutions on your own, go to:
SucculentWildLove.com/JoyfulSolutions

13. Sources of Anger and How to Transform Them

WHENEVER YOU FEEL ANGRY with someone about something, there can be three different parts, and each is resolved differently:

- You may feel the other person doesn't care about you the way you want them to.
- You may think they should behave differently.
- What they did has a practical impact and is limiting you in some way.

With intimate relationships, feeling that the other person doesn't care about us usually affects us the most. When we read in the newspaper about what the government is doing or about other world events, our strongest reaction is usually that they should act differently. When we get assigned a project that has to be completed over the weekend, that mostly has a practical impact.

"Do They Care about Me?" Evaluation and Translation

If someone leaves their clothes on the bedroom floor because they're ill, it is simple enough to pick them up. But if it's a habit they seemingly won't bother to change, it can be easy to feel angry or hurt.

If you feel that someone doesn't care enough about you to change something that is bothering you, a good way to clarify your feelings is to evaluate and translate. We call this making a Love Translation (and discuss the process further in chapter 17).

Evaluate

Take a moment to ask yourself these questions:

1. Does this person basically care about me the way I want them to?
2. Do they treat everyone this way, or is this something for me to take as a personal affront?
3. Does what they're doing say more about them than me?
4. Is there something going on with them that keeps them from doing what pleases me?

When I used to get angry with slow drivers, Jeanie, my wife at the time, would suggest, "Maybe his girlfriend just broke up with him." Implicitly, I had been taking the driver's actions as a personal rejection of my desire to go at the speed I wanted. When Jeanie suggested it might have nothing to do with me, I would usually respond at first by grumping at her, "I don't care. He shouldn't be driving like that." But I would also begin to let go and feel some compassion. (Maybe he *was* dealing with some difficult news. Maybe he didn't feel comfortable driving faster.) I would stop taking it personally, and even though the driver didn't speed up, I would stop feeling angry.

It can be tempting to assign meanings to silences from others and think that their not saying anything means they don't care. It can be incredibly transforming to simply ask the person what their silence means to them, by saying something like, "I noticed that you didn't call back after I left you that message. Is there anything you'd like me to know about this?" People will generally respond positively to being asked simply and directly about what they meant.

In an intimate relationship, if you've asked and evaluated, and you realize the person doesn't really care about you the way you want them to, as painful as that may be, it's good to know. You will continue getting hurt if you don't change your expectations, and a Joyful Solution will often involve separate paths.

Translate

If you decide they basically do care about you, see if you can translate their actions into what you believe they were genuinely communicating. Their message might have been "I'm tired and grumpy" rather than "I don't care." When you can make this kind of translation, the anger or hurt often loses its intensity.

> I'm really enjoying practicing evaluating and translating — and the positive results of doing so. I used to just react to whatever I thought it was, instead of listening carefully and taking a little bit of extra time to assess. Notice that "evaluation and translation" spells EAT. ;-) Mindfully practicing evaluating and translating in all my relationships makes all the difference. When anger comes up between John and me, I can look at him and see that he might be stuck or hasn't had a meal or is worried about something, and not take it as a sign that he doesn't care.

"Shoulding" on Each Other: Who Are You Fighting With?

When feeling angry, you might go from "I don't feel good when you do this" to "You should act differently." What you want from them might be socially accepted behavior, obeying a law, or even doing what you believe God wants.

When your reaction is "You should act differently," you are often invading the person's boundaries. For most of us, we're so sure that people shouldn't do certain things, such as murder or steal, that it seems perfectly acceptable to invade their boundaries and try to force them to act differently.

But with intimate relationships, that usually isn't a good idea. Even if you and someone in your life agree that a certain behavior is wrong — say, emotional eating and gaining weight — in a Succulent Wild relationship that doesn't mean they are required to change to try to please you.

When we feel that someone should behave differently, usually we are projecting our inner critics onto them. We wouldn't permit ourselves to behave that way, so they shouldn't be allowed to act that way either.

When we expect ourselves to behave at a certain level of competency or obey certain rules, the most common path for most of us is to think everyone else should also live up to that same standard. If we don't live up to our "should," there is something wrong with us. If they don't live up to it, there is something wrong with them.

This is one of the main benefits of recognizing our inner critics. We begin to stop identifying with them and blindly trying to live up to standards that don't really suit us (that don't feel good). And in a Succulent Wild Love relationship, we stop holding our partners to standards that don't feel right for them, even if those standards feel right for us.

I TAKE MANY THINGS PERSONALLY AND AM PRACTICING NOT DOING THAT AS MUCH BY SEEING THE OTHER PERSON'S WAY AS PERFECT FOR THEM — HAVING LITTLE OR NOTHING TO DO WITH ME. SO IF A DRIVER IS TAILGATING OR MAKES A SUDDEN U-TURN IN FRONT OF ME, I SAY, "THAT DRIVER IS DOING THINGS VERY DIFFERENTLY FROM HOW I DO THEM." THIS RELEASES ME FROM JUDGING AND TAKING IT PERSONALLY AND ALLOWS ME TO HUMOROUSLY EXPRESS OUT LOUD WHAT I'M THINKING INSIDE.

The word "should" is almost always the realm of the inner critics. They own that word and what usually comes with it: a sense of **f**ear, **o**bligation, or **g**uilt — which, conveniently, spells **FOG**.

Long-term disagreements in any relationship usually involve inner critics. One person wants the other to change. The other person doesn't want to change but feels guilty because what their partner is saying is echoing an inner critic. For example, one person may like the convenience of leaving clothes on the bedroom floor, but they have an inner critic that says this is wrong. Because they believe this is wrong (and don't have the tools in this book), they usually don't stand up for themselves and say, "I prefer this. Let's create a Joyful Solution." What they often do instead is continue to leave clothes on the floor intermittently and feel guilty.

In a situation where there isn't an inner critic — perhaps someone's partner wants them to wear their hair in an unusual way — there is no guilt. The person will usually feel free to communicate clearly how they want to wear their hair and the nagging diminishes. (See also the example given on page 97 in chapter 9.)

If you find yourself nagging, then you are likely activating an inner critic in the other person. Both you and their inner critic want them to change, but the person doesn't really want to. So they don't change, and can't admit that they aren't going to, but believe they have to live with your (and their inner) nagging.

MY YOUNGER BROTHER LIVED WITH ME WHEN HE WAS IN COLLEGE, AND HE WAS INCREDIBLY MESSY, BASED ON WHAT I FELT COMFORTABLE WITH. I TRIED ALL THE USUAL THINGS, LIKE NAGGING, BRIBES, AND TRYING TO IGNORE IT. NONE OF THEM WORKED, AND I FELT LIKE HE JUST DIDN'T CARE ENOUGH TO CHANGE.

I FINALLY ASKED HIM WHAT HAVING A MESSY ROOM MEANT TO HIM. HE REPLIED THAT HE FELT SAFEST WITH SCATTERED OBJECTS AROUND HIM. AHA! I FEEL SAFEST WITH NO SCATTERED OBJECTS AROUND ME. NOW I WAS ABLE TO UNDERSTAND THAT IT WASN'T THAT HE DIDN'T CARE ABOUT ME, AND WE WERE ABLE TO COME UP WITH A SOLUTION THAT WORKED FOR BOTH OF US.

If someone is repeatedly pressing you to do something, they are likely speaking for one or more of your inner critics. You may want to change for them, but it doesn't feel genuinely right for you. If it did, you would simply make the change, and the pressure would stop.

When you recognize that the pressure you feel is really someone speaking for one of your inner critics, you can address that inner critic directly. When you allow yourself to admit how you honestly feel and what you genuinely want to do, then you have the foundation for creating a Joyful Solution.

So if you feel pressured to behave in a certain way or feel angry that someone else isn't behaving how they "should," look for the inner critics. When you separate what each of you genuinely wants from what the inner critics want, you will be able to release the ongoing tension between you.

CHANGING THE PRACTICAL IMPACT

Often when you feel angry, it's because you feel frustrated by not getting what you want. Sometimes the frustration is immediate — they were supposed to clean the dirty dishes, and instead you have to do it or put up with a messy kitchen. Sometimes you may have a vision of something in the future — if your partner takes a job in another state, you'll have to move and you'll miss your friends.

When there are clear, practical frustrations — and you have clarified that the other person cares and identified the inner critics — then it is best to look at how to create a Joyful Solution. Look for the essence of what you each want, and help each other get it by going wide and exploring new possibilities together.

Susan and I were driving home from Carmel one night. It was dark and I wanted to use my cellphone as a GPS. Since I was driving, I asked Susan to put it in the fussy holder that clips to the windshield. After poking around with it for a few minutes, Susan said she couldn't get it in, and I was frustrated. Some thoughts went through my head:

- "Susan isn't driving and doesn't need the GPS. Doesn't she care enough about me to make the effort to figure out how to set it in the holder?"

- "What's wrong with her? She's smart. She should be able to figure this out. She shouldn't be giving up on her ability."

- "It's frustrating not to have the GPS available to me."

At first I pressed Susan to keep trying. Then I reminded myself that Susan does care about me, very much. But the turning point came when I realized I wouldn't permit myself to give up in this situation — so she shouldn't, either. I realized I was projecting my inner critic onto her.

I have an inner critic who often tells me I should be able to respond effectively in any stressful situation. If I don't, I'm not meeting my responsibilities and am not lovable. As Susan was giving up on getting the phone into the holder, my inner critic turned on her: she should be responding effectively and not giving up.

This is very common. If I don't live up to my standard of responding effectively, there is something wrong with me. Therefore, if someone else doesn't live up to it, there is something wrong with them.

As soon as I realized this, I pulled over. Susan gave me the phone, and I was able to get it into the holder. (It was easier for me because I knew its quirks.) Then I apologized. In our Succulent Wild relationship Susan is not obligated to be like me or do what I would do. I love Susan for who she is. The practical limitation I was experiencing was easily resolved once I remembered this.

While I was trying to get the phone into the holder, John was reminding me of my angry father, who would get extremely impatient with me, which often resulted in my trying to do whatever he wanted me to do — and being even more ineffective.

In the car with John, I felt spotlighted and ashamed that I couldn't easily figure out how to attach the phone, and instead of asking for help, I just kept trying and failing, and filling the role in my head of "someone who can't easily figure out simple or common things." This has been an aspect of my perfectionist inner critic for years.

After John pulled over, I realized I could have asked him to pull over. I didn't need to robotically do anything! It feels very succulent and wild to know I can live in this new way, both in my relationship with John and with others.

You can become so focused on the other person and their seeming power to block you that you lose sight of other possible solutions that wouldn't require them to change. So the key is to shift your emotional focus off them. Ask yourself, "What does this person seem to be keeping me from being, doing, or having? Is there another way I can get this?" John waiting for the woman in the mall parking lot (page 125) is a perfect example of a missed opportunity to do this.

A FABULOUS KEY IS TO SHIFT YOUR EMOTIONAL FOCUS OFF THE OTHER PERSON and CREATE A JOY♥FUll SOlution

Awareness Practice: Understanding Your Anger

When you feel angry with someone, see if you can identity the three components. Ask yourself:

★ Do they care about me the way I want them to?

◎ Should they behave differently?

✩ What is the practical impact of what they're doing?

Go deeper by asking yourself each of these questions before talking with the person who evoked your anger:

◎ Am I expecting them to care more about me?

✩ Am I expecting them to put my needs ahead of theirs?

◎ Am I invading their boundaries with my inner critics?

✩ Did I join with one of their inner critics to get them to agree to something, and then they didn't do it?

◎ What would need to change for their actions to not practically impact me or limit me?

For more support with ways of handling anger and hurt, go to:
SucculentWildLove.com/Anger

14. Moving Through Anger And Hurt

Moving Through anger and Hurt instead of Getting stuck (and keep Moving)

WHEN YOU FEEL GOOD, you want to enjoy your feelings and allow them to blossom. When you don't feel good, it's beneficial to take care of your feelings. Anger and hurt are two feelings you'll want to take good care of in a Succulent Wild Love relationship.

When I feel Angry, I tend to get loud. In my family of origin, the louder you got, the more likely you were to be heard. This style doesn't work as well with John, because although he enjoys that I have strong emotions, he's quieter than I am, and sometimes the intensity of my anger can feel overwhelming to him. We've learned to navigate this together so that I can express my anger in a way that he can hear. He'll put up his hands if the volume gets too much for him, and that's my cue to do some feelings care with myself before communicating with him again.

In the beginning of our relationship, I used to say things like, "Are you ready to reach for a thought that feels better?" or even just, "Can you calm down?" Susan did not react the way I hoped to any of these kinds of statements. In fact, it would inflame her even more, because she felt that I was trying to keep her from feeling her feelings, which indirectly I was.

But what I really wanted was not to be inundated by Susan's feelings. I would feel overwhelmed by them and frustrated because there was nothing for me to do. I would try to offer solutions, but it would be obvious that she wasn't ready to hear them.

Susan explained that if she hasn't felt the feelings first, she can't get to any solutions or even feelings of calmness. I was afraid that she was just amplifying her feelings, but it became clear to me that this was her process of allowing the storm to come and letting it pass.

Now, we have a signal to use when I get overwhelmed: I put up my hands between us or just say something like, "It's more than I can hear right now." It's really a Joyful Solution, even though at that particular moment neither of us is feeling joy.

Since I'm good at articulating my feelings and taking responsibility for them, I'm generally able to share hurt feelings more easily than anger. On a few occasions, John and I have gotten angry with each other and expressed it, and we've both gotten loud simultaneously. We have good recovery skills and are able to separate when needed and then return to solve what happened together.

I take a lot of responsibility for my experience, so I tend to get angry at myself more than at others. When I feel I have to do too many things at once, I tend to get what Susan calls "snappish." I will grump at her in short sentences. But if I get frustrated because I believe I can't get something that is important to me, I tend to withdraw or be silent for a time. Eventually I speak up, however.

The first time I visited Susan, I fell into hopelessness when I took a shower. "Hopelessness" may be too strong a word, but I was feeling pretty low. (We now call this incident "the shower meltdown.") I still hardly knew Susan but had high hopes for our relationship. Before I visited her in San Francisco, we had gotten along beautifully, but we had only been together on a cruise ship. So I didn't really know how she liked to live and what ordinary daily life would be like for us.

We called this "The Shower Meltdown"

Susan has a beautiful old claw-foot bathtub. But I don't often like to take baths. I like to shower. At the end of the tub was a handheld hose with a mostly clogged showerhead. As I sat cross-legged in the tub trying to wash my hair with the dripping water, I went into despair, thinking, "If this is how Susan likes to live, maybe I can't live with her."

After I dried off, I came back into the bedroom and was very quiet.

When John came out of the bathroom, he was quiet, but his emotions were loud. I immediately got frightened that we wouldn't be able to work through difficulties — that he or I wouldn't say anything and our unexpressed feelings would just pile up — which is what I'd grown up with and experienced in other love relationships. I resolved to do this one differently and said, "John, what's going on? What are you feeling?" And I really wanted to know.

John started explaining the symbol of the shower for him — that maybe we weren't compatible living together — and it led to us talking for several hours about daily life, how we would navigate living together, sharing upsets, and creating joyfull solutions. He was afraid that I was so attached to just my bathtub that he wouldn't be able to have both showers and me. He didn't know that I had taken out the shower years ago and had already been thinking that I would have it reinstalled.

We learned a lot about communicating with each other in that epic conversation, and that we could count on each other to share and resolve our feelings. The joyfull solution emerged easily, and we installed a new shower that we both now love.

Anger can actually feel good. If you feel helpless, anger is empowering. Anger and hurt are valuable forms of communication, both to yourself and others. When you feel them, you are saying, "I don't want this to happen again."

The idea here is to move through anger and hurt back to love. We want to let these feelings flow, get the benefit from them, and then move on to feeling better.

When some event evokes anger in us, our first impulse is usually to want to lash out at the external source of our anger (especially if it's another person). When we feel hurt, our first impulse is to withdraw. Then, after these first reactions, we want to find a way to ensure that whatever upset us doesn't happen again. The most effective way to do this in an intimate relationship is to elicit the other person's cooperation.

Most people get tripped up in handling the initial impulses, and then it's difficult to get to cooperation.

There are three ways of looking at an event or situation that evokes anger:

1.   *It's all their fault.*
2.   *It's the result of an interaction between us.*
3.   *I created my experience.*

In most of my previous relationships, I spent most of my time on numbers 1 & 2. I really didn't consider 3, because I was sure it was "their fault." Plus, I usually had collected "evidence."

As you go from 1 to 3, you are in a position of greater and greater control over what happens in your life. If it's always the other person's fault, you're at the mercy of other people's choices. The more you know how to create your experience, the more you're in charge of your own life.

The more you focus on your contribution to any given situation, and what you can do differently to get what you want, the more power and harmony you'll have in your relationships. In some situations, you might find little you could have done or can do differently. In others, you may be surprised by how much control over your experience you can actually take.

The first step in using anger or hurt effectively is to recognize when you have these feelings. This involves paying attention to how you feel. You aren't required to share this awareness with the person who is provoking the feelings, and until you're more skilled at handling your emotions, often it is best not to share them right away.

THE CONTROL STAGE OF ANGER AND HURT

Most people don't know how to use anger effectively. Some people bully others, physically or emotionally, when angry. Others put on phony smiles and then gossip negatively about the person they're angry with. Audiences cheer in movies when someone who's been hurt gets revenge. In these situations, people are in the control stage of anger, which is marked by the desire to lash out and "get" the other person, and reflects the desire to control others to get what we want.

In the control stage of hurt, someone withdraws and closes the boundary of intimacy, shutting the other person out.

running really
FAST

I useD to excel At witHDrAWinG or rUnninG AWAy. I useD AvoiDAnce wHen I felt HUrt or AnGry, BecAUse I DiDn't Know How to cAre for My feelinGs first AnD tHen commUnicAte witH otHer people.

In this stage we may be tempted to express our anger toward someone other than the person evoking our feelings. Classical examples are being frustrated at work and coming home and taking it out on our spouse or children, or expressing the frustration we feel in our relationship by telling friends what's wrong with our partner.

So the first step is to pay attention to your feelings to know when you're angry. The second is to make sure you direct your angry energy toward the source of your frustration, not someone else. Simply expressing it to someone else won't enable you to change the situation.

Confusion can also occur when little frustrations build up over time. When someone believes they've put up with enough and finally give themselves permission to lash out, the other person may feel blindsided. They think the angry person is responding to what is going on in the moment and don't understand why the response is so intense. If you find yourself in such a situation, you can let the other person know that you've been feeling frustrated for a long time.

Another impediment to clarity is when two people are arguing about one thing and then remember other frustrations. Suddenly, they are throwing out so many accusations that no one can figure out how to resolve anything. If you find yourself doing this, stop. Agree to focus on clarifying one complaint at a time. If you can't agree to do that, it's best to separate until you can.

THE INTIMACY ASPECT OF ANGER

Have you ever been involved in an activity while a child wants your attention? They may whine or pull on your sleeve. Then suddenly something is spilled or broken, and you're focusing on cleaning up the mess instead of what you were working on. As any small child knows, positive attention is best, but negative attention is better than no attention.

> I used to do this with my father. He was a salesman who traveled a lot, and when he was home I wanted to spend time with him. He wanted to see me too but wanted to spend time with his own activities, like reading the paper. I would wait until he was reading the paper and come up and poke the paper and run away quickly. He responded with irritation and sometimes yelling. I can still remember feeling satisfied that he was paying some attention to me.

Fighting with someone is an intimate experience. It can be emotionally as intimate as sex. If you learned this path to intimacy as a child or if you don't have other ways of easily being intimate, you will be tempted to create situations where you're fighting.

This is a meaningful form of intimacy, especially if you have others around you who also see fighting as a symbol of love ("my partner cares enough to fight with me"). It is an easy way for your emotions to flow and for you to feel passion. If you want to fight less, you will need to find other ways of being intimate and other ways to bring out your passion. If you don't, the desire for these will be so strong that you will be pulled back into fighting.

If regular fighting is not a path you have learned, or if you decide you want to take a different approach, then you are ready for the next stage.

THE COOPERATIVE STAGE OF ANGER AND HURT

To take charge of your painful feelings, you have to know how to release them consciously. You can do this by using the Inner Feelings Care System (see page 86) or any method that allows you to express your feelings on your terms. Once you aren't overwhelmed by anger or hurt, you can use them effectively to find cooperative solutions.

If you said or did things when you were feeling angry that you wish you hadn't, then some relationship repair is needed. This usually takes the form of letting the other person know what you genuinely meant to say and what was blown out of proportion by the intensity of your anger. The goal here is to get the focus off what you said or did in anger, and back on what upset you in the first place.

Once you have expressed your feelings to the point where they aren't overwhelming you, you can determine how intense your display of anger needs to be to convey how important the issue is to you — and avoid being so intense that all they hear is anger. For some people, if you don't yell at them, they don't believe the issue is important. For others, a clear statement is sufficient, and any more intensity might evoke feelings of guilt or shame that go way beyond what you intended.

Using "I" statements (such as "I feel angry," "I feel taken advantage of," or "I was hurt by…") to convey your feelings is much less likely to elicit defensive reactions than using "you" statements ("You shouldn't have done that," "You made a mistake," "You are wrong," etc.).

It is also best to not make blanket statements that include "never" or "always." People make these statements to support their right to be upset, but it actually backfires. In a subtle way, it tells the other person, "I expect you to behave in this negative way," which makes it more likely that they will meet this expectation.

You Always / You never / You should   *Bad Blanket statements*

I've learned that John listens very intently to me when I'm upset and that I don't need to keep repeating or get loud to be sure he heard me, as I did in my family growing up. One of the things that surprised me early in our relationship is that John rarely resists me when I feel hurt or angry in response to something he did. Rather than attacking me or defending himself, he acknowledges the validity of my feelings. And then we talk about how we could handle the situation that bothered me differently next time. I realize I now respond in the same way when he is upset about something. It's amazing to see how communicating differently with John can result in effective — and sometimes easy — resolutions.

The goal is to communicate clearly, "I want this to be different," in such a way that the other person can become aligned with you rather than recoil in defensiveness, shame, or guilt. Before you approach the other person, clearly envision how you want the interaction to turn out. Keep that vision foremost in your mind as you're talking with them. This will enable you to take the best path to what you want.

Moving Beyond Anger and Hurt

Of course, even when you use your anger to communicate effectively, the other person won't necessarily comply with what you want. A common path in our culture is to then try to force them to comply. But that is not what we recommend. We recommend inviting the other to join you in finding a Joyful Solution, either together or by separating.

Ultimately each of us is responsible for our own life. When you want someone to do something differently, you are essentially trying to get them to accept your viewpoint. If they choose not to, the next step is to determine how you can get the essence of what you want while allowing them to be who they are. You can always find a Joyful Solution for yourself, with or without the participation of any specific person.

There is always a decision point when you're angry or hurt. Do you want to make the other person feel guilty or ashamed? Do you want to punish them in some way? (You may have been taught that punishment is the best way to get cooperation, but it is much less effective than love.) Do you want to force them into your way of thinking? If you approach them with these motives, they will want to hurt you back or get away from you. Instead, it is best to use the Inner Feelings Care System or something equivalent to help these feelings pass.

Many couples release their feelings by lashing out or emotionally withdrawing from each other, and only then are they able to begin seeking cooperation. This route can work (and lashing out can be useful for people who use anger as a form of intimacy). But for a Succulent Wild Love relationship, we recommend making the effort to take charge of your feelings and spending more time feeling love with your partner.

When you know how to take care of your angry and hurt feelings and know that you can find Joyful Solutions without requiring others to change, you have true freedom in any relationship.

PRACTICES TO HELP YOU NAVIGATE FROM ANGER TO COOPERATION

1. **Take a moment after any difficult interaction to do a feelings check.**

    Being hurt or angry is an important indicator of your well-being. Give yourself permission to just simply feel hurt or angry. Remember, you don't have to tell the other person how you're feeling, and, if your feelings are very strong, it's often best not to express them until you've done your Inner Feelings Care.

2. **Tend to your hurt and angry feelings first.**

    We do not recommend trying to go to cooperation before doing your Inner Feelings Care work. If you skip this step, your feelings can be triggered and create new tension that can undercut any Joyful Solution. Or you can suppress your feelings, only to have them come springing back at a later time.

    You can also do the five-second method, where you say out loud or under your breath, "Anger, I see you, I hear you, I feel you," or, "Hurt, I acknowledge you, I see you, I know you're here." The key is to acknowledge your feelings and let them flow, so that you can respond to the situation wisely rather than either ignoring your feelings or simply reacting.

3. **See if you can communicate what you want in a way that conveys how important it is to you but not in a way that evokes defensive feelings in the other person.**

    If you're echoing an inner critic in them, it may be impossible for the person not to feel defensive at first. You can explain that you are not judging them, you're looking for a Joyful Solution. This may seem difficult at first and can take some practice. However, if you focus on wanting a Joyful Solution rather than on what they did wrong, it becomes much easier.

    If you convince the other person that they "should" do what you want, it is likely that you're creating a solution with their inner critics. This will not feel joyful to them, and they may fail to do what they agreed to.

4. **Once you are able to express your preferences rather than "shoulds," and your partner can hear you, you are ready to create a Joyful Solution.**

Anything you do to practice taking care of your feelings and to elicit the other person's cooperation will benefit your relationship and lead to feeling more love more often.

Awareness Practice: Moving Through Anger and Hurt

1. Reflect on a particular challenging situation and examine your role in it and how you could have handled it differently. Do you see it as:

   - It's all their fault.

   - It's the result of an interaction between us.

   - I created this experience.

2. Be aware of how you handle your angry and hurt feelings.

   - Do you yell?

   - Do you emotionally withdraw?

   - Can you move beyond wanting to control the other person or get revenge? It's perfectly natural to start out that way. But where you end up determines what kind of interactions you're going to have with the significant people in your life.

3. Be aware of how you might use anger or fighting for intimacy.

   - Have you ever started a fight because you felt distant from someone you loved?

   - Do you have other ways of feeling intimate in your relationships?

   - If you like to feel passion or strong emotion, do you have other ways to spark these feelings?

4. Do you know the anger symbols of those close to you?

   - Can you tell what level of intensity works to get their attention but isn't so strong that they feel overwhelmed by guilt and shame?

If you recall times that you've been angry and how you expressed yourself, you will have some idea of your anger style. It can also be helpful to replay past incidents in your mind and imagine how you would handle them differently now.

For more about dealing successfully with anger and hurt, go to:
SucculentWildLove.com/Anger

15. Your Partner Is Perfect — And So Are You: How to Give And Receive Unconditional Love

Giving and receiving unconditional Love

By "perfect," we do not mean that someone has attained an ultimate, completed state beyond the ability of others.
We mean that we don't judge them or see them as flawed in any way.
This applies to your partner and yourself.

When I first met Susan, I told her she was perfect, and any way I didn't see her as perfect was my responsibility.

When I heard John say this, I felt ecstatically happy at first — I felt like I'd wanted someone to see me this way for my whole life. Then it started sinking in that I would want to be able to see him this way too, and I felt much less certain of my abilities. Plus, I was sure that he wouldn't be able to see me that way as he got to know me better.

As we discussed in chapter 2, "How We Developed Succulent Wild Love and the Six Habits," I learned the power of seeing someone as perfect from Jeanie. Early in our relationship she told anyone who would listen that I was perfect. Though chagrined at first, I soon saw the power of what she was doing and followed her lead. But it wasn't until later that I was able to describe exactly what she had been doing to be able to love me in that way.

Jeanie had made three significant decisions:

1. I did not have to change for her to feel good. She found ways to take care of herself — because of me and sometimes in spite of me. And when we had disagreements, we often created solutions that were more satisfying than what either of us had thought of individually.

2. Her role was not to determine what was right or wrong for me but only what was right for her. She had preferences and let me know what they were, but she did not judge my actions as wrong or as representing a fault in me.

3. Jeanie would focus on what pleased her about me. She understood that someone cannot look at something they dislike and feel loving in the same moment. The only way to feel love is to focus on what is pleasing in another.

Because of these decisions, Jeanie was able to love me unconditionally, and she taught me how to do the same.

Today, I feel this way about Susan. There is nothing about Susan that I see as a flaw or lack, nothing I want or need her to change so I can feel better.

This isn't to say that I never get upset or that we don't have bumps or preferences. We do (and Jeanie and I did too). And when I get upset, I say, "ouch," and sometimes blame Susan and want her to be different. But the blaming quickly becomes humorous and doesn't last.

 or, it feels Awful and seems like it will never end. Good time to practice inner feelings care

One of the most intense examples of this occurred when Susan was helping me move from Columbus to San Francisco early in our relationship. Susan had told me that she isn't the type to put on a kerchief and pitch in for countless hours when it comes to moving. But she did offer to help and do some packing.

After Susan packed the first box, I looked at what she had done and was immediately furious. She had packed several ceramic items together, and it was obvious to me that they would be smashed in no time. The thoughts going quickly through my mind were, "If you don't want to help, fine, but don't pretend to help and then do it in a way that hurts me." But that's not what I said.

Pointing to the threatened items, I yelled, "This feels like a f--- you," and began repacking the box. Susan yelled something back at me, and we were like two cats hissing.

I've never been very good at packing or moving, plus I'm fairly impatient. In this case, it felt important to take good care of John's things, and so I wrapped each item in many paper towels, thinking that I was doing a really good job. When John came into the room and looked at me and then into the box, and told me that what I was doing was wrong, he appeared just like my sometimes critical and impatient father.

I felt so defeated, embarrassed, and angry. I snapped back at John, quit helping, and stormed off, much like I'd done as a child. Later when we were able to more calmly discuss what had happened, I was able to clarify that I did care, and in fact had been going out of my usual way, and thought I was packing things really well.

When we talked about it, I realized that Susan didn't know how rough the movers were on boxes. What she had done would have been more than enough if we were simply carrying the items from one house to the other in our car. In other words, I realized that she did care about me and my things. I repacked the box without tension, and Susan helped me get my things ready in other ways.

Now that I know the practical power of unconditional love, I always come back to the three decisions Jeanie demonstrated for me.

Once I understood Susan's perspective, I knew it had been perfect for her. It was not my place to judge her perspective. Susan was being the perfect Susan, and any way I was not able to see that was my responsibility.

My previous way of not seeing others as perfect included my noticing everything I didn't like and then making and keeping ongoing lists about the ways I thought they could or should change, so that I could feel better. These lists included items I felt angry about ("they really SHOULD CHANGE") and also items I felt resigned about ("they'll NEVER CHANGE, so why bother?") I would share excerpts of these lists with close friends — or sometimes seatmates on airplanes, people I didn't know. I found a lot of solidarity with other people who also weren't practicing unconditional love, and in fact were keeping their own lists — and were happy to share.

At that time, I didn't know about all the tools that are in this book. I didn't know about naming and caring for my feelings, consulting with my Inner Wise Self, checking to see if one or more inner critics had

Gotten Activated. I didn't know how to state my preferences and tell the difference between doing that and controlling someone. I didn't know then about sharing Microtruths or doing Love Translations (tools in upcoming chapters).

The origins of my list making were formed early. Sometimes when I would arrive home from school, my mother would announce that I was on her "shit list," and proceed to detail all the things I hadn't done or had done wrong. I remember feeling frozen and attacked, and definitely unloved. At other times she acted like a fun and loving mom, so I toggled between her two states of being, concluding that loving came with conditions.

I carried this kind of conditional love forward into all my relationships, and it got especially highlighted in my romantic and intimate relationships. My lists were a way to try to keep track of what I felt was unfair or not working, and since I didn't really know how to share what I wanted, I kept copious notes about what I didn't want.

Whenever I talked to other people about this subject, they reassured me that they had similar lists — perhaps not as voluminous or detailed as mine but usually three to six things that they wished were different or better in their relationship. And many people expressed that they were resigned to these things not changing.

if only my partner would...
if only my partner didn't...

If you believe there is something someone needs to change for you to feel better, then you cannot see them as perfect. And every time you are reminded of this part of them, you cannot love them unconditionally.

Spiritual teachers for centuries — and more recently, therapists of all kinds — have told us that unconditional love is the highest form of being with others. But, at least in Western societies, we haven't had practical tools to apply in our everyday lives that enable us to love that way on a consistent basis.

The three decisions Jeanie made — which are at the core of seeing the perfection in your partner and in all your relationships — are tools you can use to allow unconditional love to flow in your relationships. And those three decisions rest on the foundation of the other habits and tools we talked about in the earlier chapters.

If you feel someone is blocking your joy in any way, or hurting or limiting you, then you need to address this first. In the self-lovingly separate chapter we focused on the fact that in a Succulent Wild Love relationship you have the right to security, to privacy, to go on with your life as you see fit, and to be treated with respect. If you don't have these rights, there is no way you can see the other person as perfect.

When these conditions are in place, you have the foundation for a fully satisfying relationship. You can create Joyful Solutions that meet both your and the other person's needs. Once you know how to create Joyful Solutions, you are at a level where the intimate people in your life are never in a position to block your joy on an ongoing basis.

It is only from this place of clarity about what you deserve and can have, and the skill to create the relationship you want, that you are able to make the three decisions that lead to unconditional love. If necessary, go back to chapters 10 through 12, on being self-lovingly separate and creating Joyful Solutions, and practice applying their principles. When you feel confident that you can create the relationship you want, you are in a position to make the unconditional love decisions.

in succulent wild love Practice is perfect

WAYS TO PRACTICE THE UNCONDITIONAL LOVE DECISIONS

1. Deciding that someone in your life does not have to change for you to feel good. You state your preferences to others clearly, and then don't require others to fulfill those preferences.

    What this means is that if your partner or people close to you are not providing the emotional nourishment you want, you find ways of taking care of yourself.

    Ways to practice doing this:

    ⭐ Be prepared to fill yourself up — from the inside — by doing activities that nourish you. Make a list of what you know you love to do, and do these things.

    ⑥ Create new ways to do fun things by yourself — so that you practice generating what pleases you and further develop this habit.

    ◎ Join with others who naturally and freely give you the nourishment you want. These may be friends or relatives, or even a group or club whose members share your interest.

2. Deciding that your role is not to determine what is right or wrong for another person, only for yourself. You know you have preferences, and you let the people close to you know what they are, but you do not judge their actions as wrong or as being a fault.

What this means is that you do not try to be in charge of the decisions and choices others make and that you do not presume what is right or best for them.

Ways to practice doing this:

⭐ If someone you love is making choices that you wouldn't, note that you would not permit yourself to behave that way.

⭐ Realize that your way is not necessarily the best way for someone else (even if you believe it's the right way).

◉ Every time you think you see a lack in someone intimate in your life, mentally thank them for helping you see a concern about this lack in yourself, reflected in them.

⭐ Know that you do not have to participate in their decisions if they don't feel good to you. You can create a Joyful Solution that involves separate paths.

⭐ Examine yourself. Talk with your inner critics and Inner Wise Self and do your Inner Feelings Care until you are able to accept and love yourself as you are. You will know you have done this when you can look at the other person and see what was formerly a lack as simply a part of the experience of their being.

3. Deciding to make a conscious choice to focus on what pleases you about the people you love, understanding that you cannot look at something disliked and feel love in the same moment. The only way to feel love is to focus on what is pleasing in those around you.

What this means is that you literally ignore things that don't please you. We want to note again here, this is not intended for any situation that evokes anger or puts you in danger. Those instances call for Joyful Solutions, Inner Feelings Care, and other methods. This decision is for those personality styles or physical characteristics that are not pleasing to you but do not harm you.

Examples might be someone who:

⭐ is always losing their things

◉ is not as successful in their career as you would like

◉ is socially shy or clumsy

- is a pack rat
- is overweight by conventional standards, or has physical characteristics that are not appealing to you
- takes physical risks you wouldn't take
- drives in ways you wouldn't (unless you feel threatened in the car)

In each of these instances, you would be breaking their boundaries if you were to push them to change. There is nothing you need to do about them, and your best path is to ignore them and focus on the many things that do please you about your partner.

Ways to practice doing this:

- When you notice yourself focusing on something you dislike, consciously turn your attention to something you do like about the person. (It's a bit like eating a delicious apple and getting to the stem or center. You wouldn't chew on that part. You would take in the parts you like and leave the rest.)
- Do your Inner Feelings Care so you can express in private what you don't like. This will allow you to more easily ignore behaviors that don't please you.
- Allow yourself to be self-lovingly separate (for example, if someone is always hunting for their keys, you don't have to join them).
- Give yourself permission to acknowledge your preferences and then let go.

APPLYING THE THREE DECISIONS TO ANGER-PROVOKING SITUATIONS

Here are the reasons you might feel anger or frustration that we discussed in chapter 13 and how the unconditional love decisions apply in each situation.

You Feel That the Other Person Doesn't Care about You the Way You Want

To be in a state where you can give unconditional love, there has to be no sense of lack. You are not looking to your loved one to fulfill you in any way beyond how they are inherently being.

In developing the skill of unconditional love it is important to understand that you do not need any specific person to do anything for you to feel fulfilled.

> A good example of this is when I wanted to sit close to my girlfriend in bed. At first it looked like she needed to change for me to feel loved, but then I realized I could allow her to be who she wanted to be and get what I wanted too.

We want many things from a partner. We want them to be loving toward us. We want to enjoy their company, to laugh with them and have fun with them. We want to be able to count on them.

But no one is always able to give us everything we want. In a Succulent Wild Love relationship, we know that it is not the other person's job to make us happy. And we know that it isn't our job to make them happy. Each person takes responsibility for their own happiness.

I still sometimes try to make John responsible, at least in part, for my happiness. Even though I know all these habits and practice with them daily, it doesn't mean that I feel magically and unconditionally loving all the time, or even a lot of the time. And that's okay. Just practicing giving or receiving unconditional love is more love than most of us experienced growing up — or have experienced ever. And as you expand your experiences of being unconditionally loving, you'll want to do more of it.

In a Succulent Wild Love relationship you evaluate and translate. If someone cares about you the way you want them to, then this is no longer a source of frustration or anger. If they don't, then you know it is your responsibility to change your expectations, including changing or ending the relationship if necessary.

When you know this, you can make the first decision that will enable you to love unconditionally — the other person doesn't have to change for you to feel good.

You Think They Should Behave Differently

Another reason people evoke anger in us is that we believe they should behave differently. They aren't living up to social norms. They aren't engaging in what we believe is appropriate behavior. We may feel embarrassed being around them when they behave in certain ways in front of our friends or in public. They are doing things we would not permit ourselves to do.

Many years ago I was at a rehearsal dinner for a friend's wedding. For whatever reason, her father had more than enough to drink and was saying and doing things that clearly embarrassed my friend. Seeing her pain, I remember saying to her, "We know you're not your father," and other friends at our table nodded in agreement.

She felt such a sense of relief. Taking that in, most of her embarrassment faded. Our seeing her as separate helped her see herself that way, and, in turn, allowed her to let her father be.

This leads to the second decision in seeing someone as perfect. In a Succulent Wild Love relationship you focus on knowing your preferences and communicating them clearly. It means saying no to things that enter your life unwanted, without judging the rightness of them for the other person. You do not try to force someone to change by introducing God, society, or any other external authority. You do not try to force your standards on others or pounce on them with your inner critics.

In other words, you approach them with preference not righteousness. While they may do things you would not permit yourself to do, you do not judge them as bad in order to get them to be different. In a Succulent Wild Love relationship each person acknowledges that it isn't their place to judge what is right for the other — they can only judge what is right for themselves.

really really often
~~sometimes~~

I FREQUENTLY THINK THAT OTHERS "SHOULD" BEHAVE DIFFERENTLY! ESPECIALLY IF I THINK THAT MY WAY OF DOING SOMETHING IS BETTER. THE OTHER DAY, JOHN WAS EATING SOME SOUP AND COMMENTED THAT THE NOODLES WEREN'T VERY GOOD. I ADVISED HIM TO STOP EATING THEM. HE REPLIED, "YOU MIGHT BE RIGHT, BUT LET ME DECIDE."

I REALIZED THAT I'D ENTERED HIS BOUNDARIES AND WAS TELLING HIM WHAT I WOULD DO, AND WHAT I THOUGHT HE SHOULD DO. HE LATER SHARED THAT HIS STOMACH WAS A BIT AFFECTED BY THE NOODLES AND THAT HE WISHED HE'D LISTENED TO ME, BUT HE WAS ALSO GLAD HE'D FOLLOWED HIS OWN PATH ABOUT WHAT HE WAS EATING.

OTHER PEOPLE'S PATHS CAN APPEAR VERY WIGGLY!

When you decide what is right for someone intimate in your life, you are going into their boundaries. You undermine their ability to learn for themselves what is right for them. You empower your inner critics (rather than your Inner Wise Self).

Many times the intimate people in your life will make choices that appear unwise to you. In a Succulent Wild Love relationship you clearly understand that they are making the best choices they are able to at the moment. And your intent is to assist them in finding their own way to the best path for them rather than trying to impose your solutions on them.

You might not make the same choices. You would make choices that you viewed as right for you at the moment. And you would not like someone to mandate that you ignore what feels right to you and acquiesce to their solutions.

Many teachers and spiritual leaders advise us that it is beneficial not to judge. Often, we understand this advice in abstract terms, as some unattainable ideal that would be good to aspire to. Here we are presenting it as a practical approach, a decision you can make to feel more love more often.

They Do Something That Has a Practical Impact and Is Limiting You in Some Way

In a Succulent Wild Love relationship, when something doesn't feel good, the focus is on creating a Joyful Solution, with or without the other person's active cooperation. Until you know how to do this, you are not in a position to love unconditionally.

When John first introduced the concept of Joyfull Solutions to me, I didn't know how intrinsic they would become in my life. I thought I'd use them sometimes, and then go back to my secret fault-finding and list-keeping. I found out instead that I could communicate my need or desire for a Joyfull Solution ANYtime, about the tiniest or largest thing. Everything became open for discussion and revision. It was no longer "My way or the highway" or "their way or the highway." It was literally a new kind of highway.

I'm experiencing a truly blended expansion of my desires and someone else's AT THE SAME TIME — and this is miraculous to me. As I've practiced with Joyfull Solutions, I've become more and more confident that they can be created in any circumstance. I sometimes blurt it out to John — as in, "I NEED a Joyfull Solution." Other times, I can say something more welcoming and inclusive like, "I'd love to create a new Joyfull Solution together."

As a result, I have experienced hundreds of situations that I would have previously found very frustrating to be not frustrating at all, or much less frustrating. I can now identify when I'm sacrificing or trying to stop at compromising. This opens my unconditional love channels WAY UP. And this feels really, really GOOD.

The only way you can ever see someone as perfect is if you know you have the ability to create a satisfying relationship. If you feel helpless or confined in any way, then you have lost your freedom. And the other person represents that loss of freedom. And that immediately makes you see them as flawed.

For this reason, we cannot emphasize enough the importance of becoming skilled in creating Joyful Solutions before exploring viewing someone intimate in your life as perfect.

Once you know you can always create an outcome that is satisfying to you, either together or separately, where you can get your wants and needs met, you never have to pressure anyone to be different again. And from that perspective, you can allow them to be who they are and see their perfection.

But you still have preferences, and there may be things about someone intimate in your life that do not please you. When someone isn't everything you want them to be, you no longer need to see it as a flaw of some kind that they need to change. Now you can make the third decision and consciously focus as much as possible on only those things that do please you about them. Doing this, you can enjoy what you like about the other person and let them be the perfect being they are.

We Are surrounded By perfect Be-ings

When you are doing all the things described above, you will have the pleasure of loving others without reservation — and they will begin to reflect this kind of love back to you.

While we have stated these decisions in somewhat black-and-white terms — if you make them, you will have unconditional love, and if you don't, you won't — everyday life is more fluid. The two of us have been practicing these habits for a long time, and we still lose our balance. What we do have, however, is the ability to come back to them quickly. And so most of the time we are able to love each other without reservation.

I've been told all my life by other people that I tend to see things in black or white — that I often appear to be extreme in my emotions. I didn't know that those emotions could be channeled, understood, and managed differently. For instance, I never knew that I could decide to learn to love unconditionally and practice with skills that would actually allow me to feel that way.

I felt pretty sure that I would mostly conditionally love people, as

I'D BEEN ORIGINALLY TAUGHT. I DIDN'T ENVISION THAT NEW UNCONDITIONAL LOVE ABILITIES WOULD ARRIVE IN MY LIFE, AND THAT I COULD CREATE A NEW BASIS OF LOVE TO OPERATE FROM. THIS NEW BASIS HAS CAUSED A MIGHTY LOVE FOR MYSELF AND OTHERS TO FLOW AND KEEP FLOWING. AND I "LOSE MY BALANCE" FREQUENTLY AND CAN UNCONDITIONALLY LOVE MYSELF FOR THAT TOO!

No matter how often you lose your balance, each time you are able to come back to the three unconditional love decisions, you — and the people close to you — will feel more love.

1. release yourself from thinking that you need changes by someone or something else to feel good.

2. practice judging less often and deciding what others "should do."

3. focus on what pleases you about yourself or another and express it.

* giant happy thought bubble to follow you around

Awareness Practice:
You and Your Partner Are Perfect

1. Think of an area in which you have viewed your partner (or another person) as lacking or flawed in some way.

2. Write down how you could view them differently.

3. If you have lists about how people close to you should change for you to feel better, this is a good time to pull them out. Take each item on the list and see if there is something you can do, or a Joyful Solution you can create, that will remove the irritation from your life.

At this point, see if you are ready to make the three Unconditional Love Decisions:

★ No one in your life has to change for you to feel good.

Your role is only to determine what is right for yourself, not for the other people in your life.

@ You will focus as much as you can only on what pleases you about the people you love.

The main practice here is evaluating if you are ready to make the unconditional love decisions. To be clear, this does not mean allowing someone to abuse or take advantage of you. In those instances, you must create Joyful Solutions, where you are not compromising or sacrificing, before you are ready to do this practice.

We want to emphasize that "Awareness Practice" means just that: practice with your awareness and see if you can allow new habits to develop, ones that let you feel more love more often — which includes all the joys of love, given and received, as well as experiences of loving partially, sometimes barely, hardly ever, badly, or only while dreaming.

For more about giving and receiving unconditional love, go to:
SucculentWildLove.com/Love

16. Love Symbols: How Do You Know When Someone Loves You?

WHAT Are Your LOVE SYMBOLS?

IN EVERY RELATIONSHIP there are signals or symbols that indicate the other person cares about you. It may be as simple as making tea for each other in the morning, as we do, or something as dramatic as giving each other expensive presents. When you see those symbols, you feel loved; when you don't, you may feel hurt or angry. In fact, as we discussed in the chapter on the sources of anger, the basis of most hurt in intimate relationships isn't the practical things the person did or didn't do, it's the feeling that the person doesn't care.

You will have different expectations in different kinds of relationships but want to feel cared about in all of them. You expect a clerk in a store to interact with you in a different way than you would with an intimate partner, but there are still symbols that the clerk cares about you. If they don't demonstrate those symbols, you might get upset, even though you hardly know this person.

For example, if a sales clerk is chatting on the phone while you're waiting, especially about something unrelated to their job, this can feel like they don't care. You also want them to tell you what might be the best product for your needs. You want them to be honest, and so on.

Likewise, you have symbols of caring, or Love Symbols, in your more intimate relationships. One in our culture that you're probably familiar with is that a man is supposed to bring flowers and/or chocolate on Valentine's Day. Some women are hurt if he doesn't, others would much rather be surprised by his cooking dinner or doing something else.

The first time I realized that people have different Love Symbols was at around age thirteen when I went to a friend's house on Mother's Day. No one had made any special gesture for his mother, and I was sure she must be hurt, because my mother would have been. To my surprise, they told me, no, she didn't like Mother's Day and didn't want anyone to do anything.

You probably have your own version of what would be meaningful to receive or give on Mother's Day or Valentine's Day, and it would be good if both you and your significant other knew what action or gift would evoke feelings of being loved.

I AM rAther horrified At whAt I would DescriBe As "oBligAtory gifts," And VAlentine's DAy is one of the worst for this. I'm Definitely A womAn who is not looking for A gift on this (or Any other) DAte. Well, BirthDAys could Be An exception....

You may feel that your partner should know the "right" thing to do in these situations, and if they don't, they must not care. Couples from similar backgrounds tend to stay together more, in part because they were raised with the same understanding of what each is supposed to do in a relationship to be a good partner.

But in a Succulent Wild Love relationship, someone perfunctorily performing what they're "supposed" to do is not nearly as rewarding as their expressing their love for you in a way that feels good to both of you.

For me, the more creAtive or personAl the gift or gesture, the Better. one of my lovers hAD DelivereD to me A first eDition of the Book BREAKFAST AT TIFFANY'S, with A letter ABout whAt it meAnt to him And whAt he imAgineD it might meAn to me. When I first met John, he Bought me A fABulous sky-Blue JAcket, And then returneD it uncomplAiningly for A Different size. I felt so cAreD for — ABout Both the JAcket And his mAking sure I hAD the right size.

DISTORTED LOVE SYMBOLS

While many Love Symbols are pure expressions of love, most of us were raised with at least some distorted love symbols. By this we mean love mixed with fear. A common example is showing love by worrying about someone: "If I didn't care about you, I wouldn't worry about you." But worrying also involves fear about whatever is being worried about, as well as some doubt that the person is able to take care of themselves.

A mother wouldn't say to a healthy child, "I'm worried that you won't be able to lift your arms." She is fully confident that her child can do that. So when she says, "I'm worried that you...," she is implying, "I have some doubts about your ability in this area."

Another common mixture of love and fear is control: "I know what's best for you." Parents will try to control their children in a variety of ways to get them to become good citizens and to protect them. They are afraid if they don't control their children, bad things will happen.

There is often a practical benefit to this, especially when children are very young and might run across a street without looking or do something else dangerous. But frequently this control carries on into the teenage years and beyond as a form of expressing love.

These symbols of love then get translated into adult peer relationships, where one partner may try to control the eating habits of the other, tell them what to wear, or insist that they do particular tasks around the house.

In many of these instances, the people involved see what they are doing as Love Symbols. One person may feel insecure about their fashion sense and welcome the other telling them what matches. Telling someone what to do is always entering their boundaries. When it is welcome, the boundary is open. Having the other person enter can feel reassuring and enhance the intimacy of the relationship. When it isn't welcome, it is breaking into the other person's boundaries and will evoke discomfort.

If you feel good about what someone is doing, then that symbol works for you. However, it is useful to be able to separate the love and fear in any interaction, so that you can have more of the one and less of the other.

Sharing Your Love Symbols

Once you know what the symbols of love are for you, you can let the intimate people in your life know how they can help you feel loved. You can also find out what their symbols for giving and receiving love are and can be on the lookout for their particular ways of expressing love to you — and for ways they will recognize your love for them.

Love Symbols don't just occur on holidays or other special occasions, they affect you every day in your relationships. The more openly you can talk with your partner about what is meaningful to each of you, the more likely it is that you will come to joyful expressions of love for each other.

I remember when I first heard about the concept that other people weren't mind readers and would have to be told what I wanted or needed. Earlier in my life, I didn't know how to clearly ask for what I wanted — I usually expressed clearly what I didn't want, and was often quite vehement or articulate when I did so. This resulted in people "walking on eggshells" around me, afraid they wouldn't be able to live up to what I said I wanted — or didn't want. So I advise letting others know clearly — and also diplomatically, gently, or in ways that you can tell they can most easily hear.

There are also situations that might call for Joyful Solutions. If your Love Symbols are very different from your partner's, you will want to find ways to express what feels natural to you and also evokes feelings of being loved in your partner.

I briefly dated a woman who felt cared for when a man opened the car door for her. I often did this, but then started to feel resentment. I didn't want to always have to do it in order for her to feel I cared. The relationship ended before we resolved the situation, but had it not, it would have been good for me to bring this up to see if there was another way she could feel cared about when we were in a car together. At the time, I didn't have a very good understanding of Love Symbols and didn't know how to bring this up in a way that wouldn't evoke feelings of rejection.

You probably won't discover all your and your partner's Love Symbols in one conversation. So, as you spend time together — especially around holidays — whenever you notice yourself wishing your partner was doing (or not doing) something that you associate with feeling loved, you can tell them, "This as a Love Symbol for me." Then create a Joyful Solution where they can do what feels harmonious to them and you feel cared about.

Whether you're in an intimate relationship or not, you can ask yourself, "What specific things can I do to show myself that I'm loved?" You can make a list and keep it out where you can see it and add to it. If you wish, share this list with someone close to you.

When I was soulfully single, I focused on creating many Love Symbols for myself so that I wasn't waiting for a partner in order to feel romantic, or cherished, or cared about in those ways. I did a lot of self-hugging, spontaneous gift giving to myself, and taking myself out on romantic dates. I even learned how to slow dance really well with myself. And these practices still continue in my succulent wild relationship with John.

Recently we were going out, and I had gotten dressed up and wanted John to notice. He was busy getting ready and didn't compliment my clothes or appearance. I knew he would if I asked, but then it wouldn't have felt like a Love Symbol as much as my telling him what to say. So I excused myself and went into the bathroom and complimented my own appearance in the mirror, and reassured myself that I looked really good.

I ended up laughing with my reflection in the mirror and went out to the car. John was putting something into the trunk and looked up to see me and spontaneously said, "You look nice!" I smiled and said, "Thanks!"

If you want a life or love partner, you can also write a letter telling your future lover what specific things they can do to help you feel loved. As vividly as you can, imagine experiencing these. Describe in detail what will feel like Love Symbols to you. You can do this in short, simple descriptions if a letter feels like too much.

Six months before I met John, I got a special artistic box to put my wishes into. This box said "happy happy joy" on the side, and had other glad messages and drawings and art. I also bought a smaller box to go inside — on the top it said "top secret" and on the bottom it said "bottom secret."

This made me laugh and feel inspired to write a secret tiny note on a yellow piece of paper, fold it into a tiny square, and put it inside the top-and-bottom-secret box, and that into the other box. I then forgot all about it until John was moving in and I opened that tiny piece of paper. I'd written on it, "Someone to love and adore who also loves and adores me."

My Container of Joy

My secret tiny note

Annie Wright and Kyle Russell — When a Bird Dates a Fish: Learning to Love the Differences

Kyle Russell and Annie Wright

As a couple we truly couldn't be more different in terms of temperament, personality, worldview, and habits. We're so different, in fact, that when we got together, our friends and family were surprised by our pairing. Even today we both liken ourselves and our differences to what we imagine a bird and a fish might have to go through in order to be together: horizon expanding, to be sure, but also a mighty challenge.

Because of this, our relationship has included a lot of learning how to navigate and cooperate around these differences, both big and small — the conscious cultivation of a toolbox of interventions for managing friction and conflict, and ongoing softening of our expectations about "what our partner is supposed to do in the relationship." This process hasn't always been easy, and the seemingly smallest stuff — for example, Kyle's habit of leaving laundry on the floor *by the hamper instead of in it* and Annie's tendency to not close lids on jars *all the way tightly* — has often yielded the richest relational lessons.

The above-mentioned housekeeping behaviors are deeply, oddly ingrained in us and have been so since childhood (just ask our mothers!). Neither of us consciously *intends* to drive the other crazy with our habits, but during our early years together, that was certainly the impact. Along the way, we've found ways to navigate this difference of household habits: we can change the behavior itself, or we can change the meaning each of us assigns to the behavior.

The first choice — changing the behavior — seems pretty straightforward, except that it isn't because, as we said, we've had these habits since childhood and any change we make never seems to stick. So in the past few years, we've both been focused on changing the meaning we assign to these behaviors.

For example, when Kyle leaves his clothes on the floor by the laundry hamper, the default meaning for Annie in the past was "My partner isn't responsible — laundry should always go in the hamper," whereas for Kyle, the meaning of clothes on the floor symbolizes that they can be worn again; if they're *in* the hamper they need to be washed. It's an organization thing for him.

While Annie will always have a preference for seeing all the clothes in the laundry hamper, each time she now sees a pile of plaid shirts on the ground near the bin, she practices diffusing the triggering meaning by seeing the wider context of Kyle and all the *other* ways he's responsible and considerate as a partner and a housemate. It helps Annie move into a space where the meaning is no longer "My partner isn't responsible," but rather, "He's a pretty responsible guy who keeps himself organized by leaving clothes on the floor. And I love him anyway."

And as for the lids on jars, we did actually employ behavioral change there: so they won't spill, Kyle now just grabs jars from the bottom.

The household stuff seems small on the surface (and it is compared to the bigger stuff we, like most couples, face around money, sex, religion, lifestyle, etc.), but the underlying dynamic — of holding expectations and assigning meaning about each other and our actions — has been one of the richest relational lessons we've learned. The more we're learning to lean into the other's experience, the more compassion we're able to have about our differences and the more gratitude we have for our similarities.

This bird and fish are learning how to thrive together after all.

Annie is a Berkeley, CA–based psychotherapist (intern) in private practice (AnnieWright Psychotherapy.com). Kyle has created a robust career in the coffee industry and is currently pursuing a degree in business.

Awareness Practice:
Discovering and Practicing with Your Love Symbols

1. What are some of your Love Symbols? What do others do that evokes feelings of being loved in you? Do you enjoy receiving gifts? Compliments? Someone doing something for you?

2. What are some of the Love Symbols of people who are intimate in your life? Can you recognize Love Symbols for loved ones? If not, have you asked them?

3. What special Love Symbols do you have around holidays? Decorations or music or ceremonial rituals may be important to you. Create your own holiday Love Symbols if you wish.

4. Are you aware of any Love Symbols for yourself or others that involve someone entering your boundaries, such as their telling you what to do or how to act in any way? This could include "well-meaning advice," reminding you about things, advising you, or overwatching what you do or say.

5. If you feel discomfort in any area where someone enters your boundaries as a symbol of their love, can you think of new ways to respond that would feel self-loving? For example, instead of ignoring, resisting, avoiding, or forgetting, you might name how you feel, saying something such as, "I know you mean well, and I'd be more comfortable doing this on my own — thank you." Or you may become aware that you are feeling pressured or resistant to their observation or suggestion, and say something like, "That might work really well for you, and I'm just different about this." Often if you say something clearly one time, it isn't necessary to keep repeating it.

6. Do you enter others' boundaries as a way of expressing that you care about them? Can you tell if you are welcome? If you feel any resistance, see if you can find another way to show your caring.

To discover more about Love Symbols, go to:
SucculentWildLove.com/Symbols

17. Love TrAnslAtions with others And Self-Love

+ seeing with our HeARTS

How we see is WHAT we experience

EVERYONE AROUND YOU IS A UNIQUE PERSON, from your most intimate relations to strangers on the street. They have separate personalities with a variety of individual characteristics. However, your encounters with them and how you feel about those encounters often has more to do with your inner experience than their specific actions.

I often think thAt everyone is more similAr thAn DiFFerent, And sometimes Become puzzled or FrustrAted thAt they BehAve DiFFerently From How I Do or would. When John First moved in with me, I BegAn sAying humorously, "StrAngely, we Are not the sAme person...," to remind myself of our DiFFerences, And of His right to Be And BehAve DiFFerently thAn I Do. This Helps me to Be self-lovingly sepArAte And ABle to Feel more loving more oFten.

Everything is colored by our preconceptions. We tend to see the world and others in certain ways, and these often have as much to do with our expectations as the specific behaviors of those around us. In other words, we're always interpreting the actions of others, and this interpretation, more than the actions themselves, affects how we feel.

CHANGE
WHAT YOU
See BY WHAT YOU
SAY
inside to yourself
If you believe you are lovable and deserve love, you will see the actions of others in that light. If you believe you aren't loved or expect to be hurt, you'll be more sensitive to every possible slight and may not experience the love messages that are coming your way.

If you want to have more loving relationships, one of the most powerful things you can do is to change the lens through which you view the actions of others. Because if you picture yourself as lovable, then you will turn all your experiences along those lines.

I've written a great deal about how I increased the self-love in my life and how you can do the same. Here we are focusing on one very specific way to do this. Whenever you feel hurt or angry, or whenever someone sends you a not-so-loving message, literally say to yourself, "I am lovable. I deserve to have love in my life."

This will remind you of a basic truth about yourself. And from that foundation you will be able to more easily see the love that is actually all around you.

"I am lovable. I deserve to have love in my life."

If you have any difficulty saying this or believing it, ask yourself, "Why?"

This is your foundation in a Succulent Wild Love relationship. If you can see the truth in your deserving to have love in your life, then you will be able to see the love that is available to you.

When you remind yourself of this truth every time you feel less than love from someone, slowly you will find your world changing. You will be able to see others' attempts at love when before all you could see was their negativity. You will pay less attention to situations and people who are not joyful, and you will experience more loving and joyful encounters with others.

Susan and I go for a walk almost every day. Many people walk in San Francisco, especially along the bay, so we often encounter people. Almost invariably these brief interactions are fun and uplifting. When someone seems unfriendly, we either ignore them or don't take it personally (unless we don't feel good about ourselves that day).

I TAKE MANY THINGS PERSONALLY. I'VE LEARNED TO SOOTHE MYSELF SO THAT I DON'T TAKE THINGS AS PERSONALLY IF PEOPLE REACT NEGATIVELY OR IF I'VE LET THEM UPSET ME IN SOME WAY. I'M USUALLY ABLE TO SPONTANEOUSLY PLAY WITH OTHER PEOPLE AND ENJOY THEM IMMENSELY. I PRACTICE WITH THE TOOLS IN THIS CHAPTER TO GREAT EFFECT MUCH MORE OFTEN, AND THE TIMES I'M AFFECTED NEGATIVELY NOW ARE USUALLY THE EXCEPTION. Or, I do it and Feel Awful. Good CHance to re-do!

In the sources of anger chapter we talked about using evaluation and translation (see page 136) to clarify if someone cares about you when they do something that evokes anger. We called this making a Love Translation. Here we want to talk about using Love Translations in a more expansive way to increase the love you feel everywhere in your life.

A Love Translation is when you observe something another person says or does and see the underlying attempt to express love. You see what they are doing in a loving light. A gruff neighbor may lack social skills rather than being mean. Someone close to you may be pushy because they feel insecure or are afraid they won't get what they want.

Most of us have been in situations where we felt loved and unloved, powerful and powerless. Anything we focus on gets bigger in our experience. So if you pay attention to when you do feel loved, and make Love Translations when someone sends you a not-so-loving message, experiences of love will blossom in your life.

Doing this helps you approach the other person from a state of love rather than fear, making it easier for you and increasing the chances that they will have a more loving response to you. When you look below the surface actions and translate them from a loving perspective, you can often feel compassion.

See if you can look at the world through the eyes of others
when they are less than loving and see the rightness of their actions for them.

Making a Love Translation will often result in your seeing that their actions are based on being unaware of what is uncomfortable for you, or they are socially clumsy, or simply afraid. Happy people don't intentionally do hurtful things.

I recently got a new iPhone. A friend had broken hers and was still on contract, so I decided to give her my old one. When I gave it to her, she thanked me, and then flippantly said, "You saved me a couple of dollars." Of course the phone was worth a lot more, and I felt hurt by what seemed like her diminishing the value of my gesture.

On reflection, I was able to see that she felt embarrassed. She felt she didn't have the money to buy a new phone, and here I was, able to afford the latest and with enough abundance that I could just give away one that was still valuable. I was able to make the Love Translation and didn't even need to talk with her about it.

I HAVE AN INSPIRATION PHONE LINE WHERE PEOPLE FROM ALL OVER THE WORLD CALL IN AND HEAR MY OUTGOING MESSAGE, AND OFTEN LEAVE ONE OF THEIR OWN. THE GREAT MAJORITY OF THESE MESSAGES ARE POSITIVE, AND ONCE IN A WHILE, WHEN ONE IS NOT, I TAKE THE OPPORTUNITY TO DO A LOVE TRANSLATION.

A WOMAN CALLED AND LEFT A MESSAGE SAYING ANGRILY, "TIME FOR A NEW MESSAGE! I'VE HEARD THIS ONE BEFORE." HER EXPRESSION MATCHED MY INNER CRITIC PERFECTLY — I "SHOULD" HAVE ALREADY MADE A NEW MESSAGE. AFTER I INITIALLY FELT ANNOYED AND INTOLERANT, AND DID SOME INNER CRITIC CARE SYSTEM WORK, I DID SOME POSITIVE LOVE TRANSLATIONS FOR THIS SITUATION — AND OTHERS LIKE IT.

I WROTE DOWN: "SHE MUST BE FEELING SOME PAIN — HAPPY PEOPLE DON'T COME ACROSS THAT WAY. SHE EXPECTED A NEW MESSAGE AND JUST BLURTED OUT HER DISAPPOINTMENT — I'VE DONE THAT BEFORE TOO. SHE VALUES WHAT I HAVE TO SAY. SHE'D LIKE TO RECEIVE BENEFIT FROM WHAT I HAVE TO SAY. I THINK I'LL MAKE A NEW MESSAGE NOW — BECAUSE I WANT TO, RATHER THAN BECAUSE I FEEL PRESSURED BY INNER CRITICS OR AN ANNOYED-SOUNDING PERSON. I FEEL FREE."

415·546·3742 Inspiration Phone Line You're invited to call!

By "making a Love Translation," we don't mean giving someone an excuse for hurting you. If you feel frustrated or abused in any way, then this needs to be addressed with a Joyful Solution. You may understand why someone is doing something hurtful, but that does not mean you have to accept their actions. In a Succulent Wild Love relationship everyone deserves to be treated with respect and kindness.

Every action anyone takes is based on love or fear, and often a combination of both. A Love Translation highlights the love portion and ignores the fear portion.

Sometimes I operate in the world through what I would call a fear translation. For example, we had a contractor come over to look at our building because we were experiencing some leaks and wanted to get an assessment of what would needed to be done to stop them.

The guy started telling us how we needed to get the ivy off IMMEDIATELY, that it was EATING THE BUILDING, and that it SERIOUSLY needed caulking and RIGHT NOW. He said we DEFINITELY needed a WHOLE new roof — THE SOONER, THE BETTER — and that we needed a TOP-NOTCH AND EXPENSIVE PAINTER, not some cut-rate operation. He went on with further intensely worded comments.

I tried to do Love Translations — he cares about good workmanship; he wants our building to be in good shape — but I felt overwhelmed by my fears. I felt exhausted and frightened after he left, and rather hopeless about the condition of our building. Additionally, my inner critics were all over me, saying that I'd been a poor steward and that any deferred maintenance was all my fault.

Suddenly it occurred to me to ask John what he had heard the contractor say. He replied calmly, "He said our building is basically in good shape. Just take the ivy off, get it painted and caulked, and put on a new roof. That will take care of it." John's Love Translation had been going on while the guy was talking. He hadn't reacted to the drama or the fear in the ways that I had. I saw once again that we all have the choice to respond rather than react, and that we can practice Love Translations rather than fear translations.

Susan and I have an agreement in our relationship that if one of us feels more confident about something positive or has a better story, we "ride on that person's energy."

The anecdote above about the building is a good example of this. My story about the building was more positive than Susan's, so she decided to go with mine.

Susan has taught many classes on the internet, so when we decided to do a class together on relationships, I rode on her good energy. Many people ride on each other's energy in this way in relationships. I think the difference for us is that we're more conscious of it and intend that whoever has the best story takes the lead. It's possible to ride on the energy of the person who's most frightened in a relationship, and some people end up doing that.

In this book, we're offering you the choice of riding on our energy when it comes to relationships. We have a great story about what a Succulent Wild Love relationship is like, and we're confident that if you develop the habits in this book, you will be able to create a Succulent Wild Love relationship too.

The idea is to have more experiences of love in your life and fewer of fear. Everyone, and every event, represents one or the other. In Succulent Wild Love relationships you want the intimate people in your life to be symbols of love. In fact, to feel love the most, you want everyone and everything you focus on to be symbols of love.

ride your succulent wild love cycle!

Awareness Practice:
Doing Love Translations and Practicing Self-Love

Practicing with self-love means being able to feel that love flowing for yourself. If you typically feel less than loving toward yourself, you won't be able to feel love for others. Experiment with the following:

🌀 Write or contemplate the statement, "I am lovable, I deserve to have love in my life." See if any memories opposite of being loved come up. If so, write down a list of what you're thinking.

🌀 Now take two or three of these memories and write down how you would like to have been treated in those situations. Make this as realistic as possible. This will be the model for how you want to be treated from now on.

☆ If those memories included someone being less than nice to you, see if you can make a Love Translation. Also, see if you can imagine a Joyful Solution that might work if a similar situation comes up in the future.

★ In order to practice Love Translations instead of fear translations, you'll want to practice **EAT**ing more often: **e**valuate **a**nd **t**ranslate (see page 136). It can be like a fun game.

🌀 For example, if someone on the phone seems rude, you can realize that it probably has nothing to do with you, and you can say something like, "We seem to have gotten off to a bad start here — let's start over. I appreciate your help and knowledge with _____."

If someone close to you seems to be acting in an annoying or upsetting way, you can remove yourself briefly and remind yourself to EAT before you act. Maybe their blood sugar is low, or work was hard, or you know they're feeling scared. You don't need to say these things out loud to them in order to do your Love Translation.

🌀 As you go about your day, notice when you feel loved or appreciated. Notice when you're able to evaluate and translate to make your experience more loving.

✦ Then savor those experiences. Review and bask in what felt good. You can do this by thinking about what pleased you, telling friends about it, or writing it down. This will expand your abilities to feel more love for yourself — and others — more often.

To receive more scrumptious information about Love Translations, go to:
SucculentWildLove.com/Translations

18. Succulent Wild Communications

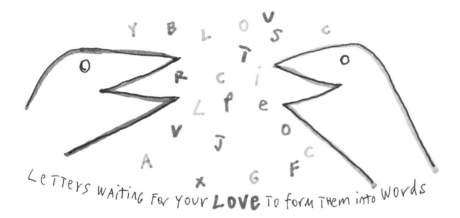

Letters waiting for your **LOVE** to form them into words

THERE ARE MANY KINDS OF COMMUNICATIONS in any relationship. Here we talk about three specific types that can resolve tension and create intimacy: Naming, Agreements, and MicroTruths.

NAMING (INSTEAD OF BLAMING)

NAMING instead of BLAMING

Have you ever gone to a doctor not sure what your symptoms meant and been given a diagnosis? Do you remember the feeling of relief when the doctor gave you a prescription with the message, "Take these and you'll be fine"?

What happened there is that the doctor "named" what was going on with you. This enabled both of you to understand and help you.

Relationships have symptoms too, usually first in the form of uncomfortable thoughts and feelings. If these are not addressed, they can turn into uncomfortable, even painful, actions.

When you name what is going on, it makes it much easier to know what to do about it.

eArly in our relAtionship, John wAs piCking me up from An Appointment thAt we hAd previously plAnned. I texted A few times to let him know thAt the time hAd ChAnged, And to give An estimAte of the time I'd be reAdy. John wAs driving while these texts were Coming in And didn't wAnt to look At them while driving, or tAke the time to pull over And review them, beCAuse he wAs running A bit lAte And wAnted to be on time.

When he pulled up, he AppeAred to be how I remembered my fAther being — grumpy, Angry, or Annoyed About the time. John bArely greeted me, And we drove off. soon After, we stopped to get some lunCh, And I sAid, "It feels to me like the timing of the piCkup is more importAnt to you thAn I Am." He just stAred At me, so I sAid, "WhAt's more importAnt to you, me or thAt you're there At the time you sAid you would be?"

He replied sheepishly, "To be on time." I felt AmAzed thAt he Admitted it! I felt suCh A rush of love for him. We were Able to tAlk About his PerfeCtionist inner CritiC in this AreA, his desire to be on time, And thAt time is importAnt to him. And of Course he understood thAt being hAppy with me wAs more importAnt thAn whAtever time it wAs. We were both Able to nAme our feelings And nAvigAte them beAutifully. Now of Course we usuAlly lAugh About time, And he's more flexible About piCkups, And I'm more understAnding About how he sometimes experienCes time.

When you name something that feels uncomfortable or hurts, it is easier to help yourself and others change what is happening.

Naming Inner Critics

Until you name an inner critic, you may feel obligated to do what it says.

Naming inner critics helps you see yourself as separate from them. Naming anything separates it from your identity and allows you to more easily examine and modify it. It helps you see that you're not that feeling or experience, that you don't have to keep it as part of your relationship.

We covered much of this in chapter 9 on the Inner Critic Care System. When you have recurrent, similar critical thoughts in your head, it can be useful to give them a name. We gave some examples, such as the Pushing One and the Perfectionist. Playfully naming these negative-message givers makes it easier not to be controlled by them.

Naming Your Feelings

When you name how you feel, it is easier to attend to your feelings.

"I feel sad." "I feel stuck." "I'm bored." Each of these feelings benefits from a different kind of response. Until you name your feelings, you can feel lost.

When you're interacting with someone and one or both of you feel hurt, naming what evokes the hurt will help you find a Joyful Solution.

As mentioned in chapter 13, we've named three general triggers when it comes to anger and hurt:

- You may feel the other person doesn't care about you the way you want them to.

- You may think they should behave differently.

- What they did has a practical impact and is limiting you in some way.

In order to name something, you need to pay attention to what you're experiencing. A simple but powerful way to start is to say — in your mind — "This feels good," or, "This doesn't feel good," about things you experience.

You may think, "Of course I know when I don't feel good," and that is probably true when you get to a certain level of discomfort. But most of us have been taught to ignore many of our feelings.

From an early age we're told to do things — go to school, study these subjects, do our homework. How we feel about doing these things is often given a low priority by the authorities around us, and soon we learn to give what we feel a low priority too.

Paying attention to your feelings can just make things worse when you believe you have to do something anyway. So tuning them out can be an adaptive behavior. But often we aren't told what we lose by doing this. We lose our inner guidance. We may be able to keep it for the larger things, like wanting a car or a lover, or when we're really upset about something. But if we aren't sensitive to our feelings in less intense situations, we can live with a significant amount of low-level discomfort and think this is just the way it has to be.

This is one of the reasons that people are often dissatisfied with their relationships. They will do things out of habit or obligation and never ask themselves, "Do I really want to do this?" This is often the adult version of learning as a child not to ask questions like, "What do I want to do in school today?" but instead expecting teachers and other authorities to make these decisions.

We have talked about the value of the Inner Feelings Care System, and if you've used it, you've likely felt some relief. But here we are talking about less intense feelings, ones that wouldn't necessarily prompt you to look for relief because you might not even be aware of them.

So the first step — and it's a powerful one — is to begin naming when something feels good and when it doesn't.

If you become aware that you aren't enjoying something, you don't necessarily have to do anything different. Perhaps you made a promise to someone and now realize you don't want to do what you promised. At this point it may be easier to simply keep the promise. But now you are more aware. You'll be less likely to offer things you don't want to do in the future — and look for Joyful Solutions instead.

Even if you only occasionally check in with yourself to see if you're feeling good, you will still receive benefit from your greater self-awareness.

Naming an Interaction

You've probably heard stories about five people witnessing a car accident and each person seeing something different. This also happens in relationships. As we talked about in the previous chapter, our preconceptions have a strong influence on what we experience.

So you may very well encounter a tense situation where someone close to you sees things quite differently. Here you can start by naming it, "We each see the situation differently — and that's okay."

Occasionally Susan and I will have a miscommunication. It may start by her saying something like, "I told you we had to leave by five," as I'm scrambling to get ready, and my responding, "No, you didn't."

But I will then often change to, "I don't know if you said anything or not. You may very well have, but I didn't hear the message," acknowledging the fact that we both have different perspectives. (Then I may try to blame her for not communicating more effectively, but that doesn't last.)

We allow each of us to cach havc our own experience. Often partners in relationships will try to force the other person to see it their way, and this can lead to endless tension. Sometimes one person can sway the other to their perception. But sometimes they can't, because the other person, given their preconceptions and experience, simply sees things differently.

What you can do is look at the situation through each other's eyes without demanding that you agree. (You may recall our story of driving in downtown San Francisco and Susan locking the car doors — to John's initial chagrin.)

AGREEMENTS

A Joyful Solution is an agreement that everyone is enthusiastic about keeping.

Often bumps in relationships arise because people have unclear agreements or someone is seen as breaking an agreement.

The principles of Succulent Wild relationships can be thought of as agreements: We will respect each other's boundaries. We will look for Joyful Solutions rather than pressing ourselves or each other to compromise. We will see the best in each other and not make the other responsible for our happiness.

You will have many other agreements, large and small, some spoken, others assumed. We used the example of Valentine's gifts in the chapter on Love Symbols. Couples may agree on certain gifts being given without ever discussing this. However, the more you discuss your agreements and bring them out into the open, the more likely you are to feel good about them and keep them.

Sometimes someone will have such a strong inner critic that they will agree to something that really doesn't feel good. A woman may have come to believe that being a good mother means always being available for her child. So rather than sharing parental duties, she may accept this uncomfortable role of the "good mother."

The father may assume everything is okay and not realize that he is making an agreement with her inner critic. Then he may be shocked to hear that she doesn't want to have the second child they had planned on. Someone abruptly wanting to change course often means an inner critic has been running the show and the person is finally fed up.

Using the same couple as an example, she may want him to do things to get a promotion at work, and he may agree because both of them were raised with the common belief that it's the man's job to provide for the family. But he often doesn't do the extra work that could get him promoted, and she often reminds (nags) him to do it. Here the agreement was made with his inner critic, that he "should" provide more financially because this is what a man does.

Usually the person who has not been keeping an agreement is so identified with their inner critic that they don't feel free to admit they don't want to fulfill their obligation. In the examples above, ideally the couple will explore what changed the mother's mind, and she will give herself permission to get support with parenting. The father will be able to admit that he doesn't want to do more at work, and they can create a Joyful Solution.

When an agreement is broken occasionally, it is generally because of a miscommunication or because one of the participants did not give it as high a priority as the other. If an agreement is broken often, or one of the participants has to constantly push the other to honor it, then it was likely made with an inner critic.

Once you name how you see an agreement being broken, the next best step is to accept where you and the other person are right now. Another way to look at this is to forgive yourself and the other person for being who you/they are. Everyone has been doing the best they can, and this is where you have both arrived.

All the tools in a Succulent Wild Love relationship work together. The partner who feels that an agreement wasn't honored can make a Love Translation and help the other look for an inner critic. They can then work together to create a Joyful Solution.

Knowing what agreements you have — and want — in any relationship, discussing them when conflicts come up, and being able to name how someone is breaking them makes it much easier to keep any relationship harmonious and loving.

TELLING MICROTRUTHS: CLEAN AS YOU GO

cleaning as you go expands
Love opportunities

In any relationship, if you can't say the little nos, you eventually have to say the Big No. In other words, if you can't ask for and get what you need in the relationship, if you don't address the small hurts and irritations, eventually you will want to leave — either emotionally or physically or both.

We have talked about creating Joyful Solutions, but before you can do so, you or your partner has to say what you want to change. When a situation feels uncomfortable, it can often be difficult to speak your truth.

Most likely, you have been taught to be polite and not hurt others. You may be afraid (correctly) that the other person will become defensive. You may be unsure of your "right" to have things be different. There are a variety of reasons why speaking your truth can be difficult. The way you can tell if you're in such a situation is if you want to say something and feel you can't.

Sometimes, the best path is not to say anything to the other person — for example, your boss. Speaking your truth to someone is a form of intimacy. It is actually a gift you give them, even though it may be painful at first. It is letting them know who you are.

You can leave them out of the process and find a way to create a Joyful Solution without them. In some relationships that is the best path, but the more you can speak honestly about what you feel and want, the more intimate your relationships become. Being able to speak your truth can also often keep you from wanting to leave the relationship altogether.

The term I use for these small, uncomfortable situations is "MicroTruths." I grew up in a family where no one spoke MicroTruths, or many truths at all. Most things were unspoken or swept "under the carpet." There were so many things under our carpet that it's a wonder we could even walk on our floor!

In many situations, speaking about what you want is easy. We do it all the time in relationships. "I would like to see this movie." "Let's put the couch in front of the fireplace." "I want to get groceries this afternoon." When there is no fear, speaking your truth is easy. MicroTruths are for those situations when you feel you can't.

Give Yourself Permission

Remind yourself that you deserve to have relationships with no ongoing tension or unresolved issues. If you have a MicroTruth, decide if you want to be intimate with the other person on this level and if you want to gain their cooperation. For example, it may be good to tell a MicroTruth to your neighbor to get their help, even if you aren't particularly intimate with them. You have the right to have security and comfort in all your relationships.

Early in our relationship, John and I went to Columbus, Ohio, to clean out his condominium and prepare it for sale. There were many emotions involved, since John had lived there for many years, including a decade

WITH HIS WIFE, JEANIE. AND HE WOULD BE MEETING HER ELDEST DAUGHTER THERE
TO CLEAN OUT JEANIE'S THINGS.

Given the feelings I still had about losing Jeanie, which I knew would be intensified as I went
through her things, and the feelings Jeanie's daughter had, Susan and I both knew it would be
risky for her to come to Columbus. (I think most people would have advised her to stay away,
and rightly so, as it could easily have turned very stressful, or worse.)

But being with Susan felt comforting, and I wanted her to come. What I valued most was
her emotional support. We talked about it and thought we could handle whatever emotions
came up.

I WENT ALONG TO HELP AND ALSO BROUGHT MY WORK WITH ME. I WAS WRITING,
MEETING WITH CLIENTS OVER THE PHONE, AND TEACHING ONLINE. AFTER WE'D BEEN
THERE FOR THREE OR FOUR DAYS, AND I'D HELPED WITH VARIOUS THINGS, WE
PLANNED FOR ME TO GO TO A HOTEL THE NIGHT OF MY ONLINE CLASS. THERE WAS
NO LANDLINE AT JOHN'S CONDOMINIUM, AND IT WAS JUST GOING TO BE EASIER
FOR ME TO TEACH IN A DIFFERENT ENVIRONMENT THAN ONE FULL OF PEOPLE AND
BOXES.

This is what Susan said at the time, but neither of us realized how much tension was evoked
in her by my mourning the loss of Jeanie as her daughter and I were going through Jeanie's
things. Since Susan was always in another part of the house, we naively assumed that she
wouldn't be affected. Looking back at it now, being in that house was intensely stressful for
everyone.

THE DAY AFTER MY CLASS, I REALIZED I WANTED TO STAY IN THE
HOTEL ANOTHER NIGHT — PURELY TO RELAX ALONE AND ENJOY THE PEACEFUL
ENVIRONMENT. I IMMEDIATELY FELT GUILTY THAT I WOULD POSSIBLY BE SEEN AS
A "BAD, UNHELPFUL GIRLFRIEND" AND AFRAID THAT JOHN WOULD FEEL ANGRY OR
HURT THAT I WANTED TO DO SUCH A THING.

I THEN STARTED ENVISIONING JOHN'S RESPONSE AS POSITIVE, AND IMAGINED
HIM FULLY SUPPORTING ME IN STAYING AT THE HOTEL. SINCE IT WAS SO EARLY IN
OUR RELATIONSHIP, AND WE REALLY DIDN'T KNOW EACH OTHER THAT WELL, I WANTED
TO BE EXTRA-CAREFUL TO COMMUNICATE MY FEELINGS AND PREPARE WHAT I
WOULD SAY, AND HOLD MY BEST VISION OF HOW HE WOULD RESPOND. I ALSO CALLED
A FEW FRIENDS FOR SUPPORT.

I THEN BEGAN TO DEVELOP A SCRATCHY THROAT, LIKE I WAS GETTING SICK,

AND THIS SEEMED LIKE THE EASIEST WAY OUT, SO I THOUGHT I WOULD JUST START BY TELLING HIM THAT.

When John answered the phone and I told him that I had a sore throat, he immediately responded as though he already knew intuitively what I was calling about, and said, "You don't need to be sick to do what you want to do." I took a deep breath and then stated clearly and lovingly that I was going to stay in the hotel another night, and asked him if he had enough help without me. He assured me that he did, and I believed him.

We said goodbye very lovingly, and my sore throat almost instantly disappeared. John told me later that when he hung up the phone, he said out loud, "Well, I was certainly very mature."

At that point I was still so involved with my own feelings that I didn't fully appreciate the tension Susan had gone through while at the house, and the relief she felt at getting away. I wanted her to come back, and I missed her support. But I had told her that the only thing I wanted from her if she came to Columbus was for her to be happy, and I knew there was no way she could support me emotionally if she felt pressured to be with me. Still, I was surprised at myself, how quickly I was able to be supportive of her doing what felt right to her, even though it meant not having her with me.

I know that my visioning work, and my not being guilty or fearing his anger or hurt, allowed me to have such a positive experience. I reveled in the bed with its white down comforter and flat-screen TV, with no moving boxes in sight. The next day, I invited John to join me for a date at the hotel so that he could enjoy that environment with me.

Things You Can Do before Telling a MicroTruth

Make a Love Translation

A powerful way to start is to look at what the other person is doing or saying and make a Love Translation. When you take a moment to look behind the obvious actions and translate them from a loving perspective, you can often feel compassion. This answers one of the three questions when we get angry, "Does the other person care about me the way I want them to?" Making a Love Translation usually results in our seeing that they do and that their actions are based on being unaware of what is uncomfortable for us, or that they are socially clumsy or afraid.

If you are angry with them, use the Inner Feelings Care System (page 86) to clarify your feelings. This will allow you to use your feelings constructively rather than being overwhelmed by them or overwhelming the other person.

See if you can look through their eyes and see the rightness of their actions for them. Are you judging them for not sharing your values? Are you invading their boundaries? When you clarify this, you can approach them on the basis of "This is what I want," rather than speaking for God, society, or the law. (In some situations, of course, you may want to invoke societal standards or the law, but this usually is not the most effective path in intimate relationships.)

Making a Love Translation and seeing the world from someone else's perspective does not mean you have to accept their actions. Doing these things helps you approach them more from a state of love rather than fear, making it easier for you and increasing the chances that they will have a more loving response.

WHAT WOULD LOVE HAVE YOU SAY?

Reduce Fear

The more you can reduce fear in yourself and the other person, the easier it will be to come to a loving, intimate resolution. Many people will tell you that facing your fear and speaking up is much better than not speaking up at all. We agree. But in a Succulent Wild Love relationship you can go one step further.

You can actually speak from a place of love rather than fear.

You can begin by imagining this. Before you speak your MicroTruth, imagine a loving outcome. In fact, we recommend not speaking your truth *until* you can imagine a loving outcome. Sometimes this will be easy. At other times you may have to make more of an effort to picture the positive outcome you want. You can ask your Inner Wise Self for help.

The more fully you can imagine a loving interaction when you talk with the person, the more likely you are to play that role and the more likely you are to receive that response. This doesn't mean there won't be some tension initially. What it means is that you can picture a path that begins the moment you approach them and ends with a loving resolution.

An easy way to start is to imagine a situation where they are relaxed and there are no time pressures or other distractions. Picture yourself stating clearly what you want. Maybe they become defensive at first, and without attacking them or making them wrong, you maintain clearly what you want. Visualize both of you wanting a positive outcome. Imagine them hearing you and joining with you in creating a Joyful Solution. Finally, imagine the relief and intimacy you feel after having given this gift to them and yourself.

Release Assumptions and Create the Right Conditions

As we discussed in chapter 11, four of the most uncomfortable words in a relationship, especially for men, are "We have to talk." They imply, "You've done something wrong, and I want to tell you about it." And the response is usually immediate defensiveness.

If you've used the steps above and are looking for cooperation rather than control, those words will probably not benefit you. It's also usually best not to call it a MicroTruth to the other person when you're sharing your feelings — especially if they're unfamiliar with the concept. It can awaken resistance, as though you're using some system against them.

If you start with, "I have a MicroTruth…," it will most likely cause immediate feelings of discomfort. If you begin by saying something like, "Would you help me with some feelings?" or, "I'm looking for a Joyful Solution," you'll be more likely to be heard.

It's really tempting to assign negative meaning to silences or actions of others who are unfamiliar to you. Early in our relationship when I was helping John move out of his condominium, he became very focused on the packing, on the emotions he was feeling, and just on his own experience.

I began to feel isolated and distant from him as I did my work and he went up and down the stairs with boxes. I experienced him as cold and distant — much like my father had sometimes been — and began to feel afraid that our emotional styles were too different to navigate comfortably.

I've learned that I'd rather communicate a MicroTruth than feel disconnected emotionally, so I shared my experience with him and my experience of his behavior. I let him know that I felt distant from him, wanted to understand more about his experience, and wanted to connect. I was able to speak from a place of love rather than fear, and John responded with love.

He listened intently and then shared more about his emotions during the packing process and that he was just very focused on the tasks. He then said, "I might appear preoccupied, but I'm very available to you. If you ask for emotional connection — if you just say, 'I want to connect' — I'll be right there, I promise."

I felt immediately close to him emotionally and glad that we had a system for similar situations in the future. As an unexpected bonus, I felt much more understanding about my father — that he had probably been similarly single-focused and just hadn't had the skills to reassure me.

Months later, we were on a vacation with my brother and his wife. We pulled into the parking lot of a state park lodge we were staying at, and John jumped out of the car and started quickly walking toward our room. It was cold and very dark, and I felt like he was just leaving me in the parking lot — until I remembered our system and called out, "John! I need to connect!" He turned, ran toward me, and hugged me tightly. He explained that he was just so focused on checking in, he hadn't thought of anything else.

Now that I know him well, I don't need to use this system often, but it's still comforting that I can ask for emotional connection anytime, and share the MicroTruth about how I'm feeling. *Asking = relief*

If you're going to speak your truth to someone you are intimate with, it helps to tell them about your experience with learning about MicroTruths and let them know your intent is to create a Joyful Solution, not to criticize them.

If you share a MicroTruth with someone who is tired, stressed, hungry, or overwhelmed, they will likely be much less cooperative. If it doesn't feel like the right time, use your Inner Feelings Care System (page 86) to share your MicroTruth with yourself. This will create the conditions for you to share it with them when the time is right.

Receiving a MicroTruth

It is easy to feel defensive when receiving a MicroTruth. After all, you were perfectly fine with what you were doing, and now someone wants you to change. If you can, loosen your idea that what the person is saying is "against" you. See if any inner critics get activated, and if they do, or other negative feelings arise, you can name what you're feeling and receive some assistance from the person delivering their MicroTruth to you.

You can ask them for clarification, or to slow down, or to say something differently. Residual feelings can occur after MicroTruth telling, so be aware that you might have a MicroTruth to share after hearing one. Consider using your Inner Feelings Care System to express your feelings to yourself before you bring them to another person.

Susan asked me if I liked her new hair clip. I said that it looked old-fashioned, and I usually favor more modern designs…and before I could say that with her curly hair she could make it work beautifully, she…

I felt annoyed with his response and just took the hair clip out. My inner critic immediately joined with him, saying to me, "See! You should have done your hair differently for this party. You should listen to him telling you how old-fashioned you look."

My favorite hair clip

I obviously didn't follow the guidelines here when communicating with John — I was overtaken by my inner critics. It shows you don't have to be perfect about it. With someone intimate, it's usually better to speak up, even if you don't do it perfectly. But if it's about something especially important, it's best to use the guidelines above.

John helped me notice that my inner critic was speaking to me and that I was then speaking sharply to him and taking out my hair clip in retaliation. I asked John to stop the car so I could let that inner critic out of the car. We drove on to the party, laughing. At the party, I asked a woman friend to admire my hair clip, which she happily did.

We can use much of the same process when receiving a MicroTruth as when telling one. If someone approaches you in a clumsy, uncomfortable manner, you can do a Love Translation, recognizing their insecurity or their inner critic.

If you begin defending yourself, you can recognize this and simply stop.

If it is difficult for you to stop, and particularly if you want to attack the other person, this is a strong indicator that they have activated one of your inner critics.

> *Ultimately, we are always fighting with our inner critics.*
> *The people around us simply represent them.*

If this is happening, it is best to stop trying to get the other person to change their perspective. Usually, at this point it is best to separate.

Use the Inner Critic Care System or some other approach to make peace with your inner critic. When you do, dealing with the other person will be easy. Until you make peace with your inner critic, you will continue to feel defensive. Once you're able to separate the other person from your inner critic, it will also be easier to see the rightness of their perspective for them. Then you can join with them in creating a Joyful Solution.

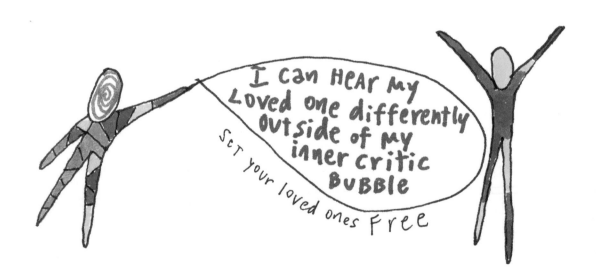

Awareness Practice: Naming, Agreements & MicroTruths

NAMING (INSTEAD OF BLAMING)

Inner Critics

Do you have consistent thoughts that seem to be inner critics speaking (ways that you are undeserving, you are limited, or there is something wrong with you)? Can you name them for yourself?

Feelings

- Write down or reflect on some things that you've discovered you really don't like doing.

- Have you discovered anything new that felt good and you want to do more of?

- Think of some situations where you were aware that you felt good or didn't feel good.

- See if you can name what you were feeling in those situations more specifically. For example:

  I felt (satisfied, excited, appreciated, passionate, loving, etc.) when

  _____.

  Or

  I felt (sad, hurt, lonely, rejected, bored, etc.) when _____.

Interactions

1. Can you think of a situation when you were upset and the other person didn't understand why or what had happened?

2. Can you think of a situation when someone did something that felt uncomfortable and you were able to name what evoked discomfort in you and resolve it?

AGREEMENTS

1. Think of a situation where an agreement was being broken. (Do you feel you have to constantly remind your partner to do anything?)

2. Talk with your partner, exploring what they feel they "should" do (their inner critic) vs. what they genuinely want to do. Revise the agreement until you have one with their adult, Aware Self rather than with an inner critic. You will know you have done this when you don't have to remind them to honor it.

3. Is your partner doing something again and again that you don't like? Talk with your partner and create a Joyful Solution, or create one on your own.

TELLING A MICROTRUTH

Be aware of any small things that feel uncomfortable in your daily interactions. Make a conscious decision whether or not to share your MicroTruth. If you decide to do so, use the steps below.

Steps for Speaking Your MicroTruth

1. Use your Inner Feelings Care System first — expressing all your feelings to yourself first and tending to them lovingly. This will allow you to speak more kindly and lovingly, and with more awareness of the importance of everyone's feelings in general.

2. Separate what actually happened from your fears about what it may mean.

3. Give yourself permission to know and speak your truth — in a Succulent Wild Love relationship you have the right to feel secure.

4. If you are talking with someone intimate in your life, tell them about MicroTruths and that your intent is to create Joyful Solutions.

5. Make a Love Translation — look for the desire for love behind the other person's statements or actions.

6. See the rightness of their actions for them — acknowledge that they may not have the same values you do.

7. Imagine the scene you want — picture them responding positively to the way you approach them.

8. Approach them when they are open to communicating and there are no time pressures or distractions.

9. Approach them with the attitude of wanting to elicit their cooperation.

10. See if you've awakened inner critics in them or in yourself. If so, talk about the inner critics as separate from you and the other person. Separate what you each want from what the inner critics want.

11. Create a Joyful Solution — look for the essence and see if there is a wide variety of ways the goal can be met.

When You Tell a MicroTruth

Use "I" statements only: "I felt _____ when this happened. It would be easier for me if you would do or say   instead."

If the recipient gets ashamed or flooded with feelings, stop, acknowledge this, and do Love Translations before going further.

Leave emotional room for the other person's reactions and responses and any residual feelings after you share a MicroTruth.

MicroTruth telling can feel messy, so be aware that it might not be received as neatly as you imagined.

Finish one MicroTruth before sharing another — don't stack them up or pile them on.

In many situations, you won't need to take time for all these steps. As you practice, you will also be able to take them more quickly. The key is getting to a place where you can speak your truth, knowing that it is an act of love and delivering it that way.

To find out even more about Naming, Agreements & MicroTruths, go to:
SucculentWildLove.com/Communication

19. TRANSFORMING ROLES AND OBLIGATIONS IN RELATIONSHIPS

rolls of another kind

MOST PEOPLE LEARN ABOUT THE ROLES they're supposed to play and the obligations they have in relationships by watching how their parents or caregivers behave. We touched on obligations in the Love Symbols chapter. There are certain actions that represent love to your partner, particularly around holidays. These can feel like obligations, but once you can see them as Love Symbols that can be adjusted, they can be part of the flow of getting to know your partner, rather than rigid requirements.

relaxing and exploring is part of the flow
if you feel like flowing isn't happening, that's okay too

HOW YOUR INNER CRITICS RELATE TO ROLES AND OBLIGATIONS

Your inner critics basically want you to play life roles in particular ways. Sometimes the role matches how you want to live. For example, you may have learned that you're supposed to go to church every Sunday. If you like to go to church, then this just feels like how life is supposed to be. If you don't enjoy going to church, you will feel ambivalent and have a nagging feeling when you don't go.

In relationships, most people subscribe to the idea that being a "good wife" or a "good husband" is positive. There are many positive aspects of what it means to fulfill a role well. We all basically want to be "good" people, to be loved and appreciated. The difficulty arises when we allow our inner critics to define what we have to do to be considered "good."

I remember feeling that I should be a "good girlfriend" and do certain things and behave in certain ways that would fill that role. Then I wrote a poem about it called "The Good Girlfriend Must Die." It's in my book SUCCULENT WILD WOMAN. I've since expanded my awareness to realize that any time I'm trying to be a "good" anything, it's usually one or more inner critics.

Another time, I was asked to make a potato salad or casserole for a potluck party, and I don't cook! I felt like I "should" cook, and considered not going. My boyfriend at the time really reassured me that he didn't expect me to cook anything, and I was able to separate from my inner critics and attend the party with joy and love. I actually painted pictures of pies for everyone, with a prosperity poem inside — now that's MY kind of cooking!

There are basically only two kinds of feelings, those based on love and those based on fear. Depending on the situation or how strong they are, we give them different names. But in terms of roles, all you basically need to know is whether you are responding from a place of love or fear.

Obligation is based on fear. If you are doing anything out of obligation (or feeling oppressed), you are acting out a (casse)role in a way that no longer serves you.

SOME QUESTIONS TO CONSIDER

⭐ *Do you feel that your relationship (or anything else) is keeping you from going where your heart leads?*

◉ *Are you so focused on pleasing your partner, taking care of a child, or being in another kind of relationship that you don't pay as much attention to the value of your self-care?*

⭐ *Are you doing some things you saw adults do in childhood that have become a model for how someone is supposed to be in a relationship? Can you see some of these as being perfect for you, and others not? It's easy to fall into a pattern of doing things that are unsatisfying in an attempt to fulfill a role.*

All of us do a lot of things that in themselves aren't enjoyable but that as part of a larger goal are fine. An obvious example would be going to get a root canal. No one is going to do that for the fun of it, but we know it's better than the alternative of losing a tooth. Other examples might be washing the dishes or getting the oil changed in your car.

Something that in itself doesn't appeal to you may be a satisfying part of a larger, desirable goal — or be a compromise or sacrifice. The distinction is how you feel as you're doing it. Are you comfortable fulfilling obligations that are a part of an overall satisfying goal, or does the role itself feel like an obligation?

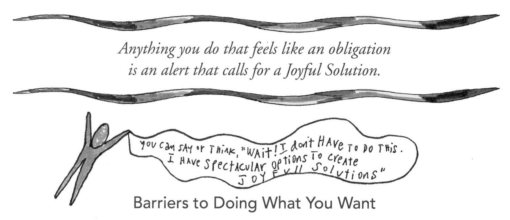

Anything you do that feels like an obligation
is an alert that calls for a Joyful Solution.

Barriers to Doing What You Want

There are three barriers to being able to play the role you genuinely want in a relationship.

The first is practical. Maybe you can't afford to hire a full-time gardener, cook, chauffeur, or — you fill in the blank. This is where you can get creative. What is the essence of the things you don't enjoy? What other ways might you accomplish these? Using gardening as an example, you might simplify the plants you use, picking ones that require less care.

> I had a patio in the back of my condo in Columbus. The people who owned it before me were avid gardeners and had planted a variety of annuals and exotic species. Over time, these melted away. What was left were perennials that grew naturally in the area and largely took care of themselves. While my garden didn't look nearly as elegant as theirs, it was satisfying enough for me.

The second barrier is your inner critics. They want you to play the role you learned and won't give you permission to change. You can use the Inner Critic Care System to separate yourself from them and give yourself permission.

The third is other people's expectations, especially your partner's — which are really a reflection of your own inner critics. You have likely surrounded yourself with people who have the same expectations of you that you have of yourself. And then it will seem as if you're doing things for them, when in reality you are doing these things to please your inner critics. Once you make peace with your inner critics, it becomes much easier to deal with others' expectations.

Understanding and Changing Roles

I've become aware that roles can get "sticky," meaning that if you've always done some specific tasks, people will expect you to keep doing them. Holidays are classic for this. My brother's mother-in-law, Kathryn, just demonstrated this beautifully when she texted to thank us for renting a house for all of us to gather for the holidays. (Our apartment is too small.)

She said how much she enjoyed being the company instead of the hostess, which is the usual arrangement during the holidays. She enjoys hosting sometimes, but not when it becomes a role or an obligation.

We all have the opportunity to tell the microtruth about what we do and don't want to do. Many of us don't because we're afraid of "hurting someone's feelings," and then we hurt our own feelings! If you become aware that you're in a role that doesn't feel good and give yourself permission to change, you can share your truth with love and kindness, and people will accept your changing roles just fine.

It is useful to separate the aspects of your roles that are intrinsically satisfying from those that you initially accepted to please your inner critics. The purpose of this is to release you from those things that they tell you are necessary for you to do but actually aren't.

For example, you might want to invite friends over for a dinner party. You're looking forward to some spirited company and delicious food. Your goal is to be a "good host." But what does that mean?

Does it mean you have to clean the house from top to bottom? That you buy expensive food? That you cook it all yourself? For some people, all these things are fine. And when they are, we don't view doing them as fulfilling a role. But if you feel a sense of obligation, your inner critics are at work.

As you think about enjoying the role of host, for example, if feelings of obligation bubble up, you can write down alternative beliefs.

Some examples:

People are coming to my dinner party because they care about me. They want to have fun and enjoy my company.

Any disapproval they may have about how I live or do things is not really my business. They probably aren't living up to their inner critics' expectations either.

This is an opportunity to use your Inner Critic Care System to address your critics' concerns. In any situation where you are feeling obligation, the more you create and listen to positive thoughts about what is right for you, the less you will be listening to your inner critics (and feeling bad).

If your partner is supportive of the new role you want to play, you can include them in this process. If not, find solutions for yourself first, with your Inner Wise Self. Once you feel the rightness of your path and can give yourself permission not to blindly follow a role you learned in childhood, you will be on much stronger ground to find Joyful Solutions with someone else.

Sam Bennett — Sacrificing in a Relationship

Sam Bennett

I married my second husband knowing he was an alcoholic. But he was very highly functioning. It was mostly under control, and I like to drink too.... So for some time it was sort of okay. And then there would be moments when it was not okay. And over time it got worse, and finally I thought — we did not talk about it much — "I will hang on for as long as I can. I'm a very tenacious girl, but I can't do this forever."

So finally I got to the point where I had to go. I ran out of rope. I left. And he got sober that very day — and has been sober ever since.

We probably could have made it past that moment, except as he started to go to sobriety meetings, I did some real thinking. "Where am I in this? How did this work for me?" And I realized that I had spent much of the relationship saying that things were okay when they were not okay. We'd spent a long time trying to get pregnant. But how can you get pregnant when your partner is passed out on the couch? And still I just kept thinking, "It's okay, it'll work. It's divine timing, it's fine."

It was not okay. And when I realized that I had sacrificed the one thing I had wanted more than anything, which was a baby, on the altar of "it's okay," I was shocked. I could not believe I had done that. I could not believe I'd let myself down that way. I could not believe I had allowed myself to be so blind.

It was one of those moments where I figured out that everything I had done in the name of being a good person, being a patient person, being a tolerant person, being an evolved person, all this stuff that I felt was doing good, was really destructive.

And it changed everything for both of us. The minute he and I separated, both of our lives went, like, BOOM! He moved to Arizona, which he had always dreamed of, and bought a little log cabin in the woods. I moved to a place I had always dreamed of — right by the beach. My income quadrupled. Every aspect of our lives went bananas, and we had the most loving, amicable divorce of all time.

You have those moments where everything burns to the ground. And I knew that it was a unique opportunity.

I had always believed that I had to earn my place all the time, and I worked really hard. The whole idea that a person could just be worthy of love because they are there — you read about these things, but I did not have any experience with that, and I put so much pressure on myself.

I know a second-grade girl who is really sassy. She is very confronting in a way that children are not allowed to be to adults — at least not in the family I grew up in. I was watching her one day and thought, "I could really stand to take a page out of her book." I was thinking back to my past. I thought, "No one will ever sexually abuse this child. She would bite their _____ off. She just would not have it." There are some children who are compliant and interested in earning your attention and affection, and other children who are hard to get along with. I sometimes wish I had a little more of her in me and could have said, "That's not okay," sooner.

Sam is a bestselling author & the creator of TheOrganizedArtistCompany.com & TheOrganized EntrepreneurCompany.com, dedicated to helping creative people get unstuck from whatever way they're stuck.

Awareness Practice:
Transforming Roles and Obligations

1. Think of the roles you play in your relationships (wife/husband, girlfriend/boy-friend, mother/father, daughter/son, friend, employee, etc.). What about these roles pleases you? List or describe some aspects. (For example, if you enjoy being a mother, you might say that you're loving, dedicated, and creative.)

    Would you like to increase or expand upon these roles? If so, describe ways you might like to do that. (If you'd like to enjoy being a mother even more, you might want to spend different kinds of time with your family.)

2. As you reflect on the roles that apply to you, is there anything about them that you don't enjoy? (Maybe you have obligations that feel constraining.)

3. What would you like to do instead? (For example, you might like to feel freer as a mother.) Describe what would support you in feeling that way. (You might communicate differently, or spend time doing something just for you, or get help with tasks you don't enjoy.)

4. Would anyone be upset or disappointed if you changed? What are your fears about that? (If you spent less time doing some things you don't enjoy, what might happen?)

    How might you transform those fears? (For example, if you don't feel like cooking every night, and you're afraid of your family's reaction, what could you do instead — go out to eat, bring dinner in, make simpler meals, have someone share the meal preparation with you, or even have them take over a few nights a week?) What Joyful Solutions can you create?

5. Use your Inner Critic Care System to give yourself permission to change. This means uncovering and caring for the parts of you that think you "should" do certain things, "or else."

To expand your awareness about roles and obligations, go to:
SucculentWildLove.com/Roles

20. Awareness of Patterns in Relationships: Bumps And Upsets & Learning to Be Kind

Practicing Being Kind

AS WE HAVE SAID, even when you use all the habits and tools in a Succulent Wild relationship skillfully, there will still be bumps, upsets, and times when you are unkind. This chapter is about moving through those moments and quickly finding your center.

Expressing Hurt and Anger in an Unkind Way

In chapters 13 and 14 we wrote about how you can use your anger and hurt effectively to gain cooperation from the intimate people in your life. However, you may be in a relationship where someone is less than kind, either because they are hurt or angry, or simply out of habit. In the chapter on boundaries we talked about being treated with respect. Part of being treated with respect is being treated with kindness.

finding exquisite balance points in the center

Sometimes people are unkind simply because they're stressed. They may be snappish or crabby with each other, but usually these are brief incidents that stop when the person becomes less tense. In these situations, separating until the person rebalances is often the best answer.

Here we are talking about a larger pattern, one where a partner is habitually unkind to you or you to them. Some examples of unkindness would be your partner making fun of you, responding with disdain when you don't know something, or being harsh or bossy with you. The way you can tell when someone is being unkind is when you don't feel good about *the way* they are saying something, even if you agree with the content.

At times, the way someone expresses their hurt or anger can be extremely unkind. In these instances, the goal is to strike a balance between listening to their genuine concerns and not being abused by the way they are presenting them. If someone is expressing anger directly, such as by yelling, it is important to let them know that you hear them and that you want to be responsive to their needs. Then it may be best to temporarily withdraw.

Talk about Anger Styles and Make an Agreement

It is important to let each other know what you're willing to accept when it comes to anger. Some people feel comfortable yelling at each other. This can feel like a great release. For others, a well-spoken communication is enough. The intent is not to suppress feelings, either yours or your partner's, but to express them in such a way that neither of you is left feeling abused.

The most effective path to a relationship of unconditional love is to use your feelings to elicit your partner's cooperation, not to pummel them. Angrily withdrawing from your partner when they are mean to you is also not a very effective way to resolve things. In a Succulent Wild Love relationship the idea is to withdraw from your partner to give them and you a chance to deal with your feelings, not as a way to punish them. This is why using your Inner Feelings Care System to rebalance is so useful if you do separate angrily.

If your partner is not being responsive in their usual, loving way, it is likely due to unresolved feelings. You can ask if those feelings are about something related to you — they may not be. In a Succulent Wild Love relationship the intent is always to open communication, to help each other get in touch with your feelings, and to express them in a way that isn't destructive to the relationship.

Being Unkind as a Habit

Acts of unkindness can also simply be due to habit, a way of relating learned in childhood.

I was often treated in a dictatorial way growing up, and this became part of my expectation in relationships. I remember dating a young woman after college. She gave me a vegetarian cookbook — I think it was for my birthday. She had inscribed a warm message in the front, but she was an artist, and I insisted (with the forcefulness I had experienced growing up) that she draw something. She acquiesced to my pressure, but that was the beginning of the end of our relationship.

In the first long-term relationship I had after graduate school, a friend would often comment on how I let my partner boss me around. I couldn't see it. To me, the way she interacted with me was normal. It was what I expected in a relationship.

When I met her, she had been raising two children on her own and was used to making family decisions with little input from anyone else. When I joined the family, that included me.

It wasn't until an incident shortly after we broke up that I was able to see the pattern. She came over to my apartment to ask me to take care of her cats while she went away for a few days. When I said I didn't want to, it quickly became clear that this wasn't a request.

She had decided it was in the best interest of everyone that I take care of the animals while she was away. And, as usual, had not consulted me in that decision.

It would have been difficult for me to take care of the cats for a variety of reasons, and in the past I would have argued with her and probably acquiesced. But all I said was, "That doesn't feel good."

She said, "Why?" looking to me to give an excuse that she could invalidate. But all I said was, "It doesn't feel good."

I remember her being so frustrated that I wasn't going along with her plan that she picked up an orange from a bowl on the kitchen counter and raised her arm, considering whether to throw it at me. She didn't and left.

The point of this story is that she wasn't to blame, and neither was I. We were both in a pattern. Over and over, I had supported the way she treated me. When I changed, she changed.

"This doesn't feel good" is a useful phrase when you're pressured to do something or aren't being treated with respect. In a Succulent Wild Love relationship it is never necessary to justify why something doesn't feel good. In our relationship, when one of us says it, the other immediately stops pushing, and we create a Joyful Solution.

and since HeALing HAppens in spirALs and lAyers, it cAn Also TAke Time To SHiFT pAiTerns

I AM A stronG, nAturAl leAder, And someTimes oTHers respond to me As being Bossy. THis usuAlly occurs wHen I've Become Bossy, ActinG out of HABit or cArelessness. I Didn't used to be ABle to tell the DifferenCe.

It's often more about the energy or vibration than the words themselves. One of my favorite games to play with others as a child was "teacher," which was thinly disguised as "the boss." I remember kids reacting to how I spoke to them and learned that kindness was much more effective.

I now know that being demanding or bossy with others is not the best way to gain their cooperation, and being aware of how I say things is very important for receiving the kind of response that I'd like. Of course, when I'm stressed or scared, I often forget.

One time, a construction crew appeared on my street and set up a massive generator outside my window. The sound was extremely loud, and since it was the end of the day, I wondered if it would go on all night and went down to ask someone about it. I was pretty scared that I wouldn't be able to sleep and thought I'd better get to the bottom of the situation by being strong and determined and ready to speak that way.

The first guy I talked to responded, "Lady, this is going to go on all night, so you just better get used to it. There ain't nothing anybody can do. And don't even think of going to the head guy." I quickly realized that being bossy was not going to work, and that refocusing on kindness was my best method.

I then went over to the head contractor and said, "I wonder if you can possibly help me — I know it isn't your fault at all, but that generator sounds like a jet plane upstairs, and I'm afraid I won't sleep all night. Is there anything you can do?" He looked at me, smiled, and said, "Sure! I'll just turn it off." Sometimes, of course, the answer isn't that simple, but kindness always feels better no matter what the situation is.

If you feel pressured or not treated with kindness, it is not necessarily an inner critic telling you that you *should* be treated this way. It may simply be a well-established habit: this is how people treat each other; it's familiar. (There are harsher instances, where inner critics are involved, and we will talk about these in the next chapter.)

If your partner is being demanding or bossy when they want you to do something, changing this is a variation of creating a Joyful Solution together. The essence is that they want you to do this thing. Going wide would be approaching you in a kinder way.

If your partner continues to speak harshly to you, make fun of you, or treat you with disdain or in any other way that feels uncomfortable, the key is for you to change — to create a Joyful Solution on your own. You have been responding to this behavior and thus reinforcing it. When you stop responding to unkindness, they will stop treating you that way.

By not responding, we mean literally that. When they say or do something that feels uncomfortable, don't reply. Stop whatever you were doing for a moment, so they can see that you heard them, then continue doing whatever you were doing.

silence

An insightful article in the *New York Times* by Amy Sutherland explains how this technique is used by exotic-animal trainers to get the animals to change their behavior: "I followed the students to SeaWorld San Diego, where a dolphin trainer introduced me to least reinforcing syndrome (L.R.S.). When a dolphin does something wrong, the trainer doesn't respond in any way. He stands still for a few beats, careful not to look at the dolphin, and then returns to work. The idea is that any response, positive or negative, fuels a behavior. If a behavior provokes no response, it typically dies away."*

You have the benefit of actually being able to talk with your partner and elicit their cooperation. But it isn't necessary that they agree with you. All you need to do is train yourself in how you want to be treated, and those around you will follow your lead.

The only time Jeanie was ever bossy with me was when she was afraid I might say something to someone that would hurt them. In those cases, I quickly understood her fear and was able to make a Love Translation.

When I first came to San Francisco, Susan often told me the best streets to take when I was driving. One day we were going to one of our regular stops, and unknown to her, I had done some map research. I had actually found a faster way that Susan didn't know about to get to one of the main streets.

As we were driving away from our home, and I began going in a different direction, I explained that I had found a new way. Susan didn't believe me and kept reiterating that the path she always took was the way to go. I just smiled and continued on the new route. Suddenly we were on the main street, and it was obvious that my way was faster.

Susan responded that she appreciated that I had stuck to my vision and hadn't let her bowl me over. Because she has such a strong personality, her past partners had often done so.

---

* Amy Sutherland, "What Shamu Taught Me about a Happy Marriage," *New York Times*, June 25, 2006, http://goo.gl/xYhCF.

One of the things I had told Susan when we met was that I can handle her. The relationships I had before helped me learn that, and how to do it in a kind way.

Sometimes, especially when she feels stressed, Susan can become bossy. But she is also extremely aware and sensitive. As soon as I mention being uncomfortable, the way she approaches me immediately changes.

WHEN I FIrST MET JOHN, I WAS SO HAPPY to HEAr tHAt HE COUlD "HAnDlE ME," AnD FElt PrETTY SKEPtICAl tHAt it WOUlD ACTUAllY WorK. I'D HAD OtHEr lovErS ClAIM tHE SAME, AnD ovEr tIME, I WOUlD EItHEr DOMINATE tHEM, or tHEY ME, AnD tHE rElAtIOnSHIP WOUlD EnD.

WHEN JOHN DrovE ME On tHIS nEW rOUtE, HE WAS SMIlING AnD rEASSUrING, AnD ACtED IMPErvIOUS to MY PrOtESTS. THIS IMPrESSED ME, AnD I lIKED HIS COnFIDEnCE vErY MUCH. I FElt DElIGHtED tHAt HE WAS StrOnG in HIS OWn WAYS, AnD tHAt I COUlD AlSO BE MYSElF AS I AM.

Negatively Mirroring Each Other

Sometimes one person in a couple is upset about something that has nothing to do with their partner. They emanate this energy outward, and their partner is the one there, so the partner feels the energy and responds to it.

Soon they are fussing with each other — they may say accusatory things, or point out something they don't like that the other is doing — when there is really no disagreement between them. They are just responding to one partner's emotional energy and bouncing it off each other.

Emotionally mirroring each other negatively can help the one who is upset release their tension about whatever is bothering them. Helping each other in this way doesn't usually lead to relationships breaking up, and it can even become a form of intimacy. But it can be uncomfortable in a relationship where the majority of interaction is more loving.

When I was in graduate school, I wanted to do my dissertation on what I called the direct transfer of emotions: situations where someone literally feels another person's emotions and acts as if these were their own.

I first got the idea for this concept in college when I was working on a psychiatric ward. I was sitting in with a psychiatrist as he was interviewing a patient in the middle of a psychotic break. The patient was sitting in front of us calmly but saying all kinds of disjointed things.

Seemingly out of the blue, the psychiatrist asked the patient why he was so angry, and the man burst into a tirade. After a few minutes he calmed down, and his thoughts became more organized.

After the session, I asked the psychiatrist what had prompted him to question the patient about being angry. I had seen no outward signs of anger. His response was, "I was feeling angry, and I knew I wasn't angry about anything."

From that day forward, I started noticing how I felt and when I might be picking up others' feelings. This has helped me greatly in my therapy work over the years, but reacting to someone else's emotions can also work against us in our intimate relationships.

When Susan is crabby, I can literally feel her crabbiness at times, and if she says something filled with tension, I feel tempted to respond in kind. Not doing so is part of the skill of being in a Succulent Wild relationship.

If I mirror the tension back to her, we'll usually get into a (brief) ill-tempered dialogue. If I don't, Susan will feel soothed, or she will leave the conversation and come back when she's in a better mood.

The same is true when I'm upset. When I'm tense or angry about something and snap at her (she says I'm "snappish"), then she has to decide how to respond. Because we're usually so loving, when we do start bouncing off each other negatively, it's really obvious, and we can catch it fairly quickly.

(Interestingly, modern brain research has discovered what are called "mirror neurons." These actually fire in concert with those of whomever we're observing and are a biological explanation for the direct transfer of emotions.)

I never get crabby — I don't know what John is talking about... ;-)))))))) Not only do I get crabby, I've written about it in my previous books and encouraged people to fly a crabby flag! I've learned a lot about tending to my own crabby feelings and sparing John whenever possible. Of course, sometimes it isn't possible, and I'm crabby around John and other people.

John and I have developed a code we call "silent running," which means that if I'm crabby, I can let him know I'm going into silent running, where we don't speak until I feel less crabby. The silence provides a sheltering space for me to be able to regroup and then communicate differently.

If you notice that you and your partner are being less than loving with each other, ask yourself, "Is there something I'm upset about? Is there something that needs to be resolved here?" Ask the same of your partner. If there is, you have the tools to do that. If not, one of you is likely feeling down about something, and it is getting between you. You can name what you see going on. Then you can talk about what is bringing one or both of you down or take some time to separate.

Amy and Rob Ahlers — Discovering Growth in a Kind Relationship

Rob and Amy Ahlers, with their daughters, Annabella and Evie Rose

AMY: In my youth I thought that going for the bad boy who treated you like crap was the only way to have excitement and passion in your life. And I absolutely know — because I have been through all sorts of relationship dynamics — that the most exciting thing you can have in your life is a relationship where your partner is kind, respectful, and loving. No more bad boys! Being with my amazing, compassionate, loving husband, Rob, has allowed me to grow and evolve more spiritually and personally. Plus, it allows me the energy and space to realize my life's calling because there is so little drama in my marriage. There is love, there is respect, there is passion, there is excitement.

I also know that some couples like to have each other be the agitator for their personal growth, and what I've learned is that the world agitates me enough, thank you very much! Having a safe harbor in my relationship allows me to grow that much more, because I do not have Rob constantly poking at me. Instead, he is my soft landing place when challenges arise.

ROB: I don't think I knew that self-awareness existed. I thought you just got into a relationship, and it would just be screwed up. People who are not self-aware tend to place a lot of…not even just blame but responsibility, that somehow it's all their partner's fault, that the partner is bringing out the worst in them.

I appreciate that I am not working as hard as I used to in order to maintain an easygoing relationship with my partner. Being with Amy has made me aware that I was always pushing so hard before, and I am so glad that I do not have to be over-nurturing, like I was before. Because I think being nurturing is a definite skill I have, and now with Amy I can just do it naturally, and it does not hurt after I have done it. I used to take on the role of over-nurturing, and it was very unhealthy for me, because my other partners clearly needed more attention than I could give. Now that I am with Amy, I feel I can really look at the things that are going on for me, and I was not able to do that before. I really, really cannot say enough how grateful I am to have had that opportunity.

AMY: Love yourself first and work on your connection to your inner wisdom, to the divine within, to whatever you call it. The more you can take responsibility for yourself, the more love you will have in all your relationships.

Amy is the Wake-Up Call Coach & a bestselling author (WakeUpCallCoach.com). Rob is a gifted musician & her beloved husband.

Awareness Practice:
Bumps and Upsets and Learning to Be Kind

1. Does your partner express hurt or angry feelings in a way that feels unkind to you?

   ⭐ If so, then make a plan about how you are going to respond in the future. Think of a way that you can be all right and support them in feeling their feelings. Create a vision of how to handle painful feelings that feels positive and doable. This may involve separating until they rebalance.

   ◉ Discuss with your partner how you both want to handle hurt and angry feelings in your relationship, and create Joyful Solutions for how you will express them.

2. Does your partner habitually treat you in a way that feels unkind? Do they make fun of you, respond with disdain when you don't know something, or act harsh or bossy?

   ✰ Do they treat others that way? If so, you know it is a style of relating for them.

   ✰ Are there people they treat with respect? This might be a good model for how you would like to be treated by them. Discuss this with them and see if you can come up with a Joyful Solution together. If they don't change, you can remind them several times, but after that it may feel like nagging.

   ◉ When they are unkind you can make a Love Translation, reminding yourself that this is simply a habit both of you can change, rather than an intent to hurt you. When they say or do something unkind, you can apply the method used by exotic animal trainers:

   • Pause, so they know you heard them.
   • Don't reply or acknowledge them.
   • Continue what you were doing.
   • Respond warmly when they are kind.

3. If you find yourself being less than loving with your partner, see if there is something that needs to be resolved between you. If not, then focus on what is bothering one or both of you. If you can support the one who is feeling down and help them feel better, wonderful. If not, then it would be best for you to separate and for whoever is feeling down to use the Inner Feelings Care System or other tools to rebalance.

For gracefully negotiating bumps in your relationships, go to:
SucculentWildLove.com/Bumps

21. Relationship Patterns Learned in Childhood

FAMILY = FAMILIAR

PERHAPS THE GREATEST CAUSE of enduring discomfort in relationships is the re-creation of negative patterns we learned in childhood. We tend to live in and re-create the world of relationships that we know. The expectations we have of what it means to be in a couple, and the roles we expect ourselves and our partners to play, were in large part learned by observing the people around us as we were growing up.

We learn to play not only practical roles, such as being a "good girlfriend" or "good husband," but also emotional roles.

Most of us, without being aware of it, are drawn to partners who represent both what we liked about the roles we observed and what we didn't like. As with many things in our lives, we are drawn to what is familiar (family = familiar). We may then resent our partners for behaving in ways that we actually expect them to.

When someone treats us in a way we don't like, usually we focus on what they're doing (the role they are playing). It is not as easy to see how we literally "invite" them to treat us that way through our behavior (the role that we are playing).

Most of the time you will initially be unaware that you're inviting someone to treat you in a way you don't like. But if you find yourself being treated in a certain way on an ongoing basis, you can be sure that you are doing things to contribute to the uncomfortable interactions.

In these situations, the person who feels mistreated will often try to change their partner, and after a while they may give up and simply resent their partner. Another way to look at this is that there is an inner critic telling the person who's being mistreated that they're supposed to be treated this way. This inner critic was usually developed in their childhood.

If you feel mistreated on an ongoing basis, the key is to address this inner critic and change your behavior. Once you learn to play a role that invites what pleases you, you will experience this on an ongoing basis.

Your invitation will be energetically accepted

My mother was a very imposing influence in my life, both in ways that benefited me and in ways that were painful. She didn't have the wisdom when she was young that she had in later years. She had been raised in a very authoritarian family environment, and that was one of the reasons she wanted to get away from Germany. (I remember her having a panic attack in her 40s when she received a letter from her mother saying she was going to visit us.)

When I was growing up, my mother considered my room an extension of her domain. I was allowed to have only one picture on the wall, painted for my parents by a friend of theirs. I never felt that my space was my own. (The first year I went to college, I put over a hundred pictures on the walls of my small room.)

I know now that my mother meant no malice. Her parents had felt ownership of her space to the extent that her father would regularly open her bureau drawers. If her clothes weren't lined up perfectly, he would throw the contents on the floor. (My mother made a point of letting me arrange my drawers any way I liked, and as an adult, her drawers were jumbled until the day she died.)

Before I met Jeanie, I was drawn to strong women who reminded me of my mother, and I felt dominated in the way I had growing up. Without being consciously aware of it, by the way I interacted with them, I actually guided them to treat me the way I expected to be treated, both negatively and positively. My mother had been demanding, but she also admired me. And this is what I experienced in these relationships.

Jeanie was extremely strong and capable but preferred to be in the background. In many ways I was the dominant one in that relationship, but I was also quite aware and sensitive to how that power could be abused. Using the habits in this book — respecting her separateness, looking for Joyful Solutions, and especially, seeing her as perfect — allowed me to take the lead in a way that didn't diminish her and was responsive to her needs.

Of course, I didn't do this perfectly. After Jeanie transitioned, I intended to continue growing, and in my relationship with Susan I'm actually even more aware. Susan is strong and capable, and is not one to stay in the background. We each take the lead at different times, resulting in the most balanced relationship I've been in.

I love that now, having healed and changed my previous negative patterns with both my parents, I'm left with the positive ones. They were happily married for 43 years. They laughed a lot, had adventures together, and were each other's biggest fans. My relationship with John has all these qualities and more.

The significant point here is that you may find yourself in some uncomfortable patterns in your relationships. If so, you have likely picked partners who feel familiar to you, both in ways you enjoy and ways you don't. Through the way you interact with them — how you approach them and react to what they do — you have also taught them how you expect to be treated.

My younger brother, Andrew, had been in relationships with dominant, critical women — much like his mother and how I often used to be. I remember saying to him, "If you can step out of this type and allow yourself to create a new pattern, you can find the love of your life." Andrew began dating online and described exactly what he wanted — saying that romance wasn't his thing, and that the person needed to be able to make herself happy rather than looking to him for this. He then met Jennifer, an artist and teacher who adores him and isn't critical or domineering, and their marriage is a happy one.

SOME COMMON PATTERNS

People engage in many types of patterns. The following are two common ones.

The Security-Freedom Pattern

In this pattern, one partner wants more freedom and the other more security.

- The one who feels insecure tries to keep the other closer.
- The one who feels a lack of freedom wants to pull away.

A good example of this is the story of wanting to sit closer to my partner in bed, in chapter 12, "Creating Joyfull Solutions on Your Own." I wanted to be closer, and she wanted to pull away. It's not that I physically needed her to sit next to me. This was a Love Symbol for me. I literally felt unloved with her a few feet away. When I resolved this by reminding myself that she loved me, I was fine — and she stopped pulling away.

I used to be scared of having a relationship with someone who was overly clinging to me — in fact, I called them "cling-ons" and developed "tests" to see if they were, by asking them in various ways if they were fine on their own. By the time I met John, I wanted someone who was not only fine on their own but self-loving and what I call a "self-entertaining unit." John was actually so much this way that it allowed me to explore the other side of the pattern, and feel my own desires to be extraordinarily close, and even sometimes like a "cling-on" myself.

If you find yourself pulling for something from your partner, identify what it means to you and see if you can give it to yourself.

If you find that your partner is trying to pull something from you, ask them if this is a Love Symbol.

Basically, you are looking to create a Joyful Solution. Look for the essence of what each of you wants, then go wide and look for ways everyone's needs can be met. You can do this on your own or with your partner. You can talk with your partner — with whoever is feeling insecure acknowledging that they also want freedom, and the one who is wanting more freedom acknowledging that they also want security. This reduces the polarization and makes it easier to come up with a Joyful Solution.

Of course, in some instances one or both partners have changed, and the one seeking freedom really just wants to get out of the relationship. That is good to know too and will become clear as both people become less polarized.

A SCAPE GOAT

The Critic-Scapegoat Pattern

In this pattern one person criticizes the other about many things, often in a self-righteous manner. The message is, "If you would improve, you would be a better person, and thus lovable." Of course, no matter how much the person improves, the criticism doesn't stop. In this case, both partners' Overachiever and Perfectionist inner critics are running wild. Neither partner feels they are good enough, with all the negative energy being focused on one of them.

Until I took a year off before I met Jeanie, I had a history of being in this kind of pattern. For example, after college I briefly lived with a woman who would get very angry with me, and I would acquiesce to her demands. I had to work one weekend, and she felt lonely with my being gone. When I returned she was extremely angry.

In this instance, I was able to stop the pattern. Because I felt proud of the fact that I had done a good job at work, I was able to quell my inner critics and not feel guilty about not being there for her. So I didn't accept her abuse. I left the house and started walking up the street. A short time later, she pulled up beside me in her car and asked me to get in. Her anger was gone. She apologized and was treating me with respect. I realized at that point that I had contributed to these painful interactions by allowing them. It wasn't that hard to get her to stop what was essentially bullying behavior. I just had to be in a place where I didn't feel I deserved it and stand up.

I engaged in this pattern in most of my previous relationships too. I had learned how to criticize from my mother and did it well. I didn't realize how critical I was also being to myself until I got into therapy and heard people say, "You are so hard on yourself." I didn't even see it — I thought I had to be tough with myself and everyone to get good results. It took me years to unwind out of this pattern, and it

STiLL SOMETiMES SHOWS UP WHEN I FeeL STreSSeD or AFrAiD. NOW I CAn reCOGNiZE iT AnD KNOW HOW TO enGAGe DiFFerently AnD More POSiTiVELY WiTH MYSELF, AnD ALL MY love reLATiONSHiPS.

we can create
new patterns

CHANGING UNCOMFORTABLE PATTERNS

One of the overriding messages in this book is that Succulent Wild Love relationships are loving and supportive most of the time. Recognizing that you don't have to have ongoing tensions, that this is not "just how relationships are," is one of the biggest steps you can take to change uncomfortable patterns.

Before reading this book, your inner critics may have convinced you that you "should" be certain ways, ways that don't fit you anymore. Your painful patterns are the result of habits and of inner critics telling you how relationships are supposed to be. As soon as you recognize that they don't have to be this way, you are free to start consciously changing them.

You can change uncomfortable patterns one Joyful Solution at a time.

Patterns can be JOY.fully rewoven

Recurring patterns are simply situations that keep repeating. If there isn't an inner critic involved — if it's just a habit — you can simply create a Joyful Solution, and each time such a situation comes up, applying it will be easier.

IN THE "SUCCULENT WiLD COMMUNiCATiONS" CHAPTer I TALKED ABOUT FEELiNG DiSTANT FroM JOHN — or FEARiNG THAT HE WAS DiSTANCiNG FroM ME. I HAD DEVELOPED THiS PATTerN WiTH MY FATHer. ONCE I WAS ABLE TO NAME it, And John And I were Able to tAlk ABout it And Develop A Joyfull Solution, And I Could let him know whenever I needed one, it BeCAme eASier to Apply it the next time it HAppened. I wish I'd known ABout Joyfull Solutions with my FAmily while I wAS Growing up And Am So GIAd I'm living them with John And everyone else in my life now. You CAn tAlk with your pArtner ABout how eACh of you is ContriButing to the situAtions, whAt eACh of you wAnts, And how you Both would like it to Be. But, As with other Joyfull Solutions, it is not neCessAry to hAve your pArtner's ConsCious CooperAtion.

we can Be ART·full and HeARt·full

There is a follow-up to the situation I described above where I was able to stop my girlfriend from bullying me. A few days later, I was shocked to observe myself baiting her to start picking on me again. The pattern, while painful, was familiar, and the changed relationship where she wasn't angry with me felt unfamiliar.

My inner critics were still telling me I wasn't good enough, and I had been using her to criticize me for not doing better in my life. In a distorted way, her criticizing me was a symbol of love and intimacy — this was one of the ways the mother of my childhood had expressed her love to me. Additionally, we had been using fighting as a form of intimacy. So, to a large extent, I now felt unloved.

While my partner had stopped, my inner critics and my draw to familiar Love Symbols hadn't. She began to criticize me again — in part at my prompting — and we finally broke up. At that time, I didn't know how to feel good in a relationship, either with someone criticizing me or with someone not criticizing me.

In the last relationship I had before meeting Jeanie, I didn't have the tools I have now, so it was easier for me to leave. It was helpful for me to take time off, both to understand what I had been doing and learn how I wanted to be in a relationship. Having done that, I was drawn to someone different from the kind of women I had been attracted to before.

This is the wAy my Brother, Andrew, ChAnGed his relAtionship pAttern. He Chose to stop Believing thAt love meAnt Being CritiCized And DominAted. He hAD repeAted the pAinful pAttern And wAS ABle to See it for whAt it wAS. He took Some spACe And time AwAy from love relAtionships And moved to A new City. He then Got A DoG, opened his heArt to new love, And

CreATeD iT. OF COUrSe, THiS iS An ABBreviATeD verSiOn OF HiS experienCe, AnD iT TOOk lOtS OF reFleCtiOn AnD neW BeHAviOrS AnD prACtiCinG BeFOre He WAS ABle tO MAke THeSe SHiFtS. BuT AS HiS BiG SiSter OBServinG, I CAn SAy THAt OnCe He MADe THe DeCiSiOn tO CHAnGe, He DiD.

To effectively change patterns involving inner critics, you may need to use the Inner Critic Care System a number of times and develop other, more positive ways of sharing intimacy. If this is too difficult, then a neutral third party can help. Often a professional therapist is best, because people close to you would be tempted to take sides.

We each have had many mentors, counselors, therapists, and teachers.
We encourage you to get whatever support you need
if you find yourself stuck in an uncomfortable pattern.

THe StAGeS Are All SpirAlS THAt MOve and SHiFt AS yOu do

We talked about the three stages of relating to your inner critics (see page 104). Similar stages apply here. In stage 1, you think that this is just the way relationships are or this is the underbelly of relationships. In stage 2, you recognize that these are patterns you learned and that you can change, but painful experiences still recur. In stage 3 you have developed new ways of being intimate, and you recognize the patterns so clearly that either you don't engage in them or, if you do, one or both of you quickly recognize this and stop. Since it takes time to come to terms with your inner critics and build new kinds of intimacy, it usually takes a while to get out of stage 2.

METHODS TO HELP YOU MOVE FROM RECOGNIZING A PATTERN TO CHANGING IT

If you are feeling bullied or criticized in your relationship in any way, or you are in any negative pattern — any type of ongoing uncomfortable interactions — the first step is to recognize that you are contributing to the situation. This recognition, in itself, will cause a shift.

Then reflect on what these ongoing uncomfortable interactions mean to you.

Is it simply a habit?

If so, just being aware of it will lead to your changing your behavior.

Do you feel you're not living up to some standard and have been inviting your partner to criticize you?

Use the Inner Critic Care System to address the inner critics your partner is speaking for. Take a stand with your inner critics that if you want to change anything about yourself, the best way is to be treated with respect and loving encouragement.

Do you feel obligated to play a role that doesn't fit you?

If so, go back to chapter 19, "Transforming Roles and Obligations in Relationships," and use the tools described there.

Is it a way you know you are loved?

If this is a familiar expression of love, then begin to look for other ways you experience your partner as loving, and focus on those. It is also helpful to actively build new forms of intimacy. What other ways could you spend time together that feel loving? Without these negative interactions, your relationship may feel less intimate at first.

Once you have made these changes in yourself, it will be easy to make changes in your relationship with your partner. You can then respond to them in the same way that you related to your inner critics using the Inner Critic Care System.

- You can literally tell your partner, "Stop!" This is like the chopping-motion inner critic technique. You can remind yourself that their treating you the way they are will not lead to you or them feeling better. Repeating, "Stop," or, "This doesn't feel good," and leaving the interaction will usually stop the bullying.

- The equivalent of reassigning your inner critic to a distant job is leaving the interaction with your partner as soon as you recognize that you feel mistreated.

- You can communicate with them. Sit down with your partner when things are calmer and listen to their concerns. Then guide them in the way you do want to be treated.

When they are simply sharing their concerns with you rather than berating you, you can do a Love Translation. Whatever they feel critical about in you, they feel just as critical about in themselves. They really don't want to hurt you but are so caught up in fear and limited understanding that they will if you let them. Once you understand your part in creating these situations and come to terms with your inner critics, you will no longer let them.

If you are the one in the pattern who is criticizing or bullying your partner, the way out is to understand that you are using them to deflect pain you feel inside. The more you turn your attention away from the person you are judging or wanting to change and toward your inner critics and resolving your own pain, the happier your relationships will be.

> In my earlier relationships, I tended to be on the critic side of the Critic-Scapegoat pattern. Later, I was more on the scapegoat side, but I would still sometimes flip to the critic side. In each case, it was more a reflection of my own insecurities and habits than a desire to hurt my partner.

There are three key things to remember:

1. Your partner isn't the "bad one." You were drawn to being with them. If you come to terms with your inner critics, your partner will be easy to deal with.
2. You may effectively get your partner to treat you differently, but if you don't change your relationship with your inner critics, and build new Love Symbols and other forms of intimacy, either the pattern will start up again with your current partner or you'll create a new bully in your next relationship.
3. If your partner doesn't want to change, you will have less and less desire to be around each other, and the Joyful Solution will be to separate.

These patterns are simply an expanded version of the kinds of effects inner critics create in most relationships. If you make the effort to understand what is happening in them, you will never again blindly allow yourself to be criticized or bullied on an ongoing basis — including by yourself.

A Succulent Wild Love relationship can feel good almost all the time. If you notice any ongoing uncomfortable interactions, you now know that they are something you learned, that they're really a distorted form of love, and that you have access to a different kind of relationship. You know more about your part in creating these types of situations and have tools to stop someone from hurting you. If you continue to feel imposed upon, and especially if you don't use the tools you have to stop it, that is a clear sign that your inner critics are still very active. In that case, you might benefit from getting support from a knowledgeable third party, such as a therapist.

Everyone has a blueprint for relationships, just like there are blueprints for building houses. If you keep building new houses using the same blueprints, even if you make some cosmetic changes here and there, they will ultimately feel the same.

One of the benefits of knowing about Succulent Wild Love relationships is that you now have a positive new blueprint for a partnership in addition to whatever you learned about relationships growing up.

Many people who don't like the type of relationship they keep creating have no other model to look to except being single. Having read this book, you now know about other, more nourishing ways to be in a relationship, and you can redesign your blueprint by creating Joyful Solutions.

Your Positive New "Loveprint"

Clark Tate — Understanding My Pattern

Clark Tate

This is more or less what takes place many times when I feel like I'm really falling in love: I feel what I believe to be pure passion, deep love, and an uncanny connection — an unstoppable longing that seems absolutely real and true. And it's driven on by the other person distancing themselves with short texts or emails with just a hint of something I want to hear. Usually never enough.

My initial interest turns to obsession. Thoughts of this person consume my day and overtake most corners of my mind. And I feel alive and justified because of it. How could this be wrong? But the pain starts when I begin to hold back — whether by expressing my reservations or playing the game of "I'm really not thinking about you all the time, so that's why I'm not in contact." This inner balance of not showing my true, consuming feelings becomes its own sad compulsion. What I'm trying to do is not scare the other off, even though they may already be at arm's length and have never given me what I feel I need.

With less and less contact and connection, I descend into stomach knots and a system contracting in upon itself. Not getting what I need and the continued distance now overwhelm the alive, passionate feelings that began it all. And all the while, to the outside world, I'm a functioning contributor humming along.

What I've come to realize in this spin is that I'm trying to fix a past injury and loss from a much earlier stage in my life. Family history in my case is the genesis: a troubled, abusive mother whose needs always trumped my own and a father who stuck with the family out of martyrdom but was rarely home.

Understanding it as my pattern is the first step — looking at my own neediness instead of the "other" as the answer to a prayer, acknowledging I will never get what I need from the person I so intensely crave. This begins with a bit of sadness. But upon acceptance, the reins around the object of desire are immediately lessened. And self-love becomes a wonderful salve. Then my experience is to ride out the wave of the addiction 'til it dissolves away. Keeping shame at bay, I try to accept this as part of myself and a grand teacher for how I need to love and care for myself.

Clark is a gifted artist and writer (ClarkTate.com).

Awareness Practice: Changing Patterns

Can you think of any recurring behaviors from your partner that are uncomfortable for you? An example would be your partner often telling you what to do, or you often feeling rejected by things they say or do. Make a note of these.

If recurring behaviors come to mind, can you identify similar situations that happened prior to the current relationship, either with other partners or in your family? You can use writing to reflect more on this.

If you can see examples of previous similar situations, this will help you recognize your part in perpetuating the pattern. But whether you do or not, the solution is the same:

1. Identify if one or more of these apply:

   ◎ It is simply a habit.

   ◉ You feel you're not living up to some standard and have been inviting your partner to criticize you.

   ☆ You feel obligated to play a role that doesn't suit you.

   ★ It is a way you know you are loved.

2. Use the methods described in this chapter and chapter 19 (page 198) to make changes within yourself.

3. Use the methods described in this chapter and chapter 9 (page 96) to stop your partner from criticizing or bullying you.

4. Use the Awareness Practices in chapters 11 (page 121) and 12 (page 131) to create Joyful Solutions.

5. Develop a new pattern of intimacy with your partner that doesn't involve criticism or fighting. You can do this by building on those areas where you feel good with each other.

   ◎ Do more of the things you enjoy together.

   ☆ Share what you appreciate and like about each other.

Simply trying to stop a pattern can be difficult. It is much easier if you build a new one to go toward. A Succulent Wild Love relationship is a model you can use.

For more about understanding and transforming patterns learned in childhood, go to:
SucculentWildLove.com/Patterns

22. JoyFull Separate Paths, in Daily Activities and in Transforming (Ending) a Relationship

ALL RELATIONSHIPS END. Even the most joyful experience has a limited life span. There comes a point in the most delicious meal you've ever eaten where you feel satiated and ready to move on. Beginnings and endings are natural parts of the flow of life.

I often feel like I hate this reality. I remember when my mother died and someone gave me a pamphlet that attempted to comfort the grieving person by saying, "remember that as you wave goodbye to your loved one, someone on the other side is waving hello." I really didn't agree with the view of this "other side" they were referencing and found the whole thing discomforting. When my cat died, many people referenced this story about the dead animal crossing over a "Rainbow Bridge" that felt equally discomforting. Of course, I don't feel this way about things that I want to end! Then I'm glad about the boundaries, conclusions, and completions.

The difference between loss and flow is resistance. Life brings us change. When we embrace it, we are on an exciting and lively journey. When we try to cling to what is, we feel life torn away from us.

I GreW UP resistinG everything AnD WATChinG My MOTHer try to DO the
sAMe. As she WAs DyinG, I AskeD Her WHAt WisDOM she WAnteD to
shAre, AnD she replieD, "I JUst WisH I HADn't resisteD everything
sO MUCH." Her leGACy to Me WAs to leArn More ABOUt not resistinG.
I'M leArninG A lot ABOUt nonresistAnce FroM JoHn. I'M reAlly HAPPy I
creAteD AnD FoUnD A PArtner WHO AllOWs More tHAn He resists. It's
AMAzinG to Feel the DiFFerences BetWeen AllOWinG AnD resistinG, AnD to
see tHAt the More resistAnce recedes, the More love FlOWs.

In my experience, nothing is more painful than the loss of a relationship that feels unfinished. My mother was the most significant person in my life growing up. The rigidity and fear of authority that she carried forward from her childhood in Germany were one side of her impact on me. The other side was someone I could talk with and whose support I valued. She was my metaphysical teacher, and in supporting my path in this area she gave me one of the greatest gifts anyone could give.

When I was an adult, our relationship drew closer to one of unconditional love and ac-ceptance. She embraced and lived many of the ideas in this book. And she helped me do the same.

My mother was not afraid of death and gave me a great deal of evidence that we are much more than our physical bodies. When she transitioned, I saw the perfection of the way she died and the rightness of her moving on. I cried only once, upon hearing that she had left. After that, I felt her being continuing. She had given me the support to move forward without her, and I felt an appreciation of her, for what she had given me and for a life well lived, more than I felt a sense of loss.

This was very different from my experience when Jeanie transitioned. I felt she was torn away from me. I knew in my heart that her leaving when she did was perfect for her. I knew that it wasn't because of any lack in our relationship. I didn't feel bad for her. I felt bad for me.

As I wrote earlier, we had agreed to always look for a solution that felt good to both of us. I felt she had hers, and it wasn't until much later that I was able to create mine.

I'm writing about these contrasting situations because there is no right or standard way to deal with loss. Feeling loss is ultimately a selfish experience (and I mean that in a positive sense). I had built my life around my relationship with Jeanie, and when she left, I felt as if she had taken part of my life with her. I even considered suicide. From my perspective, it was like my beloved had moved to Hawaii or another beautiful place. Why not join her?

As you know from reading this book, that was not my path. No one can ever replace my mother or Jeanie, but I can go on and embrace new joys.

An hour before I met Susan I had tea with a good friend, Mary, who knew both Jeanie and me and what a wonderful relationship we had. I talked with her about moving on with my life and not wanting to be disloyal to Jeanie and what we had together.

Jeanie and I had been together for 10 years, and Mary asked me if we would have been a good fit 25 years ago. No. Jeanie and I had talked about this. She was busy with her children and granddaughter and wasn't ready for the kind of relationship we had. I was much less mature and wasn't ready either.

Mary spread her arms apart at her sides and then brought her hands together at her chest. Her arms spread wide represented the rightness of Jeanie and my being apart 25 years ago, and bringing her hands together represented our 10-year relationship. Mary then continued to raise her arms, allowing her hands to separate and grow far apart again. It was like forming a giant X with her motion.

At that moment, I was able to see the rightness of what I was experiencing. It was okay for Jeanie and me to be separate 25 years ago. It was more than okay; it was perfect. And it was okay for Jeanie and me to be separate now.

I wasn't able to see the perfection of what was happening, but I was able to see that it was okay. And I was able to see the perfection of Mary reappearing in my life at that moment and giving me the gift of this perspective on my relationship with Jeanie.

I still cherish Jeanie and the time we had together. I still love her as much as ever. I have also opened my heart to love Susan and build a new life with her.

The Divine X

I love that Mary shared this giant X with John, and we've since talked about it applying to exes in our lives — that those ex-relationships are divine also, that each one helped us to be where we are now.

In every separation, whether it's for an afternoon or a lifetime, your pain and loss will depend on two things: your seeing the rightness of the change and your belief in your ability to fill the hole that has opened.

You have many separations every day. You may leave your home and go to work. You may have a brief interaction with a clerk at a cafe. You may have lunch with some friends. Separations are an integral part of the natural flow of our lives. Without them we would feel stifled.

It is only when we feel a loss of control over a separation that we feel pain. This can go in both directions. Someone staying too long can also feel like a loss of freedom — like dinner guests who stay and chat when you want to go to bed, or someone wanting you to continue in a relationship when it no longer feels good to you.

Obviously, the more you build your life around your relationship with someone, the more you have to adjust if they are no longer there. If someone can't meet you for lunch, that requires a much smaller adjustment than if you will never see them again.

Unresolved feelings can also amplify the feeling of loss. If you feel that someone has harmed you, then every time you see them, or even think of them, those feelings will come to the surface. Likewise, if there is something unsaid, you will feel the pain of not having spoken.

In cases of unresolved feelings, I use writing as a healing tool by writing what I feel but perhaps don't wish to express to that person. I write it as a letter that I know I won't send, so that I feel free to fully express myself. I then take it a deep step further by writing their reply to me — the one I wish they could offer.

I include apologies, validations, explanations, and expressions of love. I then mail or email their reply to me. Often when I read "their" mail or email, I can't tell whether they sent it or not — of course I know they didn't actually send it, but reading their words, I can feel the feelings as though they had. It's very powerfull and has led to remarkable emotional shifts in my prior unfinished relationships.

You will never be able to completely control change in your life.

I really seriously thought I could do this and can say unequivocally that it does not work.

And you will not always be able to see how a particular change might actually lead to something better. What you can do is learn how to nurture yourself, so when holes open up in your experience, you have the ability to fill them. This may mean doing solitary activities that bring you closer to nature or your Inner Wise Self. It could be knowing that you have family and friends you can count on. It can even be immersing yourself in challenging work.

I've become very skilled at doing this — I'm a rapid and creatively loving filler of gaps or holes. And I enjoy playing a game about what "new great thing" will come to fill THIS gap or hole. I remember and keep track. After my last relationship ended, and I was convinced that no new relationship could or would ever be as good or as fun, I created something magnificently beyond anything I could have ever imagined having in a relationship.

Here we are at our engagement party.

Developing this ability will not keep you from going into despair when someone you're entwined with dies or leaves. But it will enable you to flow with the daily changes in your relationships. And it will enable you to separate when being with someone doesn't feel good — whether that separation is for 15 minutes or the rest of your life.

In our relationship, we have a fairly strong emotional effect on each other. When we both feel good, it's fabulous. If one of us feels low and the other doesn't, we've made a conscious decision for the low one to make the effort to rise up rather than try to pull the other down. So when the two of us have a different story about something, we usually go with the one who has the more uplifting version.

But at times, when both of us are in a negative state, we've learned that it's best to separate, or go into silence if we can't, such as when we're in a car. As we discussed in chapter 20, if we don't, we start negatively mirroring each other. But more significantly, we actually hold each other back from rebalancing. Separating and turning the focus back to ourselves rather than on the other enables each of us to get back into balance much more quickly.

This can also be true on a larger level. Sometimes, separating or leaving a relationship can actually be the fastest path to both people rebalancing and going forward with their lives. (This is what happened for Sam Bennett and her husband; see page 202.)

There is no easy prescription we can give for whether to stay in a relationship or leave, but we can say the following:

- In any given interaction, telling your truth or removing yourself from the situation is the best thing you can do for yourself and your partner, even if it results in short-term pain.

- Allowing your partner to tell their truth or separate, even if it leads to pain in the moment for you, is the best thing you can do for yourself and them.

- Any "problem" you have with your partner is the result of your patterns and inner critics. If you don't change these, you will train the next partner to participate in the same kinds of interactions.

- Anything you do to resolve your conflicts in the current relationship will benefit you there and in any future relationship if you separate from this one.

  You and your partner may be so mutually reinforcing — with similar inner critics and patterns — that making alterations would be much easier if you separated. You may not even have the ability to make them at all in this relationship.

- As you change your relationship with your inner critics, you will be much less affected by the judgments and preferences of your partner.

- If one of you changes and the other doesn't, you will become less interested in being together.

Andrea Scher — There Is a Kiss I Wanted with My Whole Life

Andrea Scher

I've been thinking lately about our knowing — that deep, divine kind of knowing. The kind where our body tingles or we get goose bumps. The kind where we just know and we can't unknow it anymore. The kind that speaks to us in dreams. The kind that whispers at first and then gets really loud.

I've been thinking about how long we can go on ignoring our own truth. Until our body begins aching — speaking to us through pain, panic, anxiety.

A friend said to me recently, "Try this on, Andrea. Is it possible that what's best for you is actually the best for everyone else? Even if they don't like it? Even if they get mad? I want you to experiment with this. Practice telling your truth: 'I can't make it. That doesn't feel like a fit for me. This is what I want.' And trust that what is authentically true for you is ultimately best for everyone."

My husband, Matt, and I separated last fall.

It was the most excruciating chapter of my life. Unbearable at times. There were moments when I literally had to chant to myself, "You told the truth, and you didn't die. You're not dead. You survived." The terror of speaking the truth can feel so big. I was afraid my truth would kill him. Or me.

I spoke my truth imperfectly. A bit late. As best I could. It hurt.

The lessons are wide and deep and ongoing. My love for Matt is growing and changing in unexpected ways.

Today I am present to the deep knowing that I am finally beginning to honor in myself. The divine kind of knowing. The part of me that — without all the fear of troubled waters — is crystal clear.

"There is some kiss we want with our whole lives." — Rumi

There is a kiss I wanted with my whole life.
And it wasn't the kind of kiss you get from a lover.
It was the kiss from Spirit.
From Myself.
It's the kiss of living my life's true call.
It's the kiss of my own heart.
It's the kiss of joy.

Andrea is an artist, online workshop teacher & big believer in the transformative power of creativity. She lives by the motto "No capes, just courage" (SuperheroLife.com).

Awareness Practice:
Exploring Joyfull Separate Paths

1. Take a moment to reflect on times when you stayed too long in a relationship. Are you wanting to leave any relationship now? If so, what is holding you? Develop a Joyful Solution to either change what is bothering you in the relationship or decide how you can exit.

2. Are there times in your current relationships when it would be good to separate from activities sooner, such as leaving a discussion or other joint activity? This could be when one of you is feeling negative, when you're feeling uncomfortable, or simply because you want to be free to go on to something else. If so, picture how you might allow yourself to separate when you want to.

Sometimes taking a separate path is the most growthful, and ultimately the most joyful, step for all involved. For more about this, go to:
SucculentWildLove.com/Separate

23. Actively Loving: Creating Succulent Wild Love Relationships And Living Happily in Them

You can only love those around you to the extent
that you allow love to flow through you.

In a Succulent Wild Love relationship the partners most often have three kinds of feeling experiences with each other:

⭐ They are happy to see each other, actively enjoy each other's company, and frequently laugh together.

⭐ When focused on a joint project such as parenting, or spending family time together, or engaging in separate activities such as reading, they appreciate that the other is there.

@ They take moments to focus on their partner and feel the love they have for each other.

A Succulent wild Love relationship can feel Good Almost All of the Time

At the beginning of the book we used the analogy of lines on a highway. You now know how to avoid crashing into your partner or getting stuck on the side of the road. You have the tools to travel safely down the relationship highway. If you bump into your partner, you can look at the habit you broke or the pattern that came back. You know what line you crossed inadvertently and how to get back into your lane.

You know about honoring your boundaries and those of the people close to you. You know how to use your feelings constructively and how to create Joyful Solutions. You know how to separate your inner critics from your partner and make peace with them. You know how to identify patterns and change them.

We understand that knowing all these things will not instantly enable you to have stress-free relationships. We can teach you how to play golf in about a minute: hit the ball with a club until it goes into the hole; do this 18 times. Now you can take a lifetime practicing to become a better golfer. The same goes for relationships. You will have some meaningful successes with these tools fairly quickly, and then you will become more proficient over time.

As you take the Succulent Wild Love relationship journey, you will begin to feel freer and more in charge of your relationship life. This may have already begun. Every time you come to terms with an inner critic or create a Joyful Solution, your relationship shifts toward unconditional love.

As you begin to open the doorway to unconditional love, even if only for brief moments, you can consciously make the most of it by *choosing to love*. When people say "I love you" to someone, sometimes they're just being comforting and the words have no strong feeling behind them. You may state unequivocally that you love your partner, yet spend very little time actually having feelings of love flow through you when you're with them.

When we talk about feeling love for someone, we mean a unique, good feeling. In that moment, they are perfect just as they are, and you feel appreciation that they are in your life.

This is different from what we feel when someone does something we want. That is approval and an appreciation of an action, rather than feeling the perfection of someone in our life.

Most people do not know how to let love flow through them freely on an ongoing basis — or sometimes even at all — except in special situations, such as first falling in love or when there is a forced separation.

Have you ever seen the ending of a movie where someone is dying and their partner is declaring their love and appreciation? That is unconditional love flowing. The good news is that you don't have to wait for the intimate people in your life to die to tell them how much you love and appreciate them.

Susan and I consciously show our love for each other every day, through a look, a touch, hugs, words of appreciation, and many other ways small and big. We've seen that death scene in the movies and decided, "Why wait? Why not show each other that kind of love every day rather than waiting for one of us to get hurt or die?" And it feels good.

I'M A HUGE FAN OF FEELING AND EXPRESSING APPRECIATION AS OFTEN AS POSSIBLE. I PRACTICE A LOT WITH JOHN AND WITH ALMOST EVERYONE I COME INTO CONTACT WITH — INCLUDING SERVICE PROVIDERS ON THE PHONE, CLERKS IN STORES, OTHER DRIVERS, AND PEOPLE ON THE STREET OR ON HIKES.

It's SO MUCH FUN TO CONNECT IN THESE LOVING WAYS WITH OURSELVES AND WITH THE WORLD. OF COURSE, SOMETIMES I FEEL CRABBY OR INSULAR OR ANNOYED BY ANY NUMBER OF THINGS AND SHOW FEAR INSTEAD OF LOVE — OR LOVE BLENDED WITH FEAR — AND THAT'S OKAY. I LIVE IN THE "MARVELOUS MESSY MIDDLE" OF LIFE, WHICH INCLUDES THE WHOLE RANGE OF FEELINGS. I JUST SPEND MORE TIME IN FEELINGS OF LOVE AND APPRECIATION THAN THE OTHER FEELINGS, AND YOU CAN TOO, IF YOU DON'T ALREADY.

In the chapter on Love Symbols we talked about larger actions, such as buying a present on Valentine's Day or making someone tea. Here we are talking about small, spontaneous gestures and words shared throughout the day that remind you of the things you appreciate about your partner and others close to you — small expressions of love that feel good.

Some people are uncomfortable with such overt displays. If this is true for you or others around you, then you can express your love silently by consciously thinking what you appreciate about them. You can literally tell them, "I love you," in your mind. It feels good. As you do it, and mean it, you will be able to feel love flowing through you. You may have heard of spiritual masters who are able to emanate love toward everyone around them. This is what they do. They think loving thoughts and express them.

My DAD WAS one OF tHOSe "covert love opErAtors" WHo coulDn't reAlly Be overt ABout it. I leArneD to MAKe Love TrAnslAtions AnD APPreciAte HoW MUCH He WAs ABle to sHoW love in His WAy — not My WAy. It oPeneD so MAny Doors to love tHAt I Wrote A Poem ABout HiM AnD Me CAlleD "HoW to ForGive Your FAtHer." He loveD it. I reAD it At His FunerAl, AnD AfterWArD tuckeD A coPy into His suit- coAt Pocket.

poetry is A love lanGvAGe for me

Of course, feeling love for someone is impossible when you're in pain and believe they need to change for you to be happy. Every tool in this book is designed to help you move beyond this stage to a level where you and those around you can have the benefit of your love and acceptance.

Whenever your relationship is in neutral — you aren't thinking about unresolved anger or tension, you aren't feeling unexpressed hurt, and there are no important unspoken truths in your awareness — you are ready to actively choose love.

This can happen even if any of these blocks are still in your relationship, as long as they aren't in the forefront of your consciousness. It's just that until unexpressed feelings are resolved, they will spring into your awareness. In many relationships there are moments of unconditional love flowing, and then an unresolved tension will be remembered and the love flow stops.

One way some people attempt to deal with painful feelings is to try to repress them — but not in a Succulent Wild Love relationship. As they come up, you have the tools to guide your feelings and let them flow. And then you are able to love freely.

WAYS TO CONSCIOUSLY INCREASE YOUR FEELINGS OF LOVE

To increase your feelings of love, take moments each day to think about what you appreciate about the people close to you. Appreciation is an excellent doorway to feeling love. You can literally become more skilled at loving by taking time to appreciate.

Susan taught me this. We review a lot of each other's writing, and when I first started working with her, I always immediately began with what needed to be changed. Susan asked me to tell her what I appreciated about what she'd written first, and after a while I began to do that. Now it's become a habit to take a moment to appreciate something about anything I review. And I love the response I get in return.

I like to make daily GLAD or APPreciation lists and include people in them, noting specific things — tiny and large — that they did or said that I appreciate. I sometimes do this on my phone in the notes section and refer to the list again or read it to the person I'm appreciating. Everyone enjoys being appreciated, and it's such a joy to do. And the more you appreciate, the more there is to appreciate!

There is also an indirect path to appreciating someone: briefly think of what your life would be like if they were no longer in it. (If you suddenly feel better that they're gone, that's an important message too.)

When you're feeling neutral, imagine telling the people around you that you love them. If it feels right, you can even say it out loud or let them know something specific that you appreciate about them.

Look for the best in others and for opportunities to praise them.

And that includes yourself. What's the best in you? What do you appreciate about yourself? Doing this is a self-loving practice, and it allows more love to flow toward others.

Help people make Love Translations. If someone is telling a negative story, you can offer them a more positive version. (However, it's important to assess whether they're ready to shift to a more positive story. Sometimes people just want someone to listen.) If you're listening to them and feeling bad, then it's time for you to shift and either let them know that what they're saying is negatively affecting you or withdraw from the interaction.

We have some agreements in our relationship that really help:

☆ *When one of us has a more positive view of a situation, we'll agree on that view.*

◉ *When one of us feels down and the other feels better, the one feeling down makes an effort to follow the one feeling better.*

◉ *We talk about uncomfortable things with the intent of helping each other make a Love Translation and resolving the situation.*

★ *We don't invite each other to see anyone in a negative light, including each other.*

◉ *We spend very little time complaining about what is wrong with others or the world.*

☆ *We look for opportunities to appreciate each other.*

★ *We ask, "What is going on?" rather than, "What's wrong?"*

◉ *We keep a positive vision of ourselves and of the relationship, and when we don't feel that way, we do our inner work and ask for support from each other, or someone else, as needed.*

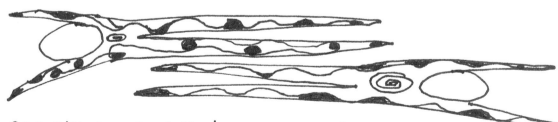

SOMETIMES we just lie down FlAttened and BreAtHe

Cliff and David Swain-Salomon — Ways We Show Our Love

David and Cliff Swain-Salomon

CLIFF: One of the things my dad taught me years ago was that to love each other and to show that love is a daily choice. And so every day, I ask myself how I am going to choose to show that to David. It could be little things, such as sending him a text message; because he's at work, I don't want to call and interrupt his day, so I'll just send a funny picture and say, "Hey, I am thinking about you." Or I'll go run errands and then create a special sacred space for us to enjoy later that day when he gets back. Every day we ensure that we always have dinner together; we always create at least one or two date times per day together.

DAVID: For me, I definitely had to grow into understanding meaningful ways of expressing myself. I get very engrossed in whatever I am currently doing, so left to my own devices, I could easily spend hours working on things for my job or playing video games. Whatever I may be focused on, when I think about Cliff (which is very often), I allow that to be my "personal escape button." That way, I remember not only to think about and feel that love for him but also to let him know that I'm thinking of him and feeling love for him right in that moment. This helps me make sure we stay connected.

We actually have a special word that we share only between the two of us. It's our word that we use in place of "I love you," because "love" is such an easily overused word. People say they love ice cream or they love puppy dogs, so we wanted to have a word that was only ours, and we only use it when we're truly feeling that deep love for each other. There are times when it will be as simple as sending a text message with just that word, and there are times when that word will prompt a midday conversation, pulling me away from my work for a moment. And on days when we're home together and feeling that love for each other well up in us, feeling that strong emotion, we just cuddle up to each other and say that word.

CLIFF: Another thing David does throughout the day is if he's between tasks at work, he'll call or text in those moments and say, "Hey, are you available?" I'll then break away from my work to chat with him. Whenever he is on a break or at lunch or walking between buildings at work, he always makes sure to have a conversation with me.

Cliff and David have been together for over eight years. Cliff is a holistic healer in Sunnyvale, California (AzHolistic.com). David is fulfilling a lifelong dream of helping teach digital devices how to speak.

Sheri and Michael Lindner —
Things That Affirm Our Love and Relationship

We do small, daily, ordinary things — kiss each other hello and goodnight; touch, pat, and squeeze each other often; ask about each other's day; do errands for each other — but these are not the defining affirmative features of our relationship.

The strength, contentment, stability, and joy of our relationship lies in the fact that we both value "Us" over all else.

From the inception of our relationship, we have shared everything — material, emotional, personal (with the exception of certain desserts!). As kids (we've known each other since we were 10 and 12), friends and family called us Ozzie and Harriet. Our contemporaries always sensed, even as we were starting out as a couple, that we were an

Michael and Sheri Lindner (1973)

established unit, and we often feel (though neither of us believes in such things) that we have been together for all time (like the strangers who meet in a museum at the start of *Aida*, who just know that they were lovers thousands of years before).

We are ambassadors for each other, bringing into our shared life not only our particular interests and gifts but all parts of the time we spend away from each other, finding that our relationship is made more fertile with this sharing. We enjoy absorbing the other's experience, both of us teachers and learners with each other, valuing both roles.

In our relationship, we are familiar with all the usual things that couples argue about (who drives too fast, who doesn't cook dinners regularly, who leaves a mess in the bathroom, who is doing more than the other, whose family members are coming — again! — to visit, or who spends money on what). But we don't end up arguing about these things; they just don't seem important when experienced side by side with "Us," with our ever-present awareness of our good luck in being together, in feeling that we have loved each other forever.

It may sound like we have each abdicated our individual identities for a shared "Us" identity. Neither of us feels that we have, but both of us value this thing that exists in us, around us, and between us, created by us, this third identity that is not Michael, not Sheri, but is MichaelSheri or SheriMichael. What makes us value it (perhaps above our individual selves) is that in that shared couple space, we each feel that we are the selves we love the most.

This was not automatic; at the beginning, each of us experienced some degree of uncertainty about how the layering of "me-you-us" would take shape within this couple identity. But we both grew to feel that our relationship was where we came to know the selves we wished to be. Within our couplehood each of our individual selves is a better self. So this is what we both protect and cherish, and in the face of this, all else is less significant.

And we play together and laugh together and talk endlessly. And we love sharing our stories, with each other and others, the stories of us, how we fell in love, how we knew we were in love, what we remember of our children's early years, and what we hope for our future.

The question, What do you do to affirm your relationship? itself suggests perhaps a set of behaviors for couples to "do." What we do affirms our love for each other, but more significantly, it is who we are that shapes what we seek and how we are.

Michael and Sheri are both psychoanalytically trained psychologists in private practice in Port Washington, New York. Sheri is also a poet and essayist.

You can love yourself in the ways that please you most

Some of you may think, "These people are lucky. My partner is never going to do all these things." It isn't really necessary for anyone else around you to do any of them. You can do them. And when you do, you may be surprised at the positive responses you receive.

When I'm uncomfortable in social situations, I've found that it helps to reflect on what I appreciate about the people around me and to imagine loving them. When I do that, love doesn't flow through me the way it does when I'm feeling comfortable, but it does shift my focus off insecurity (fear) and onto love. This enables me to feel better and most easily find the best response in the situation. I give myself the suggestion to love them and allow whatever follows.

John and I were attending a neighborhood party, and John expressed some fears about the social setting and not knowing anyone. I allowed this to affect me, and we left the party within minutes. As we walked away, I said I felt sad that we hadn't created a way to enjoy ourselves. We both then agreed to start over and returned to the party with more love than fear. We met some lovely people and appreciated the party and our time there.

LET YOURSELF FEEL "THAT GOOD"

When you start practicing these love techniques and develop the ability to love and be loved unconditionally, some additional beliefs may keep you from allowing yourself to feel the full benefit of your efforts. To feel love more often, you have to permit yourself to feel "that good."

You may be afraid if things are going too well that "the other shoe will drop" — that life or, more specifically, your relationships, simply cannot be that good. This is the voice of an inner critic. Life *can* be that good. Relationships *can* be loving most of the time. In fact, if you picture God, or Universal Wisdom, or your Inner Wise Self, they are all-loving. Life was intended for us to feel that good, to feel the abundant love available to us and everyone around us.

Another inner critic belief is "I don't deserve to have this much happiness when others are suffering." Your suffering only reinforces the idea that suffering is necessary. Your happiness is a beacon for others.

Listen to any fear thought that comes to mind from your inner critics when you feel happy or loving. Then consciously counter it. Get help from your Inner Wise Self. Your Inner Wise Self is your personal beacon of unconditional love.

 Are you "good enough" to feel unconditionally loved by others?

⭐ Are you allowed to have one joyful experience after another?

When I first heard at an Abraham-Hicks workshop that I could have one joyful event after another, I was surprised. Until that moment, I had believed that life consisted of struggle-struggle-struggle-reward. A brief moment to savor the reward, then back to struggle. Feeling good was my reward. It had never occurred to me that I could just feel good and keep creating events that felt good — or that doing things just because they felt good would enable me to achieve my goals. And yet that has turned out to be the case.

My previous version was something like "try to avoid struggle at all costs, and then have big, dramatic episodes of upsetting things until I can get back to feeling good again, which won't last because of my inner critics and limiting beliefs."

I now occupy many more feeling-good places and am committed to feeling glad no matter what — including when things are not glad at all. I find things to appreciate in every single incident — without exception. Which sometimes seems impossibly difficult.

And I have examples of doing this when my older brother died, during an IRS audit, while navigating a medical situation, and in countless other "negative" situations.

"Negative" Just Hasn't Been Processed and Shifted Yet

Feeling good and feeling love flow through you and to you can feel unfamiliar. It can feel like "This is not me" and can actually evoke fear by activating your inner critics. They are more comfortable with your old, familiar patterns. But if you address any thoughts that want to deny you joy, after a while, feeling that good will feel normal.

THERE IS NO RELATIONSHIP DESTINATION

Since we've used the analogy of driving, it may seem odd to now say that there's no destination, but it really is about the journeying.

The two of us use the tools in this book every day. And we practice the habits as best we can. We still have bumps, but we also have amazing love for each other and the people around us.

Neither of us started out this way. We've had our share of pain and inflicted our share of pain on the people close to us. Part of the reason we wrote this book is that we would have liked to have someone give us this knowledge. We wanted a book like this. We might not have read it from cover to cover or understood everything, but we would have benefited from the knowledge — and so will you.

If you're like us, you will probably still have bumps,
but you will feel more love more often.

Practicing the six powerful habits and using the tools in this book creates an uplifting spiral. You will feel less frustrated by others' choices, so will be able to give them more permission to do what feels right for them. As you begin to interact with others in this way, you and they will be able to give you more permission to do what feels right for you. And you all will then spend more of your time and energy supporting one another in creating what you each want rather than trying to change one another.

What your relationships are like is the result of decisions you make every day. You now have an awareness of what makes relationships Succulent and Wild — what makes them nourishing and expansive.

You have tools you can use when you get off balance. And you have the skills to bring your relationships back into balance. As you stay aware and practice, this will become easier and easier. And when you do have upsets, you will recover back to feelings of love and support more and more quickly. Along the way, the ongoing love and appreciation for the people around you will continue to increase as you practice what you've learned.

With much love and appreciation for taking this journey with us and being a Succulent Wild Love beacon,

Susan and John

a.k.a. Mrs. & Mr. Wonderfull

Awareness Practice: Loving Unconditionally

UNCONDITIONAL LOVE PRE-CHECKLIST

As you think of your partner, do you have a list of ways they need to change for you to be happy?

Do any incidents come to mind that evoke unexpressed negative feelings?

If you answered yes to either of these, use the Inner Feelings Care System (page 86) or talk with your partner. Create Joyful Solutions.

Do you have permission to feel "that good"? If not, use your Inner Critic Care System (page 106).

LOVING UNCONDITIONALLY

What are your partner's Love Symbols?

What are some ways you can demonstrate love to your partner every day?

Which of the things that we do in our relationship appeal to you? Of course, you can do these things with everyone around you.

With your partner or in a social situation, visualize telling each person you love them as you look at them.

To expand your experiences of loving unconditionally, go to:
SucculentWildLove.com/Unconditionally

24. What Do I Do Now?: FAQ (Fabulous and Quick) with SARK and Dr. John Waddell

SARK

Dr. John Waddell

BELIEFS AT THE BASIS OF ANY SUCCULENT WILD LOVE RELATIONSHIP

If you don't hold these beliefs, you will be limited in your ability to participate in a Succulent Wild Love relationship. If you're happy with your beliefs, you can create a unique relationship based on what you see as good for you.

★ My feelings are valuable.

✫ I can change.

@ I'm allowed to say no or, "This doesn't feel good."

◎ I can create Joyful Solutions.

@ There is always something and someone for me to appreciate.

✫ Everyone intimate in my life loves me, even if they don't know how to show it.

★ Happy people don't try to hurt others.

⊚ Hurting others is a distorted form of love.

◎ My inner critics are not me.

✫ I am lovable just as I am.

QUESTIONS

What about people who are less mature, are not bestselling authors, or don't have a PhD in psychology?

Anyone can use the principles in this book to have less tension in their relationships and even to be able to love unconditionally. The less self-aware you are, the more likely you are to bump into others. Thinking about and applying the principles in this book will make you much more self-aware.

You can choose self-awareness, and study and practice it like anything else. The results of doing this will likely astound you.

Why do you still need to do feelings care if you have this great relationship and are bestselling authors?

A woman called my Inspiration Phone Line and left a message saying in part, "You probably don't need something like an Inner Feelings Care System because it's easy for you because you're SARK. And now you're in this great relationship too." I know that it's because of doing this kind of work consistently that I feel this good this often and manifest these types of experiences.

Before developing these kinds of care systems, I was really floundering with my feelings and my inner critics and did not feel a profound connection with my Inner Wise Self. Now negative emotions don't last as long or occur as often. It's amazing to me now that I ever didn't feel this good. Anyone can do this too if they're willing to explore and practice — and you can do it badly and imperfectly, and it still works!

I had to develop my own ways for dealing with my feelings. My feelings are often not as strong as Susan's, and I tend to go into problem-solving mode fairly quickly. So my feelings care system is simpler. Susan and I still have bumps and upsets, and there will always be situations where negative feelings are triggered, no matter how briefly. But I know for certain that, no matter what method you use, allowing your feelings to flow in a constructive way makes a huge difference.

What if my partner won't read the book or do any of the Awareness Practices with me?

Once you know the creativity and power you have to change yourself, you will be much less reliant on other people changing for you. You can have complete mastery of the habits in this book and have the kinds of relationships you want, without needing anyone else to do any specific thing.

I USED TO BE BIG ON TRYING TO CHANGE EVERYONE BUT MYSELF. It rEAlly ONly WORKS PARTIAlly AND intERMITTENTly. NOW THAT I KNOW HOW TO CHANGE MYSELF, I FEEL iNCREDIBly FREE TO lovE MYSELF AND OTHERS SO MUCH MORE.

How long do you think it takes to make a good relationship great using the six habits?

Applying these habits will quickly have an impact on your relationships. How quickly you are able to master the tools depends on your interest and effort.

I lovE HOW QUICKly I WAS ABlE TO ADOPT JOYFUll SolutioNS — I WOULDN'T HAVE PREDICTED HOW SUCCESSFUll I WOULD BE AT CREATING THEM, SINCE I'M SOMETIMES SElFISH, IMPATIENT, AND SKEPTICAl. I'M AlSO SOMETIMES EAGER, WillING, AND CREATIVE, AND MY lifE IS SO MUCH MORE lovING WITH MORE APPliCATION AND PRACTICE OF THE SIX HABITS.

Why do you describe this as "a new philosophy of love and relationships for everyone"?

Most people are used to thinking that compromise, and even sacrifice, are necessary for a successful relationship. This is what we were taught, but we found out it doesn't have to be this way.

Many also think that the best possible relationship is one where you say to your partner, "I know you have flaws, but I love you anyway." What we say is, "I love you. There is nothing flawed about you. You are perfect as you are, and any way I don't see you that way is my responsibility." We believe that everyone can love unconditionally.

MARRYING OUR CORE TEACHINGS TOGETHER IN THIS BOOK, I'M AWARE OF THE SIGNIFICANCE OF THESE HABITS AND SKIllS — ESPECIAlly WHEN I SEE EVIDENCE IN SOCIETY OF THE OPPOSITE. PEOPlE GENERAlly DO NOT FEEL QUAlifIED TO lovE UNCONDITIONAlly OR TO PRACTICE DOING SO. MANY PEOPlE THINK THAT RElATIONSHIPS ARE HARD AND TAKE WORK, AND THAT YOU CAN ONly GET PART OF WHAT YOU WANT. WE KNOW THAT YOU CAN HAVE All YOU WANT.

I just can't imagine seeing my partner as perfect, or myself either. What should I do?

By "perfect," we don't mean that someone has reached some ultimate peak and will never change. We mean that we recognize that they are being perfectly themselves and it isn't our place to judge them. Your partner will never be perfect if they have to live up to your standards. You will never be perfect if you have to live up to the standards of your inner critics.

Loving yourself, seeing the perfection in yourself, loving others, and seeing the perfection in them — these are all decisions. See the three decisions Jeanie made in chapter 15 (page 154).

REDEFINING "PERFECT" IS ONE OF MY FAVORITE THINGS IN THIS BOOK. ONCE I REALIZED THAT IT WASN'T ABOUT PERFECTIONISM, I WAS ABLE TO RELAX INTO THE PERFECTION OF MY — AND EVERYONE'S — HUMANITY. I'VE DESCRIBED THIS IN MY PREVIOUS BOOKS AS "SPLENDIDLY IMPERFECT" AND NOW FEEL THAT THERE IS PERFECTION IN THE "AS IS" OF EVERYTHING THAT NEEDS NO EXPLANATION.

Do Joyful Solutions work all the time?

If you believe you can create them and make the effort, you can always create a Joyful Solution for yourself. You can't necessarily for others. If they believe that compromise or sacrifice is required, they may choose to join you or create what they're used to for themselves.

I'VE SERIOUSLY "MARKET TESTED" CREATING JOYFULL SOLUTIONS FOR SEVERAL YEARS NOW WITH JOHN, AND THERE HAVE ONLY BEEN TWO TIMES WHEN IT APPEARED NOT TO WORK. BOTH TIMES WERE BASED ON MY RESISTANCE OR BELIEF IN SCARCITY. ONCE I CLEARED THOSE UP, JOYFULL SOLUTIONS POPPED RIGHT OUT.

I liked the title and what I've read of the book, but I wonder about bringing these kinds of ideas to my community — they're kind of uptight.

The best thing you can do is model these principles and become more accepting and loving. Soon people will say, "I want some of what she's having."

BEING A BEACON OF LOVE AND JOY IS THE BEST GIFT THAT ANY OF US CAN OFFER. IT REALLY DOESN'T MATTER WHAT ROUTE YOU TAKE TO GET THERE. IF YOU SENSE THAT PEOPLE MIGHT BE OFFENDED OR PUT OFF, THEN IT'S BEST NOT TO SHARE THIS KIND OF PHILOSOPHY WITH THEM.

Do I still need therapy if I read your book?

Use whatever tools and support will help you get to accepting and loving yourself and the intimate people in your life.

"NEEDING THERAPY" IS NOT FOR US TO SAY OR RECOMMEND. I HAPPEN TO THINK THAT THERAPY CAN BE IMMENSELY VALUABLE AND TRANSFORMATIVE, AND RECOMMEND IT ON THAT BASIS.

What about sex? I thought there would be a chapter on that. What do you recommend for people who want better sex?

Sex is a sensitive subject for many individuals and couples. If you want to play tennis and your partner isn't interested, you can ask a friend or join a club. It's not the same with sex. But the principles and the six habits in this book apply to sex in the same way as to any other interactions in partnerships. It is a matter of creating Joyful Solutions and designing a relationship that is fully satisfying to both of you.

Sex is so sticky. ;-) I love sex and love being sexual with John. I've experimented tremendously with my sexuality and have considered writing a book about only that. I decided to focus my energies onto our Succulent Wild Love relationship and this book. And I know that for me, loving includes being sexual. I'm happy to say that the six habits in this book have done more for my happy sexual expression than anything previously!

How do I get my partner to change? How do I deal with them trying to get me to change?

You create Joyful Solutions. Coercion and manipulation will destroy a Succulent Wild Love relationship faster than just about anything.

Being a Succulent Wild Lover of life and other people means you no longer have much interest in changing people or reacting to them trying to change you. What a relief! This opens you up for feeling so much more love, so much more often.

QUESTIONS ABOUT YOUR INNER WISE SELF

I don't know about this Inner Wise Self stuff — seems like magical thinking to me. Is it?

You will have to decide that for yourself, but questioning its validity is actually rather unimportant. What *is* important is the emotional effect of what you receive when you explore talking with your Inner Wise Self. Do you feel better? Do you feel more loving of yourself and others? Also, do you get advice you can use? Does it give you a new, more uplifting way of looking at a situation? If so, you can credit your most mature self or your Inner Wise Self. It doesn't matter.

I believe that your Inner Wise Self is so far beyond magical thinking, and recommend that you experiment with allowing your experiences to inform your concerns.

What if I feel like I'm making it all up?

I used to feel like I was just making up answers, and then realized that it doesn't really matter.

What if I use up all the answers?

When you first begin to receive so much love and support, it can feel scary to think that you might be "using it all up." There is absolutely no scarcity with your Inner Wise Self. It is an infinite source.

What if I don't use it at all?

You won't know the feeling of internal, unconditional love and care, tuned exquisitely to your unique self.

Succulent Wild Love Concepts: A Quick-Reference List

Since this book is a whole new philosophy of love and relationships we wanted to supply you with easy reminders and definitions as you practice with and apply these concepts

Beautifull Boundaries: Boundaries that are beautifull in relationships because they are understood and acknowledged (ch. 10).

Inner Critic Care System: A system for transforming your relationships with your inner critics and their role in your love relationships (ch. 9).

Inner Feelings Care System: A self-care system for your feelings that allows you to feel more love (ch. 8).

Inner Wise Self: The wise part of you that loves you unconditionally and supports you in loving others (ch. 7).

Joyfull Solutions: Resolutions that go beyond compromise and sacrifice to where everyone can have what they want (chs. 11 & 12).

Love Symbols: Gestures or other symbols that let you know and experience love in a relationship (ch. 16).

Love Translations: Ways to transform fear into love (ch. 17).

MicroTruths: Small, uncomfortable truths that can block the flow of love if they're not expressed (ch. 18).

Naming (Without Blaming): Naming how you feel and what you're experiencing to improve communication with yourself and your partner (ch. 18).

☆ **Perfect Partner, Perfect You:** The perspective that you and your partner are perfect, which allows you to give and receive unconditional love (ch. 15).

★ **Sole-mates:** Relationships where you feel self-loving and loving with another (ch. 5).

◉ **Soulfully Single:** A way to describe and experience being single as a conscious choice (ch. 3).

★ **SPAR:** An acronym for security, privacy, activity (inner & outer), and respect, which are included in being self-lovingly separate (ch. 10).

◎ **Succulent Wild Love:** A relationship where you're self-nourishing the way a succulent plant is, and wild, as in untamed and not limited by those close to you (ch. 1).

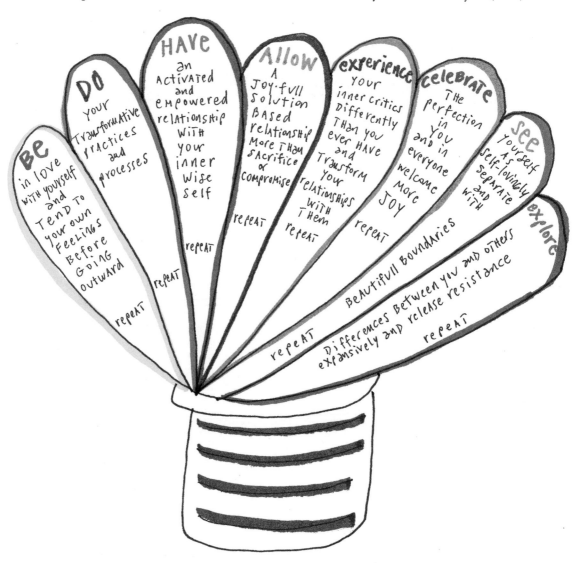

our succulent invitation to you

Dear Brilliant Reader,

It is our great joy to bring you Succulent Wild Love in this book! We have also created a special website where you can find us and other Succulent Wild Loving Souls who are empowering themselves to live this approach in their lives.

We want to help everyone have the opportunity to live and love in this way, so we have supportive tools and play-full ways to bring these concepts to life. There are juicy additional elements that we couldn't fit into the book, such as audio and video interviews with our guest essayists and information about an entire series of online programs we've developed to expand your ability to live Succulent Wild Love.

Whether you are looking for support to activate the six habits or guidance to practice them in your life, or you want to work with us in person to develop mastery of these habits, we are here for you!

You can find all this, including more of our writings, at
SucculentWildLove.com/Gifts

Of course, we love to interact with you in all ways, so you can connect with us on Facebook (Facebook.com/PlanetSARK).

On Twitter (@SusanAkaSARK) you can share your Succulent Wild Love stories at #SWL and engage with other succulents.

With Succulent Wild Love,
SARK & Dr. John Waddell

P.S. IF YOU WANT MORE SARK, YOU CAN
COME TO THE WILD HOME BASE,
PlanetSARK.COM, OR CALl THE InspirAtion
PHONE LINE: 415-546-3742
(3-5-Min. rECORDING BY SARK).

Succulent Books and Resources

There are so many incredible books and resources. Here are some of our favorites that relate to this book.

Chapter 3. Soulfully Single and Open for Love
Calling In the One by Katherine Woodward Thomas (CallingInTheOne.com)

Chapter 4. The Possibilities and Tyrannies of Soulmates and Coupling
Mating in Captivity by Esther Perel (EstherPerel.com)

Chapter 5. Longing for a Great Love: SARK's Covert Love Operation
The Desire Map by Danielle LaPorte (DanielleLaPorte.com)
> *"I accept relationships as my primary teacher about myself, other people, and the mysteries of the universe."* — Gay Hendricks

Chapter 6. Creating Your Perfect Partner for a Succulent Wild Love Relationship
Wabi Sabi Love: The Ancient Art of Finding Perfect Love in Imperfect Relationships by Arielle Ford (SoulmateSecret.com)
> *"Remember that the best relationship is one in which your love for each other exceeds your need for each other."* — Dalai Lama

Chapter 7. Your Relationship Mentor Inside: You and Your Inner Wise Self
Opening to Channel by Sanaya Roman & Duane Packer (OrinDaBen.com)
Creative Visualization by Shakti Gawain

Chapter 8. Tending to and Transforming Your Feelings So You Can Feel More Love
Love Is Letting Go of Fear by Gerald G. Jampolsky, MD (JerryJampolsky.com)
The Fear Cure by Lissa Rankin, MD (LissaRankin.com)

Chapter 9. The Critics in Your Head Are Not You — or Your Partner: Your Inner Critic Care System
Embracing Your Inner Critic and *Partnering: A New Kind of Relationship* by Hal Stone & Sidra Stone (Delos-inc.com)
Reform Your Inner Mean Girl by Amy Ahlers & Christine Arylo (InnerMeanGirlReformSchool.com)

Chapter 10. "Succulent and Wild" Means Self-Lovingly Separate and Beautifull Boundaries
Intimacy & Solitude by Stephanie Dowrick (StephanieDowrick.com)
The Invitation by Oriah (OriahMountainDreamer.com)
Inspired and Unstoppable by Tama Kieves (TamaKieves.com)

Chapter 12. Creating Joyfull Solutions on Your Own
The Work by Byron Katie (TheWork.com)

Chapter 13. Sources of Anger and How to Transform Them
No Enemies Within by Dawna Markova

Chapter 14. Moving Through Anger and Hurt
I Thought We'd Never Speak Again by Laura Davis (LauraDavis.net)
> *"When you say or do anything to please, get, keep, influence or control anyone or anything, fear is the cause and pain is the result."* — Byron Katie

Succulent BOOKS and Resources

Chapter 15. Your Partner Is Perfect — and So Are You: How to Give and Receive Unconditional Love
The Vortex: Where the Law of Attraction Assembles All Cooperative Relationships by Esther & Jerry Hicks (Abraham-Hicks.com)
Love for No Reason by Marci Shimoff (HappyForNoReason.com)
   "Love is the ability and willingness to allow those that you care for to be what they choose for themselves, without any insistence that they satisfy you." — Wayne Dyer

Chapter 16. Love Symbols: How Do You Know When Someone Loves You?
The 5 Love Languages by Gary D. Chapman (5LoveLanguages.com)

Chapter 17. Love Translations with Others and Self-Love
Go Only as Fast as the Slowest Part of You Feels Safe to Go by Robyn Posin, PhD (CompassionateInk.com)
Succulent Wild Woman by SARK (PlanetSARK.com)
   "Well-ordered self-love is right and natural." — St. Thomas Aquinas

Chapter 18. Succulent Wild Communications
Nonviolent Communication: A Language of Life: Life-Changing Tools for Healthy Relationships by Marshall B. Rosenberg, PhD (Cnvc.org)
The Seven Principles for Making Marriage Work by John Gottman, PhD (Gottman.com)
   "Love one another and you will be happy. It's as simple and as difficult as that." — Michael Leunig

Chapter 19. Transforming Roles and Obligations in Relationships
Embracing Your Inner Critic by Hal Stone & Sidra Stone (Delos-inc.com)

Chapter 20. Awareness of Patterns in Relationships: Bumps and Upsets and Learning to Be Kind
How to Be an Adult in Relationships by David Richo (DaveRicho.com)

Chapter 21. Relationship Patterns Learned in Childhood
Emotional Alchemy by Tara Brach (TaraBrach.com)

Chapter 22. Joyfull Separate Paths, in Daily Activities and in Transforming (Ending) a Relationship
I Need Your Love — Is That True? by Byron Katie (ByronKatie.com)
Forgive for Love by Dr. Fred Luskin (LearningtoForgive.com)

Chapter 23. Actively Loving: Creating Succulent Wild Love Relationships and Living Happily in Them
John & Jeanie Fly (Books 1 & 2) by John Waddell (SucculentWildLove.com)
Transformation Game by Kathy Tyler & Joy Drake (InnerLinks.com)
The Energies of Love: Using Energy Medicine to Keep Your Relationship Thriving by Donna Eden & David Feinstein (InnerSource.net)
   "You must always be a-waggle with LOVE." — D. H. Lawrence

Other Books By SARK And Dr. John Waddell

SARK's New Creative Companion

For creative spirits of all ages. A classic for energizing and expanding your creativity and sharing it with the world.

Inspiration Sandwich

Super-inspiring stories and art that contain food for your spirit and soul. Includes transformative sharing about my childhood abuse experience and also shows you how to have more daily tiny adventures in your life.

Living Juicy

365 extraordinarily juicy morsels and wisdom for you for every day of the year. Created to be perpetually nourishing.

SARK's Journal and Playbook

A guided journal with plenty of free space too — for all ages. A place for you to dream while awake and inspire yourself.

The Magic Cottage Address Book

An eccentric and extremely creative and colorfull address book for you.

Succulent Wild Woman

My statement of vulnerable self-liberation and how I came to truly love and marry myself, and guide and support you in doing the same. Succulent Wild People embrace what's in this book.

The Bodacious Book of Succulence

Bulging with succulent stories and suggestions for how you can live more succulently more often. Portraits of Succulent Wild Men too.

Transformation Soup

Healing of every description, vulnerability, and wisdom shared for all. Contains real-life healing stories and miracles you can experience too.

SucculentWildLove.com/Books

Eat Mangoes Naked

More ways to live powerfully and joyfully no matter what your circumstances are. Full of adventure stories and ways for you to feel like your life truly is an adventure.

Prosperity Pie

An abundance magnet that explores manifesting and creating money in brand-new ways. How to think and feel differently about money so you can create more of your desires.

Make Your Creative Dreams REAL

A comprehensive, 12-month "manifesting your creative dream" life program book for you and all your dreams. Includes helping you identify what your dreams are.

Fabulous Friendship Festival

How to celebrate and expand your friendships in new ways more often and understand how, when, and why to transform them.

Juicy Pens, Thirsty Paper

How I created all my SARK books and how you can share your writing and creative gifts with the world, and create the time and energy to do so.

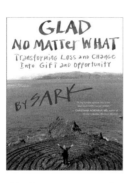

Glad No Matter What

How to really feel glad more often, no matter what happens in your life. Transformative stories about my mom and cat dying, and all about how to innovatively support yourself and others during losses and changes.

John and Jeanie Fly: Living the Law of Attraction

In this intimate story of two people who suddenly have the ability to fly, John and Jeanie are living the principles of Succulent Wild Love.

John and Jeanie Fly: Our World and the Law of Attraction

In Book 2, the couple must deal with skeptics, with many who want to elevate them to religious icons, and with others who denounce them as false prophets.

SucculentWildLove.com/Books

 **SARK** and **Dr. John Waddell**
appreciate New World Library!
(We affectionately refer to it as New Wild Library.)

NEW WORLD LIBRARY is dedicated to publishing books and other media that inspire and challenge us to improve the quality of our lives and the world.

We are a socially and environmentally aware company. We recognize that we have an ethical responsibility to our customers, our staff members, and our planet.

We serve our customers by creating the finest publications possible on personal growth, creativity, spirituality, wellness, and other areas of emerging importance. We serve New World Library employees with generous benefits, significant profit sharing, and constant encouragement to pursue their most expansive dreams.

As a Green Press Initiative Gold Certified Environmentally Responsible Publisher, we print an increasing number of books with soy-based ink on 100 percent postconsumer-waste recycled paper. Also, we power our offices with solar energy and contribute to nonprofit organizations working to make the world a better place for us all.

Our products are available in bookstores everywhere.

LET'S CONNECT

www.newworldlibrary.com

At NewWorldLibrary.com you can download our catalog,
subscribe to our e-newsletter, read our blog,
and link to authors' websites, videos, and podcasts.

Find us on Facebook, follow us on Twitter, and watch us on YouTube.

Send your questions and comments our way!
You make it possible for us to do what we love to do.

Phone: 415-884-2100 or 800-972-6657
Catalog requests: Ext. 10 | Orders: Ext. 52 | Fax: 415-884-2199
escort@newworldlibrary.com

 **NEW WORLD LIBRARY**
publishing books that change lives   14 Pamaron Way, Novato, CA 94949

OUR Appreciations for YOU the reader and...

edward + Belle

PATRICIA HUNTINGTON

Janice + JOHN

eMILY claire

CLIFF + DAVID

virginia Bell

rAY DAVI

All our non-physical FAMILY members

MAY-ree Kennedy

YoFe + DAVID

annie + Kyle

KATHRYN + AJA

Wes + JUDY

PEGGY

KATHRYN + Frank MOLLY, Schuyler

Mike COAKLEY

VAL + JOSEPH

eLissA ALex + leo

JASon + eriKA

KArin + serge

PHiLip BArbe

JOSHUA Home edwards GinA MAriA mele

our inner wise selves

BriGette

Andrew + Jennifer OTTO + Kitties

We love all of you and wish to thank and appreciate all the hearts around us.

Jeanie

MARY ursettie

russt LINDA LAURA+Todd BECKY + Brian

Leslie Lewis SAViliA Christian GAvin

VanessA

ClArK, JonAh, Tyla

MiCHAeL + SHeri

AMyt roB annaBella evie rose

To CAMperridge for HyDrATion

TArik THAMi

MALIKA + GABrielle

NiCK + LinDsAY

RObyn POSin

andreA Ben, nico MATT

every HEALTH CAring angel

LAureL+wes

MArney+Tony KAi CHArlotte

SUSie + OTTO

SHiloH + JonAthAn

MiCHon Javelosa + DAViD STAriCHA HAppy Tree Media Be THe CHange UniTED, evA, and

All previous Lovers and relation SHips

CreAtive Cove SUpporters

To Anyone we coulDn't FiT on THis PAGE

TAMA Kieves

VanDA+Frank

Vickie wArren

planet SARK DOri etter + LUKAS MAGnusson inspired income LinDA Horowitz, JoAnn, TAnyA KATie GrAnt Plume copy

Over THe MOON Group

THe WriGHT FAMiLY

THe BLETH + steele FAMiLies

edie CALDWELL

Jimmie + MArti

vAn Wise

our dear neighbors Melissa+JAy+Henry CHriSTinA MiCHAEL, JUDY CanDace+Ted nancy, ALex LinDA

PHiLip + CAroL

MiCHeLe MArtin + Steve HArris MDM MGMT

To ALL of our AuTHor Friends we couLDn't fit onTo THis PAGE!

All of our clients SUpporters and CAring professionals

LOVING IS THE WHOLE POINT

Love imperfectly keep surprise close at hand

if you feel unloved, love your self first

Transform any love "ideal" or comparison you are enough

let yourself receive love from others

Love with all of your faucets turned on

Be willing to live in between "right" and "wrong"

LOVE BOLDLY

YOU are worthy of love just as you already are- with no "improvements"

YOU Are so Deeply LOVED

Live like a full cup of self-love sharing the overflow with the world

practice exquisite self-care and self love: fill yourself up

drench yourself + others in loving

Allow yourself to be intimately seen, known and loved in your life

MAKE lots of mistakes in loving: reveal yourself Deeply

perfect timing for love NOW

See + Be in this world with love

You are seen, you are known, you are loved

love, SARK ©20

MOST of ALL, LOVE Yourself